HEALTH, WELFARE
& PRACTICE

D0569309

Also published by
SAGE Publications
in association with
The Open University

Disabling Barriers – Enabling Environments

edited by John Swain, Vic Finkelstein, Sally French and Mike Oliver

Death, Dying and Bereavement

edited by Donna Dickenson and Malcolm Johnson

All three books are Course Readers for the Open University Diploma in Health and Social Welfare

Details of the Diploma and the related courses are available from The Information Officer, Department of Health and Social Welfare, The Open University, Walton Hall, Milton Keynes MK7 6AA, UK.

HEALTH, WELFARE & PRACTICE

Reflecting on Roles & Relationships

edited by

Jan Walmsley
Jill Reynolds
Pam Shakespeare
Ray Woolfe

The Open
University

in association with
The Open University

SAGE Publications
London • Newbury Park • New Delhi

SAGE Publications Ltd
6 Bonhill Street
London EC2A 4PU

SAGE Publications Inc
2455 Teller Road
Newbury Park, California 91320

SAGE Publications India Pvt Ltd
32, M-Block Market
Greater Kailash – I
New Delhi 110 048

British Library Cataloguing in Publication data

A catalogue record for this book is available from the British Library.

ISBN 0–8039–8794–3
ISBN 0–8039–8795–1 Pbk

Library of Congress catalog card number 92–50845

Typeset by Photoprint, Torquay, Devon
Printed in Great Britain by the Cromwell Press Ltd, Broughton Gifford, Melksham, Wiltshire

CONTENTS

ACKNOWLEDGEMENTS

The editors would like to acknowledge support and comments from Clare Butler, Giles Clark, Andrew Cornwell, Robert Dingwall, Roger Gomm, Christine Jones, Robert Nicodemus, Kate Richenburg, Kate Robinson and Paul Wainwright.

The editors and publishers wish to thank the following for permission to use copyright material: Basic Books, a division of HarperCollins Publishers, for material from Donald A. Schön, *The Reflective Practitioner*. Copyright © 1983 by Basic Books, Inc; Basil Blackwell Ltd for material from Elizabeth Roberts, *A Woman's Place: an Oral History of Working Class Women 1890–1940*, 1984; Blackwell Scientific Publications Ltd for G.E. Chapman, 'Ritual and rational action in hospitals', *Journal of Advanced Nursing*, 8, 1983, pp. 13–20; British Medical Association for material from Naomi Croft, 'A feeling for medicine', *BMA News Review*, 5, 1990; and Tom Heller, 'Personal and medical memories from Hillsborough', *British Medical Journal*, 23–9 December 1989; British Sociological Association for Sara Arber and Nigel Gilbert, 'Men: the forgotten carers', *Sociology*, 23 (1), 1989, pp. 111–18; Carfax Publishing Company for material from Christopher Brown and Charles Ringma, 'New disability services: the critical role of staff in a consumer-directed empowerment model of service for physically disabled people', *Disability, Handicap and Society*, 4 (3), 1989, pp. 251–4; Critical Social Policy and the authors for material from David Ward and Audrey Mullender, 'Empowerment and oppression: an indissoluble pairing for contemporary social work', *Critical Social Policy*, Vol. 32, 1991, pp. 21–30; HarperCollins Publishers Ltd for material from Norma Pitfield, 'Making gardens from wildernesses' in *A Wealth of Experience*, ed. Susan Hemmings, Pandora Press, 1985; and W. David Wills, *The Barns Experiment*, Allen & Unwin, 1945; Harvard University Press for material from Nora Ellen Groce, *Everyone Here Spoke Sign Language: Hereditary Deafness on Martha's Vineyard*. Copyright © 1985 by Nora Ellen Groce; A.M. Heath & Company Ltd on behalf of the Estate of the late Sonia Brownell Orwell for material from George Orwell, *How the Poor Die*, Martin Secker & Warburg, 1931; Hobsons Publishing plc for material from Robert Bor, Lucy Perry and Riva Miller, 'When the Solution becomes a part of the problem in the psychosocial management of an AIDS patient', *British Journal of Guidance and Counselling*, 17 (2), 1989, pp. 133–7; Hodder & Stoughton Publishers for material from Anita Binns, 'Anita's story' in *Know*

Me As I Am, eds Dorothy Atkinson and Fiona Williams, 1990; Jessica Kingsley Publishers for material from Gillian Dalley, 'Professional ideology or organisational tribalism?' in *Social Work and Health Care*, eds Rex Taylor and Jill Ford, 1989; J.G. Kyle for material from Maggie Woolley, 'Acquired Hearing Loss: Acquired Oppression' in *Adjustment to Acquired Hearing Loss*, Centre for Deaf Studies, School of Education, Bristol, 1987; Amina Mama for material from 'Violence against Black women: gender, race and state responses', *Feminist Review*, 32, 1989, pp. 31–48; Macmillan Publishers Ltd for material from John Simmonds, 'Thinking about feelings in group care' in *Social Work and the Legacy of Freud*, eds G. Pearson, J. Treseder and M. Yelloly, Macmillan Education, 1988; and Jalna Hanmer and Daphne Statham, 'Commonalities and diversities between women clients and women social workers' in *Women and Social Work*, Macmillan Education, 1988; Don Naik for material from 'Towards an antiracist curriculum in social work training' in *One Small Step towards Racial Justice*, CCETSW, 1991; Northcote House Publishers Ltd for Maggie Potts and Rebecca Fido, 'Resisting the system' in *A Fit Person to be Removed*, 1991; The Observer Ltd for Yasmin Alibhai 'Black nightingales', *New Statesman and Society*, 7 October 1988; Oxford University Press for material from Jenny Kitzinger, Josephine Green and Vanessa Coupland, 'Labour relations: midwives and doctors on the labour ward' in *The Politics of Maternity Care*, eds J. Garcia, R. Kilpatrick and M. Richards, Clarendon Press, 1990; Piper and Marbury on behalf of William V. Hovey, representative of the Estate of Helen MacGill Hughes for material from Everett C. Hughes, *The Sociological Eye*, 1977; Routledge for material from Gerry Stimson and Barbara Webb, *Going to See the Doctor*, 1975; and Barbara Webb, 'Trauma and tedium: an account of living on a children's ward' in *Medical Encounters: The Experience of Illness and Treatment*, eds G. Horobin and A. Davis, Croom Helm, 1977; W.B. Saunders Co. for material from Ruth Purtilo, *Health Professional/Patient Interaction*, 1984; Whiting & Birch Ltd for material from Tara Mistry, 'Establishing a feminist model of groupwork in the probation service', *Groupwork* 2, 1989, pp. 145–58; John Wiley & Sons Ltd for material from Patrick Wakeling, 'Awakenings' in *Wounded Healers*, eds V. Rippere and R. Williams, 1985. Every effort has been made to trace all the copyright holders, but if any have been inadvertently overlooked the publishers will be pleased to make the necessary arrangement at the first opportunity.

NOTES ON THE AUTHORS

Sara Arber is Senior Lecturer in Sociology, University of Surrey. She is a member of the Stratification and Employment Group conducting research on ageing, older women's labour force participation, and inequalities in women's health. Recent publications include S. Arber and J. Ginn, *Gender and Later Life* (1991) and S. Arber and G.N. Gilbert (eds), *Women and Working Lives: Divisions and Change* (1991).

Anita Binns My name is Anita Binns. I am 37 years old. I have lived in my own flat in Gateshead for the last fourteen years. I've done the Open University Patterns for Living Courses, P555 and P555M and been a group leader. I am chair of a self-advocacy group 'Speaking up in Gateshead' which started three years ago. We talk about issues that are relevant to people who attend Adult Training Centres. We meet regularly with social services and help with informal interviews for staff appointments. I've travelled all over the country talking about self-advocacy. [In May 1992, a month after writing this, Anita died in hospital.]

Robert Bor is a clinical psychologist who has worked in both psychiatric and medical settings. He trained in the practice and teaching of family therapy at the Tavistock Clinic. His experience in HIV work was gained at the Royal Free Hospital, where he worked as a counsellor for five years until 1991. His training and experience have led to his recent interest in the application of systematic thinking to HIV-associated problems. He now lectures in counselling psychology at the City University, London, and is an honorary lecturer in medicine at the Royal Free Hospital School of Medicine. He is co-editor of the international journal *AIDS Care* and a clinical teacher at the Institute of Family Therapy in London. He has undertaken HIV counselling liaising with consultants in the UK and abroad, and is a Churchill Fellow.

Christopher Brown is a senior lecturer in the Department of Social Work and Social Policy at the University of Queensland, Australia. He is concerned with empowerment of marginalized people and has conducted evaluation and action research studies in which attention to the consumer voice has been central. He is also interested in dialogical approaches to social work education and to consumer-orientated research.

Graham Connelly is a lecturer in applied behavioural sciences in the Scottish School of Further Education, Jordanhill College, Glasgow. He has been a social work tutor since 1981, with residential and day care staff on CSS, ICSC, NHC in Social Care and Dip SW. He is an Open University tutor and course team member, K254 *Working with Children and Young People*. An experienced youth worker and trainer, he is a former community development worker and secondary school teacher.

Vanessa Coupland was a founder member of the Maternity Services Research Group at the University of Cambridge. She is now a social worker.

Naomi Craft was a Senior House Officer studying for her FRCS in London at the time of writing her article.

Gillian Dalley conducted the fieldwork for the article abridged here when she was research fellow at the MRC Medical Sociology Unit in Aberdeen. More recently, she has worked for the Centre for Health Economics, and for the Policy Studies Institute. She is now a senior manager with South-East Thames Regional Health Authority and maintains her interest in interprofessional working and in community care.

Gladys Elder was born in Glasgow in 1899 into a family deeply involved in the Scottish Socialist movement. Nearing seventy, after a life of great hardship, she began an Open University degree and took up the cause of older people. She died in 1976 shortly before her book *The Alienated: Growing Old Today* was published.

Vic Finkelstein is a senior lecturer in the Department of Health and Social Welfare at the Open University. He has contributed to two major Open University courses on disability, *The Handicapped Person in the Community* (1974) and *The Disabling Society* (1993). He is a former chair of the British Council of Organizations for Disabled People.

Nigel Gilbert is Professor and Head of the Department of Sociology, University of Surrey. His recent books include *Opening Pandora's Box: a Sociological Analysis of Scientific Discourse* (1984) and *Computers and Conversation* (1990). He has written many papers on stratification, the sociology of science and cognitive science.

Roger Gomm is a freelance writer and editor. Until recently, he was head of a department in a College of Further Education training community nurses, social workers and other social care staff. His main research interest is in the everyday use of language.

Josephine Green was a founder member of the Maternity Services Research Group at the University of Cambridge. She is now researching women's experiences of routine screening during ante-natal care.

Jalna Hanmer is a Reader in Women's Studies at the University of Bradford where she coordinates the MADip. Women's Studies (Applied). Her research interests and publications are in the areas of social and community work, violence against women and human reproduction. She is co-author of *Women and Social Work: Towards a Woman Centred Practice* (1988) with Daphne Statham.

Tom Heller is a general practitioner who lives in Sheffield. At the time of the Hillsborough disaster he worked in a practice adjacent to Hillsborough football ground. He also works as a senior lecturer in the Department of Health and Social Welfare at the Open University, and has been involved in the production of multiprofessional courses on a variety of health promotion issues.

Everett C. Hughes is best known for his work at the University of Chicago 1948–1961. His major research area was the sociology of work and occupations, using case studies from nursing or medicine.

Jenny Kitzinger was a founder member of the Maternity Services Research Group, a subgroup of the Child Care and Development Group at the University of Cambridge. She is now with the Media Research Group at the University of Glasgow.

Liz Lloyd is currently a lecturer in Health and Social Care at Soundwell College, Bristol, teaching on a range of access and social care courses. She is also a postgraduate student at Bristol University undertaking research into the influence of racial equality policies on the implementation of community care.

Kate Lyon is Lecturer in Applied Social Studies in the Department of Social Work, University of Bristol. She was formerly Lecturer in Criminology, University of Bath. She graduated in sociology at the LSE, and has been a research officer in the Home Office Research Unit, and a course director for NACRO. She is currently doing research on probation centres.

Amina Mama holds a doctorate in applied psychology and has taught at a number of institutions, most recently on the Women and Development Masters Programme at the Institute of Social Studies in the Hague. She currently divides her time between Africa, where she is a full-time researcher, and the UK, where she lectures at the Development and Project Planning Centre, University of Bradford.

Tara Mistry is a lecturer in social work at Bristol University; formerly she was a probation officer in Hereford and Worcester and in Avon. Her main teaching area is in the criminal justice system, probation practice and groupwork, with a particular research interest in women offenders and race and gender issues in social work practice. She is also currently bringing up her two daughters, aged two and a half years and eight months.

Audrey Mullender is Director of the Centre for Applied Social Studies at the University of Durham. She has taught on empowerment in social work practice and research in Australia, New Zealand, Canada, the USA, and in numerous European countries, including Scandinavia. She has also published extensively on the subject: notably in exploring the practice and teaching implications of anti-oppressive values in work with women, children and families, people with physical or learning disabilities, users of mental health services, and elderly people.

Don Naik is Assistant Dean, Faculty of Environment and Social Studies, Polytechnic of North London. Formerly he was Deputy Chief Social Work Adviser at the Scottish Office. He also worked as Deputy Permanent Secretary for Local Government in Zimbabwe. In London, as assistant director of a social services department, he pioneered ways of providing services appropriate to a multi-racial population. He is a Council member of CCETSW and chair of its Black Perspectives Committee.

George Orwell was a passionate crusader for socialism, producing both fictional and non-fictional books of great strength. A variety of non-fictional work emerged from his deliberate experience of poverty and hardship beginning with *Down and Out in Paris and London*. George Orwell died of tuberculosis in 1950.

Maggie Potts is a consultant clinical psychologist and manager of community services for people with learning disabilities in Leeds. She has worked in this area for the past fifteen years. In addition to psychotherapeutic work, she has also coordinated and directed research into the long-term effects of de-institutionalization on residents and staff. *A Fit Person to be Removed* was motivated by a desire to preserve the first-hand experiences of people who spent most of their lives in institutions in the hope that the mistakes and injustices of the past would not be repeated.

Jill Reynolds is a lecturer in the Department of Health and Social Welfare at the Open University. She has been a social worker and taught on qualifying courses in social work; she is interested in the use of perspectives on gender in social work education. She is the author, with Rosalind Finlay, of *Social Work and Refugees* (1987).

Charles Ringma is a professor at the Asian Theological Seminary in Manila. He founded a service for young people in Brisbane, Queensland during the 1970s. His doctoral studies at the University of Queensland examined the hermeneutic of Gadamer. As a researcher in the Department of Social Work and Social Policy, he was able to test hermeneutic theory in the arena of social research.

Elizabeth Roberts is interested in oral history, family history and women's history. She is the author of *A Woman's Place* (1984) and *Women's Work 1840–1940* (1988). She works as an administrator in the Centre for North West Regional Studies, University of Lancaster.

Donald Schön is Ford Professor of Urban Studies and Education at the Massachusetts Institute of Technology. He is well known for developing the concept of the reflective practitioner both to describe what practitioners do, and to influence the training of professionals.

Daphne Statham is Director of the National Institute of Social Work. She has been active in voluntary work and is currently chair of the National Association of Councils of Voluntary Service. Her particular research interest is in women and the personal social services, in collaboration with Jalna Hanmer.

Gerry Stimson is Professor of Sociology of Health Behaviour at Charing Cross and Westminster Medical School. He directs The Centre for Research on Drugs and Health Behaviour. He has been engaged in a wide range of research and publication in medical sociology, including work on doctor–patient interaction, and the social aspects of drug use and HIV infection.

Sheelagh Strawbridge teaches on degree and diploma courses in social work, counselling and professional studies at Humberside Polytechnic and is also a Relate counsellor. She has written articles on sociology and counselling psychology, contributed to a recent book on Victorian social values and co-authored a textbook on the sociology of culture.

Patrick Wakeling was a consultant child and family psychiatrist in North Lincolnshire at the time *Awakenings* was written.

Jan Walmsley works at the Open University in the Department of Health and Social Welfare. She is currently carrying out research with women and men with learning disabilities into how they have experienced giving and receiving care. She is a carer herself for two children, a dog, two hamsters, a horse and four hens.

David Ward is Senior Lecturer and Head of Social Work programmes at Nottingham University. With a practice background in the probation service, he has wide experience in training, research, consultancy and development work, especially in relation to groups. With colleagues, he founded the Centre for Research and Training in Social Action Groupwork at Nottingham University. The centre aims to foster the consolidation and expansion of the self-directed/social action approach. It provides a centre for contact and exchange, a range of training and consultancy services, and a base to which practitioners, trainers and researchers can be attached for study, research and professional development.

Barbara Webb was research associate at the University of Swansea Medical Sociology Research Centre from 1971 to 1978, mainly working on doctor–patient relations in general practice. She became involved in part-time consultancy work for the Community Education Department at the Open University during the period 1981–85. Since that time, she has worked independently and under contract to the Tavistock Institute of Human Relations on evaluation studies of both national schemes and local organizations in the field of health and welfare.

Jan Williams is Lecturer in Health Promotion at Manchester University Medical School. Her current work is in the education and training of specialists in health promotion. Her wider interests include adult education and professional development. She is keen to promote good educational practice in the field of professional development for health care.

W. David Wills is best known for practising and developing an approach known as 'planned environment therapy' in a number of pioneering camps and schools for maladjusted or delinquent young people between 1936 and 1969. He was committed throughout his adult life to 'love for the unloveable' as a central feature of his work. Among a wide range of published writings, three remain outstanding by any standards: *The Hawkspur Experiment* (1941), *The Barns Experiment* (1945) and *Throw Away Thy Rose* (1960).

Maggie Woolley is a past presenter and producer of 'See Hear' and has worked extensively in the arts and the media.

INTRODUCTION
ROLES AND RELATIONSHIPS
IN HEALTH AND WELFARE

This Reader has been produced as part of an Open University course, 'Roles and Relationships: Perspectives on Practice in Health and Welfare'. The Reader, and the course of which it is a part, have three distinctive features:

- an emphasis on reflective practice
- a multi-occupational approach
- a focus on roles and relationships

The book stands equally well alone and will be of interest to trainers, teachers and students working to develop and improve practice in health and welfare.

Reflective practice and the reflective practitioner

In recent years the emphasis on the training of health and welfare practitioners has shifted from the inculcation of a body of knowledge to an emphasis on skills and competence. However, competence implies the ability not just to respond to what is known and familiar, but also to respond effectively to new and unpredictable situations. In this task the ability to be a reflective practitioner – to be aware of the way problems are framed and what makes an appropriate response – has come to be regarded as a hallmark of the effective practitioner.

The recognition of 'reflective practice' is associated with Professor Donald Schön. He has drawn attention to the ability of practitioners to deal with demanding situations: 'It is this entire process of reflection in-action which is central to the "art" by which practitioners sometimes deal well with situations of uncertainty, instability, uniqueness and value conflict' (Schön, Section 1 below). This book contributes to the training of 'reflective practitioners' by bringing together a collection of articles in which academics, practitioners, theoreticians and service users themselves reflect on practice and experience through writing, through describing situations, encounters, theoretical perspectives which cast light on practice.

In putting articles together for the Reader we have been conscious to demonstrate that reflective practitioners require an awareness of their own humanity, of how their own experiences can enable them to empathize with people who seek help and use services. A number of articles, including those by Patrick Wakeling (Section 1), Tom Heller (Section 4) and Barbara Webb (Section 4) show 'experts' in their own fields using their own human experiences of illness, uncertainty and powerlessness to aid their reflective process.

Exploring a multi-occupational approach

The development of teamwork – harmonious relationships between practitioners with different backgrounds, training, organizational structures and cultures – has long been a desideratum of professional training. It is more honoured in rhetoric than in practice. This book will enable trainers and students to examine issues in interprofessional and interoccupational teamwork in two ways:

1 By directly addressing issues arising when different professions and occupations work together. The articles by Gillian Dalley and Jenny Kitzinger et al. in Section 1, and by Robert Bor et al. in Section 4, examine team work in practice settings and draw out some of the problems encountered when people from different occupations work together, as well as indicating some possible ways forward.
2 By examining a wide range of settings: probation work, disability services, child care, nursing, medicine, social work. In organizing the Reader we have deliberately avoided traditional divisions based on the health/social work divide. This makes it possible to recognize commonalities in practice across the breadth of the health and welfare fields. To take one example: in Section 3, W. David Wills describes his attempts in the 1940s to 'empower' the adolescent boys in his care which enables direct comparisons to be made with the concerns expressed by David Ward and Audrey Mullender in Section 3 in relation to empowerment in social work in the 1990s.

Why roles and relationships?

The book's subtitle is 'Reflecting on Roles and Relationships'. The concepts of *roles* and *relationships* offer a way of bridging personal individual circumstances and the wider structural forces which shape people's lives.

It [role] can provide a conceptual bridge between personality and culture or social structure, between the subjective (me 'in here') and the objective (society 'out there'). Roles are subjective, and integral to our personalities because the roles we play become part of our personal identities, the way we see ourselves and the way others see us. They are objective, part of culture and social structure; they are handed down from generation to generation; we get our roles 'off the peg', together with the cultural 'scripts' attached to them. (Strawbridge, Section 3)

Such a bridge is central to the training of practitioners as the interaction between personal circumstances and structural issues is crucial in understanding practice. It is all too easy for training to err on one side or other of this divide. A focus on individuals can overestimate the individual's ability to overcome disadvantage, regardless of broad structural issues such as poverty, unemployment, racism. Alternatively, a focus on structural issues can leave students feeling powerless: unable to see a way to make a personal contribution in the face of overwhelming inequalities within society. By sustaining a focus on roles and relationships we keep in view both the broad structures shaping our lives, the social context, and the individual's perceptions of, and contributions to, situations.

Roles and *relationships* are universal. It is almost as difficult to imagine oneself outside role, outside relationship, as it is to imagine a world without time. The concepts of roles and relationships therefore enable us to look at all the actors in health and welfare. Users and workers, professionals and informal carers *all* have roles, *all* have relationships. This is reflected in the Reader. We have selected articles by people with a variety of roles. Attention is drawn to the relationship that the author has with the material. Some authors explicitly acknowledge that relationship. You will find an article by a woman with learning disabilities writing about her own life and experiences (Anita Binns, Section 3). Anita may be said to have an intimate relationship with what she is writing; she is describing her own immediate experiences. Similarly, Barbara Webb, a sociologist by occupation, made use of a personal experience as mother of a child in a burns unit to write 'Trauma and tedium' (Section 4). It makes an interesting combination.

By contrast, it is perhaps more normal in an academic Reader to find papers where the role of the writer is not explicit, and the relationship s/he has with the material is not mentioned. Roger Gomm (Section 3), for example, does not explain why he has chosen to write about empowerment, nor does he refer to the capacity in which he wrote the article. In the context of roles and relationships you may become inquisitive about such matters, and wonder what impact the writer's role has on the subject matter and the way it is presented.

The sections

In structuring both the Reader and the course, we were aware that 'roles and relationships' offered particular perspectives on practice in health and welfare. Another interpretation is that they could leave us with no boundaries at all. Roles and relationships *could* encompass the whole of human life and experience. In drawing the boundaries we have made use of three key themes to structure the first three sections:

- experience and expertise
- diversity and discrimination
- empowerment and power

The final section, reflecting on practice, provides a synthesis of the themes.

The themes are not 'opposites': we do not mean to imply that 'experience' is good and 'expertise' bad or vice versa. Rather, they have become organizing categories which can act as bridges between the individual and the structural and support the development of reflective practice. They have the additional advantage of providing a means to bring contemporary concerns to the fore in the wider discussion of perspectives on practice.

The first theme, *experience and expertise*, draws attention to current debates on professionalism. A professional worker has both experience and publicly recognized expertise. Yet others also have valuable experience – informal carers, unqualified workers, service users. Their experience does not necessarily carry the cachet 'expertise', but is not necessarily inherently less valuable.

The second theme, *diversity and discrimination*, enables us to address anti-discriminatory issues. Discrimination is a neutral term; it can be helpful to discriminate, rather than offer indiscriminate services, regardless of the needs of the users of a service. However, negative discrimination on the grounds of gender, race, disability and other ascribed characteristics has been recognized as endemic in the provision of services. To counterpose this, effective discrimination can reflect diversity and allow it to flourish. This section of the Reader draws on examples from the experiences of women, black people and older people.

The third section, *empowerment and power*, explores the sources of power, and the meaning of empowerment. Empowerment is currently a buzz word in health and social welfare services. Practitioners are exhorted to 'empower' service users. But this can mean different things to different people. 'Empowerment' is a politically contested term. Our Reader section furnishes examples of different approaches to empowerment, shedding much-needed light on a subject which is often victim to muddled thinking.

The final section is *reflecting on practice*. In developing the course we were consciously trying to help students to become reflective, to stand back from their immediate situation and consider it in wider contexts. The articles in this section are written principally by practitioners who are doing just that: standing back and thinking about practice.

Although we have organized the Reader into sections, the issues raised overlap section boundaries. You will find that many, perhaps the majority, of articles have something to say which relates to two or more of the section themes. For example, Vic Finkelstein's article in Section 3 is also of immediate importance in considering diversity and discrimination. We ask you to make your own connections and think about the links between the Reader themes as you use the book, and develop your own perspectives on practice in health and welfare.

SECTION 1

EXPERIENCE AND EXPERTISE

The terms *experience* and *expertise* provide an organizing focus for this section of the Reader. The distinction that is often made between the two is that while the latter involves experience, it also involves the possession of specialist knowledge and skills derived through a formal period of training leading to certification. This places the topic of professionalization very much at the core of the debate and raises the issue of how public recognition and validation have come to be crucial in attributing the label 'expert' and thus perceiving those individuals to whom the label is attached as possessing 'expertise'.

The end product of this process is that financial rewards are attached to work which is done on the basis of professional expertise. Unpaid carers for sick, old or disabled people frequently acquire a vast amount of experience and skill in carrying out tasks for the people for whom they care. The skills they practice may be very similar to those carried out by professionals, yet the term 'expert' tends to be reserved for the latter, even if it is their first week in the job. Such a distinction between experience and expertise runs counter to the contemporary emphasis on competence in performance, irrespective of the way in which the knowledge and skills which underlie that competence were gained.

However, while attempts to value experience may be applauded, there is a risk that expertise comes to be devalued. Attempting to place the experience of the service users on the same footing as the expertise of the professional can lead to a kind of 'false equality' where the expertise of the service provider is devalued or even denied.

The first three articles in this section by Jan Williams, Donald Schön and Everett C. Hughes respectively address the question 'what makes a profession'. Jan Williams argues that it is the claim to a body of expert knowledge which characterizes the professions. Yet that claim is now being challenged. For the helping professions at least, the relationship the professional develops with the service user is more important than his/her role as expert.

Some of Jan Williams' concerns also appear in Donald Schön's article. He emphasizes the role of the professional as 'intuitive artist' rather than 'technical expert'. In the extract we have selected, Schön discusses how professionals 'reflect-in-action', making a connection from the theory to the realm of practice.

The extract from Everett C. Hughes' classic article 'License and Mandate' adopts a different angle on professions. He focuses on the profession's ability to set the terms of a debate, this being an important aspect of the power they possess. The profession itself influences the kinds of questions that are asked in its particular domain. The professional is allowed to possess 'guilty knowledge', knowledge which for the lay person would be impermissible. For example, the doctor can ask the patient details rarely shared in the closest of relationships; the nurse assists with intimate personal care; the counsellor can take a 'sex history'. Thus professionals are set apart, licensed to possess knowledge and to seek information which the individual normally conceals.

Jan Walmsley's article takes up some of the contradictions which exist in the domain of caring. She explores the overlap between the tasks performed by paid and unpaid carers and sets out some of the paradoxes that this gives rise to, particularly among professional carers.

The relationships between different professional groups is the theme of the next two articles. Teamworking between different professionals has long been seen as desirable, yet appears to present considerable practical difficulties. Gillian Dalley's article shows some of the reasons for this in her examination of relationships between professionals in the health service and social work: the effects of different organizational practices, ideologies and cultures. In their article 'Labour Relations: Midwives and Doctors on the Labour Ward', Jenny Kitzinger, Josephine Green and Vanessa Coupland examine relationships between midwives and doctors on wards with different management structures. They highlight the issues posed by overlapping roles. Identifying what is doctor work and what is midwife work can be fraught with difficulty but the task is not insurmountable given appropriate attitudes.

The next three articles take different perspectives on the relative roles of workers and users. Ruth Purtilo's 'Meaningful Distances' is a discussion of boundaries between personal and professional roles. She illustrates how the role of the worker is distinct from that of a friend or colleague, and how setting appropriate boundaries is an important skill in worker–user relationships.

Patrick Wakeling's article describes a role reversal, based on his own experience. When a psychiatrist becomes a patient in a psychiatric hospital much of his experience is denied. His behaviour is rationalized as resulting from overwork and stress. The reality of his mental illness is devalued. Through the experience of being a patient, Wakeling describes how he increased his understanding of depression and his expertise as a practitioner.

Gerry Stimson and Barbara Webb offer an account of doctor/patient consultations. While at first sight it may look as if the doctor has a monopoly of expertise, the patient emerges as an active participant in the encounter, who is by no means powerless. The authors describe how the patient draws on his/her own sources of experience and information to make choices which are not necessarily those the physician prescribes.

We complete our examination of different aspects of experience and expertise with two historical perspectives. In 'Pregnancy and Childbirth', Elizabeth Roberts uses personal accounts by women and constructs a picture of how one kind of expertise, that of the traditional untrained midwife, was replaced by another, that of the qualified midwife. Finally, George Orwell's 'How the Poor Die' takes us back to the grim reality of health care for the poor of Paris in the 1930s. The doctors' interpretation of their role as experts took little account of the quality of the experience for the patients.

1

WHAT IS A PROFESSION? EXPERIENCE VERSUS EXPERTISE

JAN WILLIAMS

What is a profession?

The question of what constitutes a profession has long been debated; and attempts have been made to identify a set of distinct traits which characterize all professions. Freidson (1986) centres on the issue of self-direction or autonomy, suggesting that central to a profession is the power to regulate its own affairs – a power which is usually statutorily granted.

Millerson (1964), surveying the work of twenty-one authors on the definition of professions, extracted a total of twenty-three elements used by them to define a profession, though there was little consensus among them. Certain key characteristics are, however, frequently cited. These include:

- skill based on theoretical knowledge
- the provision of training and occupation
- tests of the competence of members
- organization
- adherence to a professional code of conduct
- altruistic service

With many different perspectives on the traits which characterize professions, there can be no one 'ideal type' profession. Different occupational groups conform more or less closely to the above criteria – and they change over time.

An important element of the professional–client relationship, it is proposed, is that of 'mystification': professionals promote their services as esoteric. They create dependence on their skills and reduce the areas of knowledge and experience they have in common with their clients. In this

Abridged from 'Family life, education and the training of professionals', PhD thesis, University of Manchester, 1989 way they increase the 'social distance' between themselves and their clients, and so gain increasing autonomy (Johnson, 1989).

While a small number of occupations have long held the status of professions, in the past forty years, with growing knowledge and technology, many more have started to 'professionalize'. Occupations such as social work, nursing, health visiting, midwifery and teaching – often referred to as the semi-professions – have sought to enhance their status and earn recognition as full professions.

Expert knowledge as the basis of professions

As suggested above, a key characteristic of traditional professions is the body of theoretical knowledge which forms the basis for applied specialist skills. Hoyle (1982: 48) described the academic community's criteria for valid knowledge as: 'codified, systematized, universalistic knowledge generated by experimentation and independent sceptical scholarship and, where applied to practical and personal problems, applied in a rational and detached manner'.

The possession of such a systematized, theoretical body of knowledge is seen as an essential foundation for any occupational group aspiring to professional status. A professional group's body of specialist knowledge forms the foundation for developing whole philosophies and systems; for example, lawyers define the nature and function of law and the way to administer justice; and doctors define sickness and health and the distribution of medical services. The claim to specialist knowledge is central, for on it rests the professionals' claim to be qualified to advise, the claim to 'know better' than their clients – and hence the claim for autonomy, for being trusted by the public, for reward and prestige.

The traditional professions of medicine, law, architecture etc. have a well-established base of expert knowledge. In recent years aspiring professions such as social work, nursing and teaching have similarly attempted to define and emphasize the body of theoretical knowledge underpinning their work; they have sought to extend the length of initial training, and grounded it more firmly in academic disciplines; they have argued for all-graduate entry; attempted to remove unqualified personnel; and developed a growing body of research and scholarship to underpin their occupations. In these ways they have sought 'professionalization', attempting to gain full status and recognition as professionals (Hoyle, 1982).

An expert knowledge base, then, is the foundation on which professional status is built; and the purveying of that knowledge is the means by which power and control is maintained. All professions offer a service; and that service includes 'giving advice'. The claim to be qualified to give that advice, like everything else claimed by the professional, rests on the claim to specialized knowledge. According to Hughes (1975: 249) 'Professions *profess*. They profess to know better than others the nature of certain matters, and to know better than their clients what ails them or their affairs.'

Traditionally, therefore, the professionals' approach to client advice, or education, has been a prescriptive one – that is, the professional, as expert, prescribes what the client needs to know, passes on that information/advice and expects compliance. The emphasis is on a one-way transmission of knowledge from expert to lay person: 'knowledge is a gift bestowed by those who consider themselves knowledgeable upon those whom they consider to know nothing' (Freire, 1972: 46). This prescriptive approach to client education conforms to the traditional educational model of pedagogy. Its theoretical basis is rationalism: a belief in scientific objectivity, a belief that knowledge is certain and absolute, and has a status and origin independent of individual human beings.

Yet knowledge is not absolute, but socially constructed. Values are implicit, if not explicit, in these professionally defined bodies of knowledge, and in the selection of knowledge for transmission. With a prescriptive approach to education, these values too are afforded the status of knowledge, and held to be absolute. In this way professionals impose their perspectives and values on the rest of society – and education becomes a means of social control. This is what Jarvis (1985) has termed 'education from above'.

The relevance of expert knowledge to professional practice

Increasingly today, professional knowledge is being challenged. Professional prescriptions of what constitutes valid knowledge are being called into question; and the concept of knowledge as absolute and value-free no longer holds sway. There is criticism that professions are out of touch with the perspectives and needs of their clients; and the value of the theoretical knowledge underpinning professions, and the relevance of theory to practice, are being questioned.

The field of health promotion offers some useful illustrations of this. Kemm (1991), for example, discussing the health education advice professionals give to their clients, questions the validity of the knowledge base for this advice. He suggests that knowledge is one class of belief – the others being opinion, dogma, myth and fallacy – and that knowledge differs from the others in that accepting it as true can be justified. But, he suggests, in practice it is a difficult distinction to make:

> Describing the beliefs of health promoters as knowledge rather than opinion is frequently justified by appeal to science. This implies that these beliefs are firmly founded on the failure of attempts to refute them, and that they are the only interpretation admitted by the observational evidence. Alas the reality is more complex and in health promotion it is hard to draw the dividing line between knowledge and opinion. (Kemm, 1991: 292)

Considering the question of lifestyle and health, he goes on to suggest that what is accepted as knowledge in this field has changed over time, and that much of the 'knowledge base' for health promotion falls far short of evidence tested and proved 'beyond reasonable doubt', and is usually closer to the 'balance of probability'. So, he proposes, rather than talking of the 'knowledge base' which underpins health education advice, health professionals should describe it as 'best available opinion'; opinion which, while providing a reasonable basis for action, should not be assumed to be infallible nor equated with knowledge (Kemm, 1991).

A growing interest in 'lay epidemiology' again illustrates the limitations of 'expert' knowledge alone. Lay epidemiology looks at the ways in which lay people perceive issues of health and illness and how they incorporate professionals' health messages into their own health culture. Frankel et al. (1991: 430), reviewing health education messages regarding coronary heart disease, suggest that health professionals simplify the messages to the point of distortion, and that this brings them into disrepute – so that 'there is public delight when the experts are seen to have "got it wrong" '. The importance for professionals of recognizing and understanding lay epidemiology is stressed, since one-way communication, based on health professionals' prescriptions alone, results in health education messages being widely ignored.

As the professional knowledge base for health education is being challenged, so too is the *way* in which expert knowledge is being used by professionals. Harding et al. (1990), discussing the educational role of the pharmacist, warn against the traditional didactic approach as being too narrow, and failing to take account of the sociocultural context in which people operate. Drawing on a critique by Rodmell and Watt (1986) of traditional health education practice, they suggest that: 'an implicit assumption of the traditional health education philosophy is an absence or inappropriateness of the lay person's own health knowledge. Thus health educators may assume that their interpretation of health and illness is better or more appropriate than the interpretation of lay people' (Harding et al., 1990: 89). They criticize health education which is not tailored to the clients' needs, and in which clients are told not what *they* want, or need to know, but rather, what the professionals want to tell them. Failure to accept and act upon inappropriate health education messages is then deemed irresponsible or intransigent.

An alternative approach to the use of expert knowledge

An alternative approach is one based on partnership, in which professional and client together identify what the client wants and needs to know. Instead of a one-way transmission of knowledge from professional to client, there is a two-way transaction, building on the existing knowledge and experience of the client, according to the client's perceived needs, and the professional's response to these.

This approach recognizes that knowledge is socially constructed, and acknowledges the value-laden nature of the definition and transmission of knowledge. No longer is the professional seeking to impose her view of what constitutes knowledge on her clients, with the goal of attaining compliance. Her role has changed from one of controlling to one of supporting and enabling, helping the client to draw on and think through his own experiences, and sharing her expert knowledge to help him develop his understanding. The goal of the professional becomes the personal growth and development of the client. Thus the professional–client relationship changes from one of superior–subordinate to one of partnership; it becomes, in Jarvis' terms (1985) the 'education of equals'.

It can be seen that an approach to education based on the philosophy of the 'education of equals' poses a challenge to the way in which the professional's expert knowledge is viewed and utilized. Thus it strikes at the heart of professionalism. Approaches to education based on the 'education of equals' recognize clients' experiential knowledge as the foundation for learning, with the professional's expert knowledge at the *service* of the client. For professionals who have trained for many years to acquire a body of expert knowledge, who have passed examinations to gain qualifications and entry to the profession, to challenge the pre-eminence of their professional knowledge base constitutes a grave threat. It removes power from them and hands it over to the client; and locates their base of power with their clients rather than with their professional body.

A new foundation for professional practice

If traditional professional practice is being called into question, and the place of expert knowledge is being challenged, what is the foundation for the professional–client relationship? Halmos (1965) has suggested that personal service professions in fact belong to a single profession – that of 'counselling' – a profession which includes all those people whose principal means of helping their clients is through the medium of the personal relationship. In personal service professions, it is suggested, professional effectiveness depends more on the quality of the relationship between professional and client than on a body of expert knowledge.

In social work, for example, it is being suggested that expert knowledge has been given false precedence; that in reality, 'to do social work is to do purposefully and deliberately that which is primarily intuitive' (England, 1986: 39). England describes the central process in social work as the 'intuitive use of self'. He suggests that the social worker's central function is to develop an understanding of her client, his needs and his worldview. He goes on to suggest that the basis for that understanding is the social worker's own personal experiences; that the worker uses her intuition to understand and communicate with her clients – and that to achieve her intuitive self, she needs self-understanding, understanding which comes from *within*, not from external, generalized, expert knowledge.

In nursing, too, it may be suggested that the central function is the creation of a relationship – that 'nursing is a special case of loving' (Jourard, 1971). Jourard suggests that technical care – the hygienic surroundings, medicine and rest – is insufficient, and that patients need 'human warmth, love and responsive care'. The healing relationship is the relationship between nurse and patient which makes the patient feel valued as an individual, offers him understanding and empathy, and serves to 'increase his sense of identity and integrity'. The same healing relationship, Jourard suggests, is central to the role of physicians, teachers, clergymen, dentists, lawyers, counsellors, psychotherapists and every other helping profession.

From this perspective, the most important foundation of the helping professions – and one which they all have in common – is the 'self' of the professional, the way in which she relates to her client, and the interpersonal skills she brings to the transaction.

Professional practice from this perspective has less to do with the application of esoteric knowledge, more to do with intuition, common sense, techniques for helping and interpersonal skills – a core of skills which should be common to all helping professions. The primary focus of professional training thus becomes, not the inculcation of a body of expert knowledge, but the identification and development of personal and interpersonal skills; and professional knowledge has a lower priority than the quality of the professional's relationship with the client. Thus a shift is apparent from seeing the foundation of the helping professions as scientific rationalism to recognizing it as art. In emphasizing the personal qualities needed for effective professional practice, this is not to suggest that expert knowledge has no relevance, but to see its role as being to *support* the helping relationship. Very few, Hoyle (1982) suggests, have as much genuine hard, scientific knowledge as they profess as the foundation for their practice. Rather, it is suggested, professionals have 'dressed up' common sense as theoretical knowledge to enhance their own status. The traditional professional emphasis on a body of academic knowledge has been designed, not to enhance the effectiveness of professional practice and hence to benefit clients, but to advance the cause of professionalization. Expert knowledge gives an image of omniscience: it is this which gives professionals power and control over their clients. As Cohen (1985: 175) expresses it: 'Most of the terms used by the helping professions combine a high degree of unreliability (in their diagnoses, prognosis and prescription of the right treatment), with an unambiguous set of constraints upon clients.'

Professionalization or professional development?

The quest for professionalization has led to an emphasis on scientific absolutes and material precision. The new approach to professional practice calls for a broadening of perspectives on what constitutes knowledge, and the recognition of the validity of experiential knowledge and intuition. Where, then, is the place for theoretical knowledge? England suggests that theoretical knowledge is valuable only in so far as it serves the professional's intuition and understanding of her clients. It is valuable in so far as it is *indistinguishable* from personal knowledge. Theoretical knowledge, as he sees it:

> is useful only in as much as it is incorporated into the worker's general . . . knowledge and available to inform his intuitive knowledge and intuitive behaviour. The real test of the worker's learning is never in his ability to show mastery of abstract knowledge, but in the way such knowledge is plundered and fragmented to inform his practice; his formal learning becomes useful in as much as it is inseparable and indistinguishable from his colloquial learning. (England, 1986: 35)

Theoretical knowledge, as the philosophy of the 'education of equals' proposes, thus loses its centrality in the professional–client interaction. It moves from a position of dominance to one of support. This has implications for the whole of the nature of the professional–client relationship. When expert knowledge ceases to be central, the professional's worldview no longer takes precedence over the client's. Nor does the professional have the right to set the terms of the relationship, to prescribe behaviour and to expect compliance. The relationship is now a negotiated one; and the role of the professional is to develop an understanding of her client's perceived needs, and to share her expert knowledge and skills, in so far as they serve these needs.

However, this development poses a dilemma for professionals. In order to further the cause of professionalization, professional training needs to focus on a body of expert knowledge as the foundation for professional practice. But for professional development – to develop practitioners who are more effective at helping their clients – the need is for training which focuses on personal and interpersonal skills, on building on experience, developing intuition and common sense. Thus, there are forces pulling in two different directions. The question is, will professionals and aspiring professionals see this new development as threatening their professional identity? Or can it offer a new model for professional practice?

References

Cohen, Stanley (1985) *Visions of Social Control: Crime, Punishment and Classification*. Cambridge: Polity Press.

England, Hugh (1986) *Social Work as Art: Making Sense for Good Practice*. London: Allen & Unwin.

Frankel, Stephen, Davison, Charles and Smith, George Davey (1991) 'Lay epidemiology and the rationality of responses to health education', *British Journal of General Practice*, 41: 428–30.

Freidson, Eliot (1986) 'Professional dominance and the ordering of health services: some consequences', in P. Conrad and R. Kern (eds), *Sociology of Health and Illness*, 2nd edn. New York: St Martin's Press.

Freire, Paulo (1972) *Pedagogy of the Oppressed*. Harmondsworth: Penguin.

Halmos, P. (1965) *The Faith of the Counsellors*. London: Constable.

Harding, Geoffrey, Nettleton, Sarah and Taylor, Kevin (1990) *Sociology for Pharmacists: An Introduction*. Basingstoke: Macmillan.

Hoyle, Eric (1982) 'The professionalisation of teachers: a paradox', in P. Gordon, H. Perkin, H. Sockett, E. Hoyle (eds), *Is Teaching a Profession?* Bedford Way Paper 15, University of London, Institute of Education.

Hughes, E. (1975) 'Professions', in G. Esland, G. Salaman and M.A. Speakman (eds), *People and Work*. Edinburgh/Milton Keynes: Holmes McDougall/Open University.

Jarvis, Peter (1985) *The Sociology of Adult and Continuing Education*. Kent: Croom Helm.

Johnson, T. (1989) *Professions and Power*. London: Macmillan.

Jourard, Sidney M. (1971) *The Transparent Self*, 2nd edn. New York: D. Van Nostrand.

Kemm, John (1991) 'Health education and the problem of knowledge', *Health Promotion International*, 6 (4): 291–6.

Millerson, Geoffrey (1964) *The Qualifying Associations*. London: Routledge & Kegan Paul.

Rodmell, S. and Watt, A. (1986) *The Politics of Health Education*. London: Routledge.

2

REFLECTION-IN-ACTION

DONALD SCHÖN

When we go about the spontaneous, intuitive performance of the actions of everyday life, we show ourselves to be knowledgeable in a special way. Often we cannot say what it is that we know. When we try to describe it we find ourselves at a loss, or we produce descriptions that are obviously inappropriate. Our knowing is ordinarily tacit, implicit in our patterns of action and in our feel for the stuff with which we are dealing. It seems right to say that our knowing is *in* our action.

Similarly, the workaday life of the professional depends on tacit knowing-in-action. Every competent practitioner can recognize phenomena – families of symptoms associated with a particular disease, peculiarities of a certain kind of building site, irregularities of materials or structure – for which he cannot give a reasonably accurate or complete description. In his day-to-day practice he makes innumerable judgments of quality for which he cannot state adequate criteria, and he displays skills for which he cannot state the rules and procedures. Even when he makes conscious use of research-based theories and techniques, he is dependent on tacit recognitions, judgments, and skilful performances.

On the other hand, both ordinary people and professional practitioners often think about what they are doing, sometimes even while doing it. Stimulated by surprise, they turn thought back on action and on the knowing which is implicit in action. They may ask themselves, for example, 'What features do I notice when I recognize this thing? What are the criteria by which I make this judgment? What procedures am I enacting when I perform this skill? How am I framing the problem that I am trying to solve?' Usually reflection on knowing-in-action goes together with reflection on the stuff at hand. There is some puzzling, or troubling, or interesting phenomenon with which the individual is trying to deal. As he tries to make sense of it, he also reflects on the understandings which have been implicit in his action, understandings which he surfaces, criticizes, restructures and embodies in further action.

Abridged from *The Reflective Practitioner*, Basic Books, New York, 1983

It is this entire process of reflection-in-action which is central to the 'art' by which practitioners sometimes deal well with situations of uncertainty, instability, uniqueness and value conflict.

Knowing-in-action

Once we put aside the model of technical rationality, which leads us to think of intelligent practice as an *application* of knowledge to instrumental decisions, there is nothing strange about the idea that a kind of knowing is inherent in intelligent action. Common sense admits the category of know-how, and it does not stretch common sense very much to say that the know-how is *in* the action – that a tightrope walker's know-how, for example, lies in, and is revealed by, the way he takes his trip across the wire, or that a big-league pitcher's know-how is in his way of pitching to a batter's weakness, changing his pace, or distributing his energies over the course of a game. There is nothing in common sense to make us say that know-how consists in rules or plans which we entertain in the mind prior to action. Although we sometimes think before acting, it is also true that in much of the spontaneous behaviour of skilful practice we reveal a kind of knowing which does not stem from a prior intellectual operation.

In examples like these, knowing has the following properties:

1 There are actions, recognitions and judgments which we know how to carry out spontaneously; we do not have to think about them prior to or during their performance.
2 We are often unaware of having learned to do these things; we simply find ourselves doing them.
3 In some cases, we were once aware of the understandings which were subsequently internalized in our feeling for the stuff of action. In other cases, we may never have been aware of them. In both cases, however, we are usually unable to describe the knowing which our action reveals.

It is in this sense that I speak of knowing-*in*-action, the characteristic mode of ordinary practical knowledge.

Reflecting-in-action

If common sense recognizes knowing-in-action, it also recognizes that we sometimes think about what we are doing. Phrases like 'thinking on your feet', 'keeping your wits about you', and 'learning by doing' suggest not only that we can think about doing but that we can think about doing something while doing it. Some of the most interesting examples of this process occur in the midst of a performance.

Big-league baseball pitchers speak, for example, of the experience of 'finding the groove'.

Only a few pitchers can control the whole game with pure physical ability. The rest have to learn to adjust once they're out there. If they can't, they're dead ducks.

[You get] a special feel for the ball, a kind of command that lets you repeat the exact same thing you did before that proved successful.

Finding your groove has to do with studying those winning habits and trying to repeat them every time you perform.

From technical rationality to reflection-in-action

I do not wholly understand what it means to 'find the groove'. It is clear, however, that the pitchers are talking about a particular kind of reflection. What is 'learning to adjust once you're out there'? Presumably it involves noticing how you have been pitching to the batters and how well it has been working, and on the basis of these thoughts and observations, changing the way you have been doing it. When you get a 'feel for the ball' that lets you 'repeat the exact same thing you did before that proved successful', you are noticing, at the very least, that you have been doing something right, and your 'feeling' allows you to do that something again. When you 'study those winning habits', you are thinking about the know-how that has enabled you to win. The pitchers seem to be talking about a kind of reflection on their patterns of action, on the situations in which they are performing, and on the know-how implicit in their performance. They are reflecting *on* action and, in some cases, reflecting *in* action.

When good jazz musicians improvise together, they also manifest a 'feel for' their material and they make on-the-spot adjustments to the sounds they hear. Listening to one another and to themselves, they feel where the music is going and adjust their playing accordingly. They can do this, first of all, because their collective effort at musical invention makes use of a schema – a metric, melodic and harmonic schema familiar to all the participants – which gives a predictable order to the piece. In addition, each of the musicians has at the ready a repertoire of musical figures which he can deliver at appropriate moments. Improvisation consists in varying, combining and recombining a set of figures within the schema which bounds and gives coherence to the performance. As the musicians feel the direction of the music that is developing out of their interwoven contributions, they make new sense of it and adjust their performance to the new sense they have made. They are reflecting-in-action on the music they are collectively making and on their individual contributions to it, thinking what they are doing and, in the process, evolving their way of doing it. Of course, we need not suppose that they reflect-in-action in the medium of words. More likely, they reflect through a 'feel for the music' which is not unlike the pitcher's 'feel for the ball'.

Much reflection-in-action hinges on the experience of surprise. When intuitive, spontaneous performance yields nothing more than the results expected for it, then we tend not to think about it. But when intuitive performance leads to surprises, pleasing and promising or unwanted, we may respond by reflecting-in-action. Like the baseball pitcher, we may reflect on our 'winning habits'; or like the jazz musician, on our sense of the music we have been making; or like the designer, on the misfit we have unintentionally created. In such processes, reflection tends to focus interactively on the outcomes of action, the action itself, and the intuitive knowing implicit in the action.

Practitioners do reflect *on* their knowing-in-practice. Sometimes, in the relative tranquillity of a postmortem, they think back on a project they have undertaken, a situation they have lived through, and they explore the understandings they have brought to their handling of the case. They may do this in a mood of idle speculation, or in a deliberate effort to prepare themselves for future cases. But they may also reflect on practice while they are in the midst of it. Here they reflect-in-action, but the meaning of this term needs now to be considered in terms of the complexity of knowing-in-practice.

A practitioner's reflection-in-action may not be very rapid. It is bounded by the 'action-present', the zone of time in which action can still make a difference to the situation. The action-present may stretch over minutes, hours, days or even weeks or months, depending on the pace of activity and the situational boundaries that are characteristic of the practice. Within the give-and-take of courtroom behaviour, for example, a lawyer's reflection-in-action may take place in seconds; but when the context is that of an antitrust case that drags on over years, reflection-in-action may proceed in leisurely fashion over the course of several months. An orchestra conductor may think of a single performance as a unit of practice, but in another sense a whole season is his unit. The pace and duration of episodes of reflection-in-action vary with the pace and duration of the situation of practice.

When a practitioner reflects in and on his practice, the possible objects of his reflection are as varied as the kinds of phenomena before him and the systems of knowing-in-practice which he brings to them. He may reflect on the tacit norms and appreciations which underlie a judgment, or on the strategies and theories implicit in a pattern of behaviour. He may reflect on the feeling for a situation which has led him to adopt a particular course of action, on the way in which he has framed the problem he is trying to solve, or on the role he has constructed for himself within a larger institutional context.

Reflection-in-action, in these several modes, is central to the art through which practitioners sometimes cope with the troublesome 'divergent' situations of practice. When the phenomenon at hand eludes the ordinary categories of knowledge-in-practice, presenting itself as unique or unstable, the practitioner may surface and criticize his initial understanding of the phenomenon, construct a new description of it, and test the new description by an on-the-spot experiment. Sometimes he arrives at a new theory of the phenomenon by articulating a feeling he has about it.

When he finds himself stuck in a problematic situation which he cannot readily convert to a manageable problem, he may construct a new way of setting the problem – a new frame which, in what I shall call a 'frame experiment', he tries to impose on the situation.

When he is confronted with demands that seem incompatible or inconsistent, he may respond by reflecting on the appreciations which he and others have brought to the situation. Conscious of a dilemma, he may attribute it to the way in which he has set his problem, or even to the way in which he has framed his role. He may then find a way of integrating, or choosing among, the values at stake in the situation.

When someone reflects-in-action, he becomes a researcher in the practice context. He is not dependent on the categories of established theory and technique, but constructs a new theory of the unique case. His inquiry is not limited to a deliberation about means which depends on a prior agreement about ends. He does not keep means and ends separate, but defines them interactively as he frames a problematic situation. He does not separate thinking from doing, ratiocinating his way to a decision which he must later convert to action. Because his experimenting is a kind of action, implementation is built into his inquiry. Thus reflection-in-action can proceed, even in situations of uncertainty or uniqueness, because it is not bound by the dichotomies of technical rationality.

Although reflection-in-action is an extraordinary process, it is not a rare event. Indeed, for some reflective practitioners it is the core of practice. Nevertheless, because professionalism is still mainly identified with technical expertise, reflection-in-action is not generally accepted – even by those who do it – as a legitimate form of professional knowing.

Many practitioners, locked into a view of themselves as technical experts, find nothing in the world of practice to occasion reflection. They have become too skilful at techniques of selective inattention, junk categories and situational control, techniques which they use to preserve the constancy of their knowledge-in-practice. For them, uncertainty is a threat; its admission is a sign of weakness. Others, more inclined toward and adept at reflection-in-action, nevertheless feel profoundly uneasy because they cannot say what they know how to do, cannot justify its quality or rigour.

For these reasons, the study of reflection-in-action is critically important. The dilemma of rigour or relevance may be dissolved if we can develop an epistemology of practice which places technical problem solving within a broader context of reflective inquiry, shows how reflection-in-action may be rigorous in its own right, and links the art of practice in uncertainty and uniqueness to the scientist's art of research. We may thereby increase the legitimacy of reflection-in-action and encourage its broader, deeper and more rigorous use.

3

LICENSE AND MANDATE

EVERETT C. HUGHES

An occupation consists in part in the implied or explicit *license* that some people claim and are given to carry out certain activities rather different from those of other people and do so in exchange for money, goods, or services. Generally, if the people in the occupation have any sense of identity and solidarity, they will also claim a *mandate* to define – not merely for themselves, but for others as well – proper conduct with respect to the matters concerned in their work. They also will seek to define, and possibly succeed in defining, not merely proper conduct but even modes of thinking and belief for everyone individually and for the body social and politic with respect to some broad area of life which they believe to be in their occupational domain. The license may be merely technical; it may, however, extend to broad areas of behavior and thought. It may include a whole style of life, or it may be confined to carrying out certain technical activities which others may not carry out – at least not officially or for a reward. The mandate may be small and narrow, or the contrary.

License, as an attribute of an occupation, is usually thought of as specific legal permission to pursue the occupation. I am thinking of something broader. Society, by its nature, consists in part of both allowing and expecting some people to do things which other people are not allowed or expected to do. Most occupations – especially those considered professions – include as part of their being a license to deviate in some measure from some common modes of behavior. Professions, perhaps more than other kinds of occupation, also claim a broad legal, moral and intellectual mandate. Not only do the practitioners, by virtue of gaining admission to the charmed circle of the profession, individually exercise a license to do things others do not do, but collectively they presume to tell society what is good and right for it in a broad and crucial aspect of life. Indeed, they set the very terms of thinking about it. When such a presumption is granted as legitimate, a profession in the full sense has come into being. The nature and extent of both license and mandate, their relations to each other and the circumstances and conflicts in which they expand or contract are crucial areas of

Abridged from *The Sociological Eye*, Aldine Press, Chicago, 1977 study, not merely for occupations, but for society itself. Such licenses and mandates are the prime manifestation of the *moral* division of labor – that is, of the processes by which differing moral functions are distributed among the members of society, as individuals and as categories of individuals. These moral functions differ from one another in both kind and measure. Some people seek and get special responsibility for defining values and for establishing and enforcing sanctions over a certain aspect of life; the differentiation of moral and social functions involves both the area of social behavior in question and the degree of responsibility and power. Since this is the aspect of occupations to which I give most emphasis in this article, I will illustrate it in a manner which I hope will stimulate discussion and research.

Many occupations cannot be carried out without guilty knowledge. The priest cannot mete out penance without becoming an expert in sin; else how may he know the mortal from the venial? To carry out his mandate to tell people what books they may or may not read and what thoughts and beliefs they must espouse or avoid, he must become a connoisseur of the forbidden. Only a master theologian can think up really subtle heresies; hence Satan is of necessity a fallen angel. A layman would be but an amateur with a blunderbuss where a sharpshooter is wanted. The poor priest, as part of the exchange involved in his license to hear confessions and to absolve and his mandate to tell us what's what, has to convince the lay world that he does not yield to the temptations of his privileged position; he puts on a uniform and lives a celibate existence. These are compensating or counter-deviations from the common way of dressing and living; they would not be admired, or perhaps even tolerated, in people who have no special function to justify them. The priest, in short, has both intellectual and moral leeway, and perhaps must have them if he is to carry out the rest of his license. He carries a burden of guilty knowledge.

The lawyer, the policeman, the physician, the reporter, the scientist, the scholar, the diplomat, the private secretary, all of them must have license to get – and, in some degree, to keep secret – some order of guilty knowledge. It may be guilty in that it is knowledge that a layman would be obliged to reveal, or in that the withholding of it from the public or from authorities compromises the integrity of the man who so withholds it, as in the case of the policeman who keeps connections with the underworld or the diplomat who has useful friends abroad. Most occupations rest upon some bargain about receiving, guarding and giving out communications. The license to keep this bargain is of the essence of many occupations.

The prototype of all guilty knowledge is, however, a different, potentially shocking, way of looking at things. Every occupation must look relatively at some order of events, objects or ideas. These things must be classified, seen in comparative light; their behavior must be analyzed and, if possible, predicted. A suitable technical language must be developed in which one may talk to one's colleagues about them. This technical, therefore relative, attitude must be adopted toward the very people whom one serves; no profession can operate without license to talk in shocking terms behind the backs of its clients. Sometimes an occupation must adopt this objective, comparative attitude toward things which are very dear to other people or which are the object of absolutely held values and sentiments. I suppose that this ultimate license is the greatest when the people who exercise it, being guardians of precious things, are in a position to do great damage. (No one is in so good a position to steal as the banker.)

Related to the license to think relatively about dear things and absolute values is the license to do dangerous things. I refer not to the danger run by the steeplejack and the men who navigate submarines, for that is danger to themselves. (Even so, there is a certain disposition to pay them off with a license to run slightly amok when the one comes down and the other up to solid ground.) I speak, rather, of the license of the doctor to cut and dose, of the priest to play with men's salvation, of the scientist to split atoms; or simply of the danger that advice given a person may be wrong, or that work done may be unsuccessful or cause damage.

License of all these kinds may lie at the root of that modicum of aggressive suspicion which most laymen feel toward professionals, and of that raging and fanatical anger which burns chronically in some people and which at times becomes popular reaction. Many anti-vivisectionists do not love beasts more but love doctors less, suspecting them of loving some parts of their work too much. It is a chronic protest. Of course, there are people who believe that they have suffered injury from incompetent or careless work or that they have been exploited by being acted upon more for the professional's increase of knowledge or income than for their own well-being.

Herein lies the whole question of what the bargain is between those who receive a service and those who give it, and of the circumstances in which it is protested by either party. Of equal or greater sociological significance is the problem of a general questioning of license or mandate. Social unrest often shows itself precisely in such questioning of the prerogatives of the leading professions. In time of crisis, there may arise a general demand for more conformity to lay modes of thought and discourse.

One of the major professional deviations of mind, a form of guilty knowledge, is the objective and relative attitude mentioned above. One order of relativity has to do with time; the professional may see the present in longer perspective. The present may be, for him, more crucial in that it is seen as a link in a causative chain of events; the consequences of present action may be seen as more inevitable, rippling down through time. The emergency, in this sense, may appear greater to the professional than to the layman. In another sense, it appears less crucial, since the professional sees the present situation in comparison with others; it is not unique, and hence the emergency is not so great as laymen see it. In time of crisis, detachment appears the most perilous deviation of all, hence the one least to be tolerated. Their deviation, in these cases, consists in a drastic reversal of what many laymen consider the urgent as against the less urgent aspects of our situation. And it arises from their license to think in different terms.

Militant religious sects give us an instructive illustration. They ordinarily, in Christianity at least, consist of people convinced that they are all in imminent danger of damnation. So long as they remain militant sects, they are in chronic crisis. It is perhaps not without sociological significance that they do not tolerate a clergy, or much differentiation of function at all. It is as if they sense that professionalizing inevitably brings some detachment, some relative and comparative attitude. In a large society the clergy are generally more ardent than the laity; a sect might almost be defined as a religious group in which the opposite is true. Inquisitions to the contrary, it is probable that the professional clergy tend to be more tolerant than ardent laymen. Although it may seem paradoxical to suggest it, one may seriously ask under what circumstances religious people tolerate a professional clergy.

The typical reform movement is an attempt of laymen to redefine values and to change action about some matter over which some occupation (or group of occupations or faction within an occupation) holds a mandate. The movement may simply push for faster or more drastic action where the profession moves slowly or not at all; it may be a direct attack upon the dominant philosophy of the profession, as in attempts to change the manner of distributing medical care. The power of an occupation to protect its license and to maintain its mandate and the circumstances in which licenses and mandates are attacked, lost or changed are matters for investigation. (And one must not overlook movements within a profession.) While there has been a good deal of study of the political activities of occupational groups, the subject has been somewhat misunderstood as a result of the strong fiction of political neutrality of professions in our society.

One can think of many variations of license and mandate, and of the relations between them. School teachers in our society have little license to think thoughts that others do not think; they are not even allowed to think the nastier thoughts that others *do* think. Their mandate seems limited to minor matters of pedagogy; it does not include definition of the fundamental issues of what children shall be taught. Educational policy is given into their hands very grudgingly, although they have a good deal of power by default.

Study of the license of artists and entertainers could also yield much knowledge concerning the degrees of conformity possible in a society and the consequences of trying to reduce deviation to something like zero. For these occupations seem to require, if they are to produce the very things for which society will give them a living of sorts (or, in some cases, unheard-of opulence), at least some people who deviate widely from the norms more or less adhered to and firmly espoused by other people. Their license is, however, periodically in a parlous state, and there seems no guarantee that it will not, at any moment, be attacked.

4

IT'S NOT WHAT YOU DO BUT WHO YOU ARE: CARING ROLES AND CARING RELATIONSHIPS

JAN WALMSLEY

It is perhaps a truism by now that unpaid carers are unsung heroines, or heroes, whose unremitting hard work often compares favourably with the shifts worked by paid carers. This article seeks to explore three interrelated themes:

1 The fact that in caring work the relationship between the carer and the dependent person is the crucial determinant of whether payment is made.
2 The difficulties posed for paid carers by the similarities in the tasks performed by paid and unpaid carers, and the way paid carers deal with those difficulties.
3 The impact payment has on the caring relationship; and whether unpaid care is 'better' than paid care.

It's the relationship that counts

> Mum, she got confused you know. I used to do everything . . . I was in the kitchen, in front of the stove, cookin' milk or something and she used to say 'come in here, don't you dare go out there and do the milk' . . . I just couldn't go anywhere. I had to stop in every weekend and look after her, she was a handful. ('Gwen', research interview with author, 1989)

Gwen is a woman with learning difficulties. She attends an Adult Training Centre as a client, but was, for a time, the primary carer for a woman with dementia. This was not because of her skill or her professional qualifications but because the woman was her mother. Ironically, Gwen has always been excluded from paid employment; yet no one questioned her duty to perform the task of caring for her mother within the confines of the family home.

Compare this with the following:

An elderly patient – a lady in her seventies – confided to her primary nurse that she was badly missing her dog, her only companion for many years . . . This feeling of separation wasn't helping her to get any better. The nurse discussed the problem with the patient and together they arrived at a solution. With the patient's agreement the nurse phoned the neighbour and arranged for the dog to be brought to the hospital. (Nursing recruitment advert, 1991)

Nursing is a skilled job, for which applicants require academic qualifications and extensive training. Yet the advert emphasizes the nurse's human caring qualities. An advert may seem trivial, yet it carries an image the profession seeks to impart about itself to potential recruits.

Caring implies both an activity and a relationship: 'care comprises a social relationship as well as a physical task' (Qureshi and Walker, 1989). Interestingly, the case of Gwen, the unpaid carer, highlights the labour of caring, while the nursing advert suggests the importance of the care relationship for the skilled professional. Caring is, as Hilary Graham (1983) puts it, both love and labour.

It is not uncommon for relatives – daughters, daughters-in-law, sons, spouses – to care for highly dependent relatives. The extent and the burden of unpaid care has been well documented (Nissel and Bonnerjea, 1982; Baldwin, 1985; Briggs and Oliver, 1985; Lewis and Meredith, 1988). Recent figures from the Equal Opportunities Commission show that 14 per cent of all adults are carers (EOC, 1991).

It is paradoxical that because of the kin relationship, a person, often but not always a female relative like Gwen, acquires the role of 'carer'. Whether or not Gwen had an affectionate relationship with her mother was immaterial. By contrast, the worker who has the role of carer, such as the nurse quoted above, is often expected to develop a relationship with the cared-for person which is 'caring'. There are two contrasting meanings of the term 'relationship': the quality of care crucially depends on the *affective* relationship between carer and cared for, yet the role of carer can be assigned to someone because of their *kin* relationship rather than because of any affection, or any wish to care.

This confusion is highlighted by schemes which pay 'ordinary people' to provide caring services (Ungerson, 1990). These include payments to people for fostering highly dependent people, such as disabled people or people with mental handicaps (Leat and Gay, 1987), and the Kent Community Care Scheme (Challis and Davies, 1986). Hazel Qureshi sees such schemes as exploitative of the carers employed, almost invariably women (Qureshi, 1990). Such is the ideological commitment to care being done for 'love' rather than money, and such is the economic commitment to providing care on the cheap, that people employed in these schemes are given not wages, but payments. They are expected to develop a caring relationship with those they care for. They are not unionized, and have no occupational pensions, sick pay or holiday pay, or any of the benefits associated with employment.

There is no overtime payment for foster carers, though they are on duty 24 hours a day; they can claim no expenses for food, outings, respite care, wear and tear, clothing, laundry, extra space (Williams, 1990). The common-sense view that care is done for love is so pervasive that hardly anyone, including foster parents, questions the poor conditions of work.

These schemes illustrate the importance attached to care as a relationship, rather than care as a role. Carers are expected to be motivated by altruism rather than cash. As Clare Ungerson describes it (1990: 20): 'the assumption is that nominally paid workers will provide better-quality care since they are doing the work for love rather than money.' In this way they are similar to unpaid carers who are also deemed to be caring for altruisitic, not financial, motives.

Workers as carers

Many people are paid a wage for the type of caring work others undertake out of a sense of love or duty, or for the nominal payments offered to foster parents and others. Clare Ungerson (1990) argues that the distinction traditionally drawn in Britain between paid and unpaid caring work is misleading, and that in Scandinavian countries there is no such distinction. In Scandinavia the term 'care-giving work' encompasses all types of work where the care-giver provides consistent and reliable care for a person who, through age, infirmity or youth is unable to care for herself (Waerness, 1990). The dichotomy in Britain between formal and informal (paid and unpaid) care is, Ungerson says, one which perpetuates the public/private split, in which work undertaken in the domestic (private) context is invisible and unappreciated.

Clare Ungerson (1987) analysed the skills possessed by mothers as carers. It is an impressive list: it includes social and communication skills, skills in domestic tasks, information gathering, punctuality and reliability, and the ability to act autonomously over long periods of time. Such an analysis reinforces Phillips and Taylor's (1980: 82) statement that 'far from being an objective economic fact, skill is often an ideological category imposed on certain types of work by virtue of the sex and power of the workers who perform it.' That is, skills do not exist in a vacuum with one skill inherently more valuable than another, but are valued according to who is using them. Possession of the skills employed by carers, might, in another context, stand a person in good stead in the employment market.

What does this mean for paid carers? Many, perhaps most, health and social welfare workers make a living from 'caring'. Indeed, 'the caring professions' is a term often used to describe social work, nursing, physiotherapy, occupational therapy and even primary school teaching. However, any claims such workers may have to professional status is challenged if their sole *raison d'être* is to care. How can they command respect, high salaries, autonomy and all the other benefits that come from being professional if what they do is the sort of work that 14 per cent of the population do for nothing? There is a variety of responses: for convenience, examples have been selected from the world of nursing, but that is not to suggest that only nursing is beset by these contradictions.

One response is to emphasize technical aspects of the work: as Hewa and Hetherington (1990: 179), writing in a North American context put it, 'the burgeoning mechanistic approach to the human body makes modern health care services increasingly devoid of human values.' In a recent recruitment advertisement for nursing the glossy photograph shows a young woman in a nurse's uniform sitting next to a patient in a hospital bed with a computer at her side. The advert cleverly juxtaposes the traditional image of the nurse caring for a sick person with a high-status, high-technology gadget. Clearly, the photo tells us, nurses don't just 'care', they are also highly specialized, highly trained users of the latest in computer technology.

Another response, illustrated by the nursing advert cited earlier, is to portray the nurse as a sensitive and caring person, able to overcome the normal assumptions of her role by inviting the patient's dog into the hospital. The professional nurse can construe it as her duty to look after strangers with real care and compassion, regardless of the individual's personal qualities – what Campbell (1984) calls 'moderated love'.

A third response, perhaps more characteristic of care assistants and home helps than of qualified staff, is to blur the boundaries of the paid caring role so that services are rendered over and above the time and duties paid for. Care is both labour and love. Caring, whether formal or informal, is not always susceptible to the dictates of the shift. Hazel Qureshi (1990: 76) says of the helpers in the Kent Community Care Scheme (in which neighbours are paid a small sum for caring tasks) 'it is possible for helpers to become trapped into continuing to provide care for an individual even though they may no longer feel they are receiving sufficient returns.'

Recent discussions in the nursing literature show the profession agonising over the true role of the nurse. Jean McFarlane (1988: 11): writes 'Because of the lack of scientific precision in the concept of caring it fails to provide a blueprint for scientifically based professional action in modern health care.' Alison Kitson (1988) accuses nurses of concentrating on their instrumental role (helping patients get better) as opposed to their expressive role (helping patients feel better): 'I believe that the confusion which affects the nursing profession in its thinking and its service is related to the domination of rational objective technological modes of thought over the emotional, subjective, more personal expression of life' (Kitson, 1988: 26).

Members of the caring professions have very real skills and knowledge, as have other paid carers such as home helps and care assistants. It is, however, perhaps unfortunate that the apparently everyday mundane qualities required to provide affective care are so undervalued as to be frequently ignored in both the training and the practice of those professionals (see Craft, Section 4; Middleton, 1987; Brechin and Swain, 1989). Kitson is not alone in recalling that when you are ill or in pain you are in need of both care and cure. It is perhaps a consequence of the undervaluing of unpaid care as an activity which has led to a tendency on the part of some professionals to emphasize 'technical rationality' (Hewa and Hetherington, 1990; Schön, 1991) at the expense of the domain of the emotions which is characteristic of good-quality care in the widest sense.

Paid care versus unpaid care

Why is paid care sometimes seen as inferior to unpaid care? This assumption is pervasive in 'common-sense' attitudes to, for example, putting an elderly person into a home rather than having him or her cared for by relatives; or parents employing a childminder rather than staying at home to care for young children. Such is the hostility to the alternatives that it is no surprise to find Netta Coston saying of her handicapped son 'I pray to God he dies before I do' (the *Guardian*, 24 June 1991). It is a view that has been reinforced by politicians – 'Caring families are the basis of a society that cares' (Jim Callaghan, quoted in the *Guardian* 23 May 1978) – and by government policy documents such as the Griffiths Report which sees community care as having the aim of maintaining the individual in his or her own home (see Qureshi, 1990). Feminists such as Janet Finch and Dulcie Groves have pointed out that 'informal care' provided in the home is ideologically convenient because it is care on the cheap, carried out primarily but not exclusively by women (Finch and Groves, 1983: 221–4).

Recipients of care are rarely asked what they prefer. Research by Lewis and Meredith (1988) and Qureshi and Walker (1989) shows a pervading assumption that older people want their relatives to take on the task of caring for them when they are no longer able to care for themselves. In many cases this is correct. However, Qureshi (1990) quotes research findings which suggest that at least some elderly people prefer paid helpers to family help, and that payment for services offers a dignity and a sense of control which is absent from care by family members.

Yvonne Hall, a contributor to the Open University (1991) pack 'Disability – Identity, Sexuality and Relationships', echoes this point: 'although there are a great deal of hazards and difficulties in being placed in residential care it's frequently the first opportunity that a disabled person has to get away from the family home.' Disabled people have been critical of the way paid care is provided, but still see it as desirable to have alternatives to relying on the help of relatives to perform the tasks of daily living (Morris, 1991).

Conclusion

I set out to describe some of the contradictions in caring. Caring implies both a set of tasks and a relationship, whether the carer is paid or unpaid.

Good-quality care requires that the carer develops an affective relationship with the person they are caring for so that care can be offered in a way that is sensitive and maintains the dignity of the person being cared for. Arguably, the skills required by carers are similar whether the carer is paid or not.

Various solutions have been promulgated to resolve the contradictions inherent in care. Ungerson (1990) argues for payment of carers regardless of the relationship, thus obliterating the distinctions between formal and informal care: all care becomes paid-for care. Service brokerage is an alternative formulation which envisages the cared-for person as the 'employer' of the carer, thus subverting the dependency which caring entails (Brown and Ringma, Section 3). And, in earlier times, institutionalization was on offer to certain dependent people, such as those with learning difficulties, the advice to parents being to 'put him away and forget about him' (Walmsley, 1991).

None of the 'solutions' is unproblematic, and it is not my purpose to resolve the contradictions. Rather, at this point, it is appropriate to return to the three interrelated themes set out at the beginning of this article.

In caring work the relationship between the carer and the person in receipt of care determines whether payment is made for the work. Relatives, if they accept the task, are expected to care as a part of their relationship, not as paid workers. Furthermore, Qureshi and Walker (1989) have shown that the availability of a relative to care makes it less likely that professional support services will be available to the carer. There is rarely a partnership between informal and formal care to sustain the carer and to offer her relief.

Similarities between the tasks performed by paid and unpaid carers have posed some difficulties for professional carers. These have sometimes inclined professionals to emphasize the attributes they possess which set them apart from unpaid carers, such as a body of professional knowledge and technical skills; or, alternatively, to blur the boundaries so that they become more like unpaid carers, and emphasize the relationship they have with the person, rather than their role as paid worker.

It is not axiomatic that unpaid care is superior to paid care. Some elderly people quoted in research studies, such as Qureshi and Walker's *The Caring Relationship* (1989), indicate a preference for paid care; and for younger disabled people the provision of paid care may be essential to offer them an opportunity to leave the family home. A choice of options both for carers and people requiring care is a more attractive proposition than the assumption that wherever possible families care for their own.

Perhaps what is most important for vulnerable people is the care relationship, regardless of who undertakes it. Sensitivity to the needs and wishes of the dependent person, empathy and acceptance, are hallmarks of good-quality care and it is those aspects of the role of carer which we should seek to promote. There is no 'right' answer. The ability to negotiate the type of care offered is a skill worthy of respect, whatever the status of the person offering it.

References

Baldwin, S. (1985) *The Costs of Caring: Families with Disabled Children*. London: Routledge & Kegan Paul.

Brechin, A. and Swain, J. (1989) 'Creating a "working alliance" with people with learning difficulties', in A. Brechin and J. Walmsley (eds), *Making Connections*. Sevenoaks: Hodder & Stoughton.

Briggs, A. and Oliver, J. (eds) (1985) *Caring*. London: Routledge & Kegan Paul.

Campbell, A. (1984) *Moderated Love: a Theology of Professional Care*. London: SPCK.

Challis, D. and Davies, B. (1986) *Case Management in Community Care*. Aldershot: Gower.

Equal Opportunities Commission (1991) *Care to Work*. London: EOC.

Finch, J. and Groves, D. (1983) (eds) *A Labour of Love: Women, Work and Caring*. London: Routledge & Kegan Paul.

Graham, H. (1983) 'Caring: a labour of love', in J. Finch and D. Groves (eds), *A Labour of Love: Women, Work and Caring*. London: Routledge & Kegan Paul.

Hewa, S. and Hetherington, R. (1990) 'Specialists without spirit: crisis in the nursing profession', *Journal of Medical Ethics* 16: 179–84.

Kitson, A. (1988) 'On the concept of nursing care', in S. Fairbairn and G. Fairbairn (eds), *Ethical Issues in Caring*. Aldershot: Gower.

Leat, D. and Gay, P. (1987) *Paying for Care: a Study of Policy and Practice in Paid Care Schemes*. London: Policy Studies Institute.

Lewis, J. and Meredith, B. (1988) *Daughters who Care: Daughters Caring for their Mothers at Home*. London: Routledge.

McFarlane, J. (1988) 'Nursing: a paradigm of caring', in S. Fairbairn and G. Fairbairn (eds), *Ethical Issues in Caring*. Aldershot: Gower.

Middleton, S. (1987) 'Carers' relationships with people with mental handicaps: the need for guidance', *Mental Handicap*, 16: 140–2.

Morris, J. (1991) *Pride against Prejudice*. London: The Women's Press.

Nissel, M. and Bonnerjea, L. (1982) *Family Care of the Handicapped Elderly: Who Pays?* London: Policy Studies Institute.

Open University, Department of Health and Social Welfare (1991) *Disability – Indentity, Sexuality and Relationships*. Home Study text and Audio cassette, K665Y. Milton Keynes: Open University.

Phillips, A. and Taylor, B. (1980) 'Sex and skill: notes towards a feminist economics', *Feminist Review*, 6: 79–88.

Qureshi, H. (1990) 'Boundaries between formal and informal care giving work', in C. Ungerson (ed.), *Gender and Caring*. Hemel Hempstead: Harvester Wheatsheaf.

Qureshi, H. and Walker, A. (1989) *The Caring Relationship*. Basingstoke: Macmillan.

Schön, D. (1991) *The Reflective Practitioner*. Aldershot: Avebury Press.

Ungerson, C. (1987) *Policy is Personal*. London: Tavistock Publications.

Ungerson, C. (1990) 'The language of care', in C. Ungerson (ed.), *Gender and Caring*. Hemel Hempstead: Harvester Wheatsheaf.

Waerness, K. (1990) 'Informal and formal care in old age: what is wrong with the new ideology in Scandinavia today?', in C. Ungerson (ed.), *Gender and Caring*. Hemel Hempstead: Harvester Wheatsheaf.

Walmsley, J. (1991) 'People with learning difficulties: experiences of care', PhD research in progress, Open University, Milton Keynes.

Williams, F. (1990) 'Media notes', in *Mental Handicap: Changing Perspectives*. Milton Keynes: Open University.

5

PROFESSIONAL IDEOLOGY OR ORGANIZATIONAL TRIBALISM? THE HEALTH SERVICE–SOCIAL WORK DIVIDE

GILLIAN DALLEY

Central government policy has, in the past two decades, accepted the stream of recommendations about teamwork coming from a variety of reports. The need for effective teamworking in the provision of coordinated services was stressed by the report of the Butler-Sloss Inquiry (1988) into child abuse in Cleveland. It recommended the establishment of multi-disciplinary teams with the 'intention to foster teamwork and co-ordination of activity without undermining primary professional responsibility or agency function'. The team, then, has been and still is seen by policy-makers and planners as the main instrument for achieving collaborative relationships between professions and between agencies in the provision and delivery of integrated care.

But just as central government was making a commitment to the concept of the team and to teamworking, reports from practitioners and from academic research began to demonstrate the problems arising from attempts to initiate teamworking. Evidence taken by the Harding committee and cited in the report (Harding Report, 1981) from practitioners and managers in the field saw problems arising from three different sources: one was to do with poor accommodation and lack of resources which imposed too great a burden on health visiting and district nursing staff; another was the structural problem – GPs were independent contractors while nursing staff were part of the health authority management structure; the third was the difference in outlook between the different professional groups involved and the lack of understanding of each other's roles and orientations that this involved.

Much has been written specifically on the workings (and failings) of 'the team' in the health and social services worlds (see, for example, Lonsdale

Abridged from R. Taylor and J. Ford (eds), *Social Work and Health Care*, Jessica Kingsley Publications, London, 1989 et al., 1980; Bruce, 1981), often using the concept of ideology as an explanatory factor in describing why teams often do not work well. Writing about the relationship between health visitors and social workers, Dingwall (1977) suggested that differences in attitudes and beliefs had created a climate of hostility which had become self-fulfilling. Huntington (1981), in a study of social work and general practice, describes the two 'occupational cultures' which each of the professional groups inhabits and which inhibit practitioners from developing collaborative working relationships. A study of collaborative relationships in the primary health care setting by Cartlidge et al. (1987) concludes that levels of collaboration are low.

The view, then, is widely held that differences in the belief systems and attitude sets of the various professional groups inhibits cooperation. The medical practitioner is seen to be held deep in the grip of the 'medical model'; the social worker cleaves to a psychosocial perspective on the world which contests the individualized, disease-centred medical view. Nurses, of all sorts, are trapped in a deferential relationship with doctors which they resent but from which they cannot escape. This, of course, caricatures the position to a certain degree but much of the evidence available points towards this interpretation.

The research evidence

In research conducted by the present writer to examine professional attitudes to a number of policy issues (concerning, in particular, community care and policies for the priority groups) patterns of views which were distinctive of particular professional groups certainly emerged. Further, many instances of difficulties in interprofessional working were also described. Two hundred and thirty-six people were interviewed in three Scottish locations; they were drawn from a wide variety of professional groupings within the health and social services: hospital consultants, GPs, health visitors, district nurses, ward sisters, NHS managers, basic grade social workers and social work managers of all levels.

Interprofessional working

The most numerous instances of incompatibility in working together arose between GPs and social workers; but there were many other difficulties recorded, between social workers and health visitors, between health visitors and GPs, between GPs and hospital consultants and between hospital-based social workers and consultants. Difficulties were expressed in both the practical terms of organizational and structural issues and the abstract terms of orientation and attitudes. For instance, one GP found difficulties in working with social workers because of the way their work was organized: 'I think again one of the difficulties is that the way the social work teams are arranged – one of them has a particular responsibility for the elderly, one for the handicapped, one for children, so that again tends to cut across what we do.' Another GP referred to the competition between medicine and social work in the definition of problems: 'doctors and social workers – again you vie for whether a problem is a social or a medical problem . . . to establish precedence there'.

In the case of a district nurse, difficulties in working with both GPs and social workers were described:

> I feel it very much . . . it's very frustrating . . . You're a buffer in the fact that you've got the doctor you liaise with, she comes back and says I want this that and the other, you go to the social work department and get nothing from them. And I feel, well, you know, I thought it was teamwork and here's me going in, and I just felt nothing was being done.

In the case of social workers, hostility towards health visitors was sometimes expressed by them in terms of differences in fundamental attitudes:

> Yes, I think there is a difference between our attitudes certainly, from our experience with health visitors. And their whole training has been to take a person into care and to – in many ways take away their rights, I suppose – and our training leans to the opposite point of view almost and I think there is some kind of friction in our attitudes on many points.

Similar hostility was felt by some social workers towards GPs:

> I think that there certainly is a lack of understanding by a large number of GPs of the social work role. It's a suspicion and it's also at its worst (because they think) that if they do begin to develop a relationship then there's a floodgate opening . . . that's again to do with the structure and the pressure they can be under as much as any real recalcitrance.

Evidence such as this, then, demonstrates a widespread sense of discontent with regard to the success of interprofessional working. Explanations of the failure to collaborate successfully is put down both to structural difficulties – the way the services operate, differences in organization, lack of understanding about the pressures under which colleagues in different professions have to work and so on – and to differences in approach and orientation. Just as academic analysts have identified 'professional ideology' as a barrier to cooperation, so practitioners recognize the same constraints. A senior social worker, who led a team working exclusively in a primary care setting in a health centre with attachments to a number of group practices, expressed her disappointment at their failure to establish successful interprofessional working:

> I have felt disappointed in the level of coordination – you know, I feel that things should be better coordinated in a primary care team, and that patient management

ought to be optimum – but, I mean, dreadful things happen – and people fall between, even where there's a nurse, a health visitor, a doctor and a social worker. And everybody is assuming that somebody else is doing it . . . I think professional orientation (causes it). Partly the problem is that health visitors and nurses feel they can do nothing without asking the doctor.

The role of professional ideology

Practitioners may *believe* and report that they view things differently from those in other professional groups; it is important from an analytical standpoint, however, to investigate how far such ideological cleavages exist in reality. The interview study covered a wide range of topics concerning both the politico-moral domain (questions, for example, about the balance of social responsibility for the care of dependent people, as between family and state; the role of voluntarism in welfare) and the practical issues of resource allocation for the priority groups (covering, for example, the relationship between institutional and community care; the degree to which resources should be invested in prevention or withdrawn from the acute sector).

When responses to the politico-moral issues are examined, it is clear that significant differences between professional groups emerge. Most striking was the contrast between GPs and many of the other groups in respect of their views about the question of responsibility. More than three-quarters of GPs interviewed felt that it was predominantly the responsibility of families to care for dependent members, as opposed to just over a third of basic grade social workers and half of health visitors. In contrast, almost two-thirds of social workers felt it was a matter of state responsibility or joint responsibility (between the state and families) as did almost half of the health visitors and social work and NHS managers. District nurses were more like GPs though less overwhelmingly supportive of the 'family responsibility' position.

The following remarks of one GP were characteristic of many: 'Morally it should be the family (taking responsibility) but then we're not living in a very moral age. And the families just don't want to know – the hard fact is that people really don't want to have this burden.' A majority of district nurses mirrored this view: 'I see it in this country the way we run things, then I see it's got to be the family has the prime responsibility often the family should and could help a lot more – because it's their folks, they should have a responsibility to their own people.'

Social workers, on the other hand, viewed things rather differently: 'Well I think we live in a society which has admitted by stating it's a democracy . . . that the community is responsible for the community . . . well, actually, well the state, I think I have to say the community and the state.' Health visitors spoke in a similar vein: 'I have great sympathy for relatives. I think it should be a state responsibility. Um, it would be nice to see relatives getting more involved with the elderly – er – but it can be very difficult for them. They can be made to feel very guilty if they don't look after their relatives.'

Perceptions about the public tended to match views about the issue of responsibility. Those who believed it was a family responsibility to care tended also to believe that the public in general was reluctant to care and that too much was expected of professionally provided services. A number of GPs appeared very judgemental in their views of the public: 'I would say the majority [of the public] opt out. Fewer and fewer folk are going to upset their own lives at all to cope with their own relatives. I think they're being selfish and not accepting of the position.' But those who saw a greater responsibility lying with the state, tended also to be less judgemental of the public. They were more ready to see the strain and stress that is often involved in caring for a dependent relative and felt that the public had the right to expect more from the services. A social worker said: 'I find the majority of them are [willing to care]. It's surprising the amount of wives, spouses, that accept the nature of their spouse's illness – mental or whatever . . . and stand by them.' Some health visitors felt similarly:

> I don't think so [that people expect too much of the services]. I feel that the people I've come across who have some quite hard jobs with elderly relatives, I think actually sometimes put up with quite a lot more than perhaps I would expect to myself . . . yes, I think the majority of them are [willing to care]. I mean, saying that, I have come across people who just don't want to know at all. But again, few and far between.

Fewer district nurses were so sympathetic. Most were more sceptical about the public: 'they're liable to say "Oh get the nurse in, you should have a nurse to do that." I think people become selfish – they don't realize just how many dependent people there are . . . Nowadays a number of them are not [prepared to care] – people are too busy with their own lives now.'

On the evidence derived from the interview study, it seems clear that ideological differences emerge on these issues between some groups of 'front-line' practitioners located in both the health and social services. At one extreme are the GPs who hold strong and judgemental views about the moral responsibility of families to care; at the other extreme are social workers who have a more open view about the moral position: the state has an underlying responsibility, although families also have a role. They tend not to 'judge' the public by perceiving it as morally deficient in failing to accept responsibility. Located somewhere midway between the two are health visitors and district nurses.

Force of circumstance: the conditioning of everyday action

Further investigation of front-line workers' attitudes demonstrates a degree of *similarity* in views on some issues. This is often most clearly revealed

when their views are set against the views of other categories of respondents
– managers and hospital-based staff, for example. Managers in both the
health and social services, for example, frequently showed a greater
empathy for the public than the community-based front-line practitioners
who, in fact, had the greatest contact with them. In spite of the ideological
contrasts between, say, GPs and social workers, or health visitors and social
workers, these were frequently cross-cut by contrasts between all of them on
the one hand and managers, removed from the field, on the other.

Thus managers could express positive feelings towards the public
untempered by direct knowledge of the reality of the circumstances – both
the difficulties faced by, and created by, the public and the heavy strain
placed on some field staff by those difficulties. Field staff were often torn by
feeling sympathy for their clients but also frustrated and pressured by them.
A sector administrator, for example, recognized that he did not have direct
experience of the problem: 'As I say, not coming directly in contact with a lot
of them, but I do obviously speak a lot to nursing officers and medical
people . . . but you do hear of families doing this and that . . . and who do
realize that they have a role to play.' This respondent thought highly
of the public but tended to be critical of some practitioners. He recounted a
case where a family had requested the use of a particular sort of bed – in his
view, legitimately – but the nurse involved had felt them to be too
demanding; he was critical of GPs, suggesting that they did too little for
dependent people.

In contrast, were the views of practitioners who held more jaundiced
views of the public. A health visitor, for example, said:

> I think it's because the great wave of unemployment and whatnot has tended – I'm
> talking about the people in this area, not about the people outwith it, but in this
> area the dependency on state aid is vast and they do an awful lot of taking and not
> a lot of giving, I'm afraid . . . They don't want to take responsibility for themselves.
> Not here. My caseload is made up of people who have not taken responsibility for
> their own lives, therefore that's why they run into social problems, because they
> don't think.

And yet this was a respondent who believed firmly that the state was
responsible for providing care and support to those who were dependent.

In respect of issues which were the direct concern of managers and more
removed from field staff – issues of resource allocation and strategic policy,
for example – front-line practitioners tended to be able to offer answers
directly, while managers responded in a much more circumscribed way. For
them, the dilemmas were real; for practitioners, the problem of decision-
making in these matters was hypothetical and therefore less charged with
complexity. On the question of support for central government's priority
policies (favouring the priority groups over the acute sector), front-line
practitioners were more firmly in support than their managers who, while
coming out in support, were much more equivocal in their responses. An
NHS manager, for example, supported the policies in principle:

Yes, I'd agree with that policy provided that you have to have – you still have to have acute medical, sufficient acute medical services so that they can cope with the needs of the community . . . I mean, it's said in Glasgow that there are too many acute beds, too many acute medical wards and that this should be run down a bit to make priority for these dependency groups. All I know is that every winter, it's the same story. Every hospital has difficulty in finding a bed to take people into.

But a front-line social worker answered much more directly:

Yes, I think we have a responsibility to cater for the disabled . . . the elderly, the chronically sick, the people who do require additional support and services . . . Old age is something that happens, chronic, mental or physical disability, these are things over which people have very marginal control . . . we should spend a good percentage of our time concentrating on these people . . . Mine happens to be a very personalised view because I work in this field.

The evidence seems to suggest, then, that although professional ideology is a strong and binding influence in contributing to group identity, the factor of circumstances is also at work, cutting across ideological ties. The experience of working at the front-line, at the interface between the public as clients and the services, confers a commonality of attitudes about certain issues amongst practitioners, just as the responsibility of managerial decision-making binds managers together in their views irrespective of their agency or professional background.

Tribal ties: beliefs or allegiances?

Individuals belonging to the same professional group exhibit many attitudes in common especially, as has been discussed, at the ideological level. Similarly, individuals working under common circumstances, in the same or parallel structural positions, hold certain views in common, cutting across professional boundaries. But further examination of responses shows yet another dimension; it relates to respondents' perceptions about themselves, their attitudes and about others.

The strength of what Huntington (1981) calls occupational culture, or what here could well be called corporate identity or *organizational* culture, fuels whatever cleavages or bondings already exist. Huntington tends to see professional ideology as a part of occupational culture; it is perhaps more helpful to separate them as constructs. Professional ideology relates to particular sets of values and moral attitudes, generally acquired implicitly over time through the training and induction processes of professional qualification; organizational culture is a means of drawing explicit boundaries around a group, imbuing the group with a view about itself that proclaims its distinctiveness as being characterized by particular behaviours and attitudes (whether or not it really is distinctive). It is the certainty that it is, and the allegiance to the group which that stimulates, that is significant – hence the label 'tribalism'.

In some instances, professional ideology and organizational culture (or tribalism) may act to reinforce each other; the profession may also be the group. This is perhaps true of social work since it tends to be a single profession department (although that is to ignore the differences which are known to exist between levels of qualification and spheres of work: CQSW/CSS; casework/residential care work, for example). In the case of the health service, there are a number of professional groupings located within the larger organizational space, often with clearly articulated differences in ideology. But those professional groupings tend to coalesce when set against another organization or agency, such as a social services or social work department. The cleavage then becomes an inter-agency rather than an interprofessional one: one of culture rather than of ideology.

Conclusion

The very multiplicity of factors militating against the success of inter-professional working has consequences for attempts to improve collaboration. While a commonality of experience sometimes confers similar attitudes and reactions on disparate groups of professionals, it frequently goes unrecognized; fundamental differences existing at the ideological level ensure that the gulf – and concomitant hostility – remains. This may then be exacerbated and, at times, superseded by ties of tribal allegiance which are not necessarily grounded in genuine differences of view but are, rather, the product of unfounded and sterotypical assumptions about those located outside the inclusive boundaries of organization and culture. Attempts, therefore, to overcome ideological differences – through joint pre-qualifying or in-service training, for example – may fail because the strength of 'tribalism' goes unrecognized.

References

Bruce, N. (1981) *Teamwork for Preventive Care*. Chichester: John Wiley.

Butler-Sloss Inquiry (1988) *Report of the Inquiry into Child Abuse in Cleveland 1987*. Cm 412. London: HMSO.

Cartlidge, A., Bond, J. and Gregson, B. (1987) 'Interprofessional collaboration in primary health care', *Nursing Times*, 83 (46).

Dingwall, R. (1977) *The Social Organisation of Health Visiting Training*. London: Croom Helm.

Harding Report (1981) *The Primary Health Care Team*. (Report of the Standing Medical Advisory Committee and Standing Nursing and Midwifery Advisory Committee, DHSS.) London: HMSO.

Huntington, J. (1981) *Social Work and General Medical Practice: Collaboration or Conflict?* London: Allen & Unwin.

Lonsdale, S., Webb, A. and Briggs, T. L. (1980) *Teamwork in the Personal Social Services and Health Care*. London: Croom Helm.

6

LABOUR RELATIONS: MIDWIVES AND DOCTORS ON THE LABOUR WARD

JENNY KITZINGER, JOSEPHINE GREEN and VANESSA COUPLAND

In this article the authors describe some of their conclusions from a study of six hospitals to assess the implications of different medical staffing structures in domestic units. They investigated the effects of replacing the traditional three-tier structure of consultant, registrar and senior house officer (SHO) with a two-tier medical hierarchy that cuts out the registrar.

As one obstetrician declared: 'The system will not work unless it is to the patient's detriment; it is legally and morally indefensible, unless the consultant numbers are trebled' (Valentine, 1983). Many consultants felt that working without intermediate-grade staff would downgrade their role, partly because of the necessity to come in more often when on call. As one three-tier consultant in our study said: 'I came in once for two simultaneous caesars, but only because the baby would have died otherwise. My job is not to come in but to be consulted.' The debate in the medical press centred on the effects of two-tier staffing on *consultants*; little was said by or about the other remaining members of the obstetric team: SHOs and midwives. Doctors, when referred to at all in discussions of midwifery and obstetrics generally, tend to be lumped together without considering the very different positions, both in terms of role and status, of consultants and SHOs. These differences imply quite distinct relationships with midwives, and it is therefore worth considering how these roles are traditionally construed before we go on to look at interstaff relationships.

In National Health Service hospitals the consultant is usually given the role of manager and leader of the medical team – someone who sets policy, is

Abridged from J. Garcia, R. Kilpatrick and M. Richards (eds), *The Politics of Maternity Care*, Clarendon Press, Oxford, 1990 there to be consulted, but only does a very limited part of the routine work. In this 'consultant-led' model, day-to-day obstetric difficulties are the domain of the registrar. The registrar, however, is technically a doctor in training, and as such will telephone the consultant before making any major decision. The SHO works under the direct supervision of the registrar.

The constant factor is that there are three grades of doctors, with much of the everyday hands-on obstetrics being performed by the middle grade. The removal of this linchpin grade inevitably leads to changes in the roles of the remaining staff. Most of what a registrar does (e.g. operative deliveries) cannot be done safely by an inexperienced SHO, and must therefore be done by the consultant. This means that consultants in two-tier hospitals might be expected to spend more time on the labour ward, and consequently see far more of the midwives. In the absence of the registrar, day-to-day decisions on the ward can become the midwives' responsibility, as they will usually be the most senior and experienced personnel on the spot. The shifts in role may, in turn, affect relationships because of the opportunity to develop closer rapport between midwives and consultants, and because, if midwives take on more decision-making power, there must be repercussions for their interactions with SHOs.

The context of doctor–midwife relations

The relations between doctors and midwives are highly charged and traditionally antagonistic (Donnison, 1977). A particular potential for conflict arises out of the coexistence of two separate, yet interdependent, hierarchies. The relationship between the two is not rigidly structured, and medical and midwifery staff at all levels often have conflicting views of each other's legitimate spheres of concern. Negotiation about roles is apparent throughout the hierarchy, be it about the consultant's and the Director of Midwifery's relative influence on policy, or the SHO's and staff midwife's relative qualifications to suture. Many such disputes crystallize around the disputed territory of 'normal' versus 'abnormal birth', 'midwives'' versus 'doctors'' cases.

Normal versus abnormal: drawing up the lines of battle

'A midwife is a person who is trained to . . . conduct normal labours on her own responsibility . . . She must be able to recognise the warning signs of abnormal or potentially abnormal conditions which necessitate referral to a doctor' (World Health Organization, 1966). This is part of an internationally accepted definition of a midwife. However, the definition of 'normal labour' is political. There are two major competing models of labour, each of which implies a different professional relationship. One model assumes that labours are normal until proved abnormal. Most therefore start off as the responsibility of the midwife, and it is up to her to decide if and when to involve a doctor.

However, the usual medical model implies a quite different professional relationship. This model adopts the basic premiss that every labour is potentially abnormal until it is over, and that childbirth is 'the most dangerous journey in a person's lifetime'. The consultant must therefore take responsibility for the progress of labour, and the junior doctors and midwives must act as the consultant's deputies and in accordance with his policies. There is no room for the midwife as an independent practitioner for normal labour, since a 'normal labour' can only be recognized in retrospect.

'Normal = natural' or 'normal = common'?

Normality is not a single or fixed concept for midwives. In particular, we identified two distinct ways in which they interpreted 'normal labour': as 'statistically common' and as 'natural'. In the first case, normality includes such common procedures as episiotomy, intravenous drips, artificial rupture of the membranes and electronic fetal monitoring. These are part of 'normal labour', and therefore, some midwives argue, they are the responsibility of the midwife. On the other hand, 'normal' may be used to mean 'natural' – a definition which includes breech and twin deliveries but excludes the common procedures listed above.

Natural and common: complementary or conflicting definitions of normality?

The two uses of the concept of normality are in some ways complementary: together they can combine to expand the midwives' role. A midwife would need to call a doctor less often if the definition of her role as a 'practitioner in her own right for normal birth' included breeches and twins, rupturing membranes, and setting up drips.

However, the 'natural' and the 'common' definitions of normal labour can also conflict. There was concern that a strictly 'natural' interpretation could lead to some midwives 'abandoning' women once they required the slightest form of medical intervention. The 'normal = natural' definition could thus be seen to restrict the midwife's role and circumscribe the care she gives to women in labour.

On the other hand, some midwives argue that a strictly 'common' definition of 'normal' can distort traditional midwifery values. Anxiety was expressed that as midwives became proficient in the use of technology, they would lose the ability to 'use their ears, eyes and hands' and to support women to give birth naturally.

Midwives and SHOs: conflicting expectations

The SHOs and 'shop-floor' midwives are the members of the medical and midwifery staff who work most closely together on the labour ward; it is here that some of the general issues about doctor–midwife relations are brought sharply into focus.

In the highly status-conscious environment of the hospital, the relative position of midwife and SHO can become a matter of group negotiation. SHOs, by virtue of being doctors, take precedence over the midwives, who may be seen as 'just nurses'. However eighteen out of twenty-four SHOs in our study were GP trainees, and thus spent only six months in obstetrics. By contrast, the midwives had specialized in obstetrics for at least eighteen months as well as having substantial practical experience: the sisters we interviewed had, on average, seventeen years' practical midwifery experience, while the staff midwives had practised for an average of six and a half years. It is in this situation that the hierarchy of 'doctor' over 'nurse' most obviously runs counter to the hierarchy of skill and experience. As one consultant said: 'It's like the NCO and Lieutenant – the midwives have the experience even though the lower status.'

There was often a mismatch between SHOs' and midwives' evaluation of their own and each others' relative skills. SHOs were variously characterized by midwives as 'green as green', 'still wet behind the ears', and not knowing 'one end from the other'. Many midwives spoke pityingly of SHOs' 'illusions of superiority'. The SHOs did indeed sometimes give high priority to their own medical training over and above the midwives' experience, and resented midwives' views of them as less knowledgeable.

SHO–midwife interaction is thus framed both by conflicting views of each other's expertise, and by the traditional medical versus midwifery attitudes towards childbirth. Added to this is the fact that their roles overlap to some extent. Those tasks which midwives have been seeking to reclaim, such as suturing and setting up intravenous drips, are tasks which would otherwise be performed by the SHO. The SHOs in our study did not experience this loss as particularly threatening, since they saw such jobs as 'tedious and petty interruptions to sleep'.

The allocation of decision-making responsibility generates far more controversy than the issue of task distribution. This is because decision-making is seen as critical to the roles of both midwives and SHOs. Midwives in two-tier units tend to have a more extended decision-making role than their three-tier colleagues (for example, deciding when to call the consultant), and also to have more formal input into such decisions as when to accelerate a labour, and when to send a woman home.

In most hospitals, however, midwives make far more of a decision-making contribution than is formally acknowledged. SHOs may be officially responsible for many decisions but, as one midwife said: 'You're usually putting it into *their* hands to do what *you* want them to do.' The midwives' low status inhibits them from openly expressing opinions, a situation that is exacerbated by some SHOs who argue that they, as doctors, are the only competent decision-makers: 'midwives are not medically trained so can't interpret what they see.'

This type of attitude has led most midwives to develop definite tactics for dealing with particularly arrogant SHOs. Most midwives stated that they tried to guide SHOs without undermining their confidence or status. Midwives, like nurses (Rushing, 1965; Stein, 1967; Hughes, 1987), have developed particular strategies to avoid provoking overt conflict. They sought to advise the SHO without challenging the hierarchy or negating the SHOs' medical training, and they emphasized the need for gentleness and diplomacy: 'You want what's best for your woman and you're not going to get it if you say directly. You just have to make them feel important and learn how to pull the right strings.'

Almost every midwife could immediately provide a list of tactics of 'how to get the SHO to do what you want'; it was as if they had all read the same manual on 'Gaining SHOs' Compliance': 'Instead of saying "this woman should have . . ." you get a lot more done if you watch your phraseology and say "do you think we might perhaps think about doing . . .?" ' With some individual exceptions, midwives emphasized the politics of approaching the SHO tactfully. Some presented this as a process of humouring the junior doctors; others presented it as an elaborate game ('you have to learn to be devious') or as common politeness ('you do it as a courtesy'; 'it doesn't lower a midwife to be tactful'). Whatever the interpretation offered by different midwives, the end-result was that they were involved in a great deal of what we chose to call 'hierarchy maintenance work'.

Consultant–midwife relations

The consultant post represents the highest point of the medical hierarchy, and the incumbent of this position has most control over the way in which she or he wishes to work. Consultants in British hospitals have, on the whole, a common background (as far as class is concerned, and usually as far as race and gender are concerned too). However, they differ in age and experience, in their obstetric policies, in their obstetric workloads, and in their attitudes to junior doctors and midwives. Naturally, they also differ in the extent of their other commitments; for example, their gynaecological workload, their private workload, their families and their outside interests. Tied up with all of these is personality: some are easier to get on with than others.

The consultant's path crosses that of the midwife in two ways – as policy-maker and through direct contact. The consultant determines the policies that affect the midwife (and labouring women), and thereby attracts midwives' approval or disapproval, affection or dislike. It is here that the standard issues of normal midwifery versus abnormal medical cases come to the fore again. It is the consultant who defines, in principle, when a doctor should take over from a midwife, when drugs should be administered and procedures carried out. These policies may be seen as vague and allowing the midwife a great deal of autonomy, or as rigid and limiting the midwife's freedom. They may be seen as flexible and allowing normal (natural) labour to take its course, or as aggressive and interfering. Where consultants within the same unit had different policies, midwives sometimes felt like 'piggies in the middle'. One three-tier midwife was dismayed at the thought of working without registrars because she felt that an increase in the number of consultants in the unit would add to the number of conflicting policies. She was rather horrified by the suggestion: 'You mean two extra consultants with different ideas!' However, in the two-tier system we found that better communication between consultants could lead to a convergence of policies.

The consultants also differed considerably in their attitudes towards midwives. Two-tier consultants were more positive about midwives' power on the labour ward: 'It really behoves the midwives to run the show . . . they are in charge of the labour ward'; while some of the three-tier consultants did not even see the midwives as having an independent role at all: 'the days of the midwives – in my view – managing cases themselves . . . is gone. I consider the midwives to be my juniors, my deputies.' Three-tier consultants were also generally less aware of what midwives were actually doing, let alone what they wanted. For example, one three-tier consultant said that he did not know whether or not the midwives in his hospital put up drips or took blood: 'Isn't there something against it in their training? I don't think they're allowed to stick needles in people.'

These differences in consultants' perception of the midwife's role are to a large extent a result of two-tier consultants spending much more time on the labour ward. Initially we had thought that this might result in midwives feeling that consultants were breathing down their necks. Midwives in three-tier units certainly shied away from the idea of a two-tier structure partly because they did not want the greater contact with consultants that this would imply. Two-tier midwives, on the other hand, accepted the greater consultant involvement because they had less reason for wanting their consultants to keep away; they were less often at odds with 'the doctors' orders'. Contrary to the fears of the three-tier midwives, then, those working in the two-tier structure did not appear to find their consultants intrusive.

No longer in awe of their consultants, two-tier midwives felt confident to talk with them relatively freely, something that few three-tier midwives could even imagine. One two-tier consultant, commenting on the advantages of frequent visits to the labour ward as opposed to the traditional consultant behaviour of just rushing in for emergencies, said: 'You can discuss things over a cup of tea with the midwives – I have a closer relationship with them than [other consultants] do. The midwives . . . really know me and like me.' The midwives in two-tier hospitals were proud of this intimacy. One told us a story of how amazed midwives from other hospitals were to see her chatting to her consultant at a conference: 'No wonder your system works if you can talk to your consultants like that', they declared.

The two-tier system itself, imposed on unwilling consultants, would not guarantee better midwife–consultant relations or increased midwifery autonomy, because the consultant's attitude is a key factor. The two-tier units that we explored represented living structures that were mediated by staff attitudes, and these units had assembled some atypical staff: quite a few independent-minded midwives had been attracted to the highest profile two-tier unit in our sample, and some traditionally minded consultants had certainly avoided two-tier units. However, at least in theory, the relationship between the staffing structure and the staff's views could be a two-way process. Midwives who accept posts in two-tier hospitals might find that the experience of working without registrars helps them to develop their skill and confidence as independent practitioners. Similarly, consultants might develop greater respect for midwives. As one consultant commented: 'In the two-tier structure you're more dependent on the midwives so you *have* to respect them.' Some two-tier consultants also come to enjoy their increased contact with women in labour, even though they did not originally choose to work in that way (Pentecost, 1983).

Relations between midwives and doctors are constantly under informal negotiation on the labour ward. The relationship between midwives and SHOs is, in particular, the focus of subtle manipulation as a result of the mismatch between midwives' skills, and the SHOs' status in the traditional unit.

The innovative two-tier system contains the potential for developing a more autonomous and powerful midwifery role within the hospital structure. It can also result in an increase in overt conflict between midwives and SHOs, and may be associated with improved midwife–consultant relationships. However, whether or not this potential is developed, and how specific problems arise and are resolved, depends on the attitude of the staff involved. The power of the consultants to determine the details of labour ward working means that their attitudes are crucial. The two-tier structure can provide a framework for change, but it is not, in itself, sufficient to promote midwifery autonomy or particular changes in interstaff relationships.

References

Donnison, J. (1977) *Midwives and Medical Men: a History of Inter-Professional Rivalries and Women's Rights*. London: Heinemann.
Hughes, D. (1987) 'When nurse knows best: some aspects of nurse/doctor interaction in a casualty department', paper presented at BSA Medical Sociology Group Conference, 25–27 September 1987.
Pentecost, A. (1983) 'Is there another consultant lifestyle?', *British Medical Journal*, 287: 305–6.
Rushing, W.A. (1965) 'Social influence and social-psychological function of deference: a study of psychiatric nursing', in J.K. Skipper and R.C. Leonard (eds), *Social Interaction and Patient Care*. Philadelphia: Lippincott.
Stein, L. (1967) 'The doctor–nurse game', *Archives of General Psychiatry*, 16: 699–703.
Valentine, B.H. (1983) 'Is there another consultant lifestyle?', *British Medical Journal*, 287: 914.
World Health Organization (1966) *The Midwife in Maternity Care*. Technical Report Series, 331. Geneva: WHO.

7

MEANINGFUL DISTANCES

RUTH PURTILO

In human interaction, distance and closeness are highly relative. At one pole there is a complete lack of interaction, while at the other there is intimacy. At any point along this continuum certain professional and personal qualities are put into play, while others remain in the background. When the relationship becomes more intimate, other combinations of the qualities predominate. Behavior of health professional and patient will vary accordingly. There are some specific situations in which interpersonal distance should be consciously created.

Patient loneliness

The first situation is often precipitated by patient loneliness, which almost every patient experiences. Quite often, a professional person who wishes to help the patient overcome loneliness becomes his or her companion. A problem arises only when the health professional and patient relate over a period of time. One-time encounters may enable the health professional to perceive the potential for responding to a patient's loneliness, but they do not create a problem like that illustrated in the following story:

> Jack Simms is a paraplegic. He has been a patient at University Hospital for six months. His affable, optimistic spirit has made him very popular with the staff. At 23 years of age, he was involved in a car accident in which his fiancée was killed. Some health professionals have long suspected that Jack's optimism is a veneer for the deep sorrow and frustration resulting from this sudden, dramatic change in his life. One day he tearfully tells Karen Morgan, a health professions student who has been treating him, that he is depressed and desperately lonely. Up to this point, their interaction has been full of banter and they have felt quite comfortable with each other. Karen does not divulge to the rest of the staff Jack's expression of depression and loneliness, but that night on the way home, she stops by his room to see him.

Abridged from *Health Professional/Patient Interaction*, W.B. Saunders, Philadelphia, 1984

In the following weeks, she begins to visit him more often. She finds him attractive, they share common interests, and he is obviously happy in her company. But during this time, Karen also leads her own private life, going on dates and interacting with a world of other people. But Jack lies in bed thinking about her and, in the afternoons, he counts the minutes until she arrives.

During her Christmas vacation, Karen goes to visit friends in a distant city and has a marvelous time. When she returns, bursting with enthusiasm, she finds Jack sullen and angry at her for staying away from him for so long.

Jack's reaction indicates that he feels she has rejected him. He has now reached the point where leaving her to go to his own home will mean relinquishing an immediate, perhaps his only, enjoyment. Karen has thus unwittingly fostered detrimental rather than constructive dependence. In her attempt to be a bright spot in Jack's life, she has become for him life itself.

Her subsequent attempts to explain or her sudden withdrawal may have profound, lasting effects on Jack's entire recovery process. Instead of being an intimate friend as he had hoped she was, she becomes just another of a long line of rejections he has experienced. He has thus become far more dependent on her than she had intended or was able to manage. Karen's well-intentioned response to Jack's loneliness initiated the events leading to this tragic state of affairs. She responded with a combination of professional and personal qualities that led to behavior Jack did not understand.

Pity

The second situation in which distance may have to be considered involves a professional person who, in an attempt to respond well to a patient, gets so entangled in the apparent futility of the patient's plight that it becomes impossible to think about or act rationally toward the patient.

Most health professionals can name at least one type of illness or injury that involves them emotionally. Sometimes their feelings are so strong that they cannot bear to treat patients with that particular condition. In one study, fifty-four health professionals named blindness as the condition they felt would be the hardest for them to cope with (Janicki, 1970). This group may have had difficulty treating blind people because they felt so sorry for their patients. Other health professionals might have named cancer, severe burns, aphasia or psychoses instead of blindness.

It is not at all unnatural for health professionals to become periodically so involved in the patients' dilemmas that they take these problems home with them. Almost any health professional can recall the time he or she had trouble falling asleep, or was moved to tears or laughter by a sudden tragic or joyful announcement touching a patient's life. There is, however, a significant difference between this depth of caring, which stimulates a purely human response, and fruitless or destructive entanglement. Again, the problem can be illustrated with a story:

Michael Kader was admitted to the psychiatric ward of City Hospital after the police brought him there from his apartment. The police found him unconscious after a friend reported that he did not respond to her phone calls. Michael is a 26-year-old heroin addict, and a Vietnam veteran. His mother died when he was 12 years old, and he left home to live on the streets shortly after that. He recently learned that his father died of a heart attack shortly after he ran away from home.

Craig Hopkins, a health professional student in clinical education, is 29 years old and is also a Vietnam veteran. His similarity to Michael Kader, however, ends here. Craig Hopkins grew up in an upper middle-class home and served in Vietnam as an officer. He has never had close contact with an addict before, but he finds Michael very warm and human. They both chat when Craig has a few minutes, and over the weeks, Craig arrives at the conclusion that Michael has had more than his share of misfortune.

One day when Craig goes into Michael's room, he finds the patient doubled up, writhing in agony. With a trembling voice, Michael tells him that the doctor has withdrawn his drug completely. To Craig's surprise, Michael grabs him by the wrist and pleads, 'Please, Please, I can't stand this pain. If you will lend me five dollars, I can get just enough to make it over the hump. If I can't get a little relief, I will kill myself. The doctor is a sadist.'

Craig Hopkins tears himself away and leaves the room. That night, however, he cannot sleep. He is haunted by the picture of an asthenic man who has survived the death of his parents and the horror of war but has succumbed to the needle; he sees clearly the beads of sweat that cling to Michael's face as he speaks.

The next day when Craig goes towards Michael's room, a nurse stops him, saying that Michael is asleep as he has been given a heavy sedative. 'Last night he tried to hang himself in the bathroom by tying a sheet to the shower pole', the nurse says. 'You've got to watch those fellows on the needle. They'll do anything to manipulate the staff to give them more of the drug. I think he was just trying to scare us.'

Craig remembers Michael's pleading eyes the day before and is overcome with a desire to make a sharp retort to the nurse's statements. He goes instead to Michael's room and deftly slips five dollars into the drawer of the bedside stand. He is not sure why he does this, but he quickly turns and leaves.

Clearly, Craig Hopkins has reached the point where he is responding instinctively rather than rationally because the situation is so painful to him. Such a feeling exceeds sympathy and is more closely related to pity. Because pity distorts the objective perspective necessary to resolve the real problem, he ceases to be of help. In fact, he may include himself among the patient's many problems.

The health professional cannot solve a problem arising from pity simply by acting aloof and 'professionally' competent. The pity is in response to a real need of a patient. What is called for, therefore, is a combination of personal and professional qualities that allows the patient to know that his or her dilemma is acknowledged with sympathy. The problem occurs when the health professional, overcome by feelings about the dilemma, uses both professional and personal qualities to try to solve the problem in some irrational manner that results either in damage to the relationship or, as in the case just cited, in no help for the patient.

Overidentification

The third situation in which distance must be maintained can also manifest itself at the first meeting between patient and health professional. The problem arises when the health professional has trouble seeing the patient as an individual, for a number of reasons:

1   The patient so perfectly embodies a stereotype that he or she becomes the stereotype.
2   The patient so reminds the health professional of someone else that the patient becomes that person.
3   The health professional has had an experience so similar to the patient's that he or she believes the experiences to be identical.

In all three instances such a reaction is called overidentification.

Having had similar experiences may actually *hinder* the effectiveness of health professional–patient interaction at times. Everyone has had the experience of beginning to relate a traumatic (or exciting) event only to have the other person interrupt with, 'Oh! I know *exactly* what you mean!' and then go on to describe his or her own story. One feels cheated at such times, thinking, 'No, that's *not* what I meant, but you are more interested in telling me about yourself than in listening to me!' The way such overidentification works within the health professions can be illustrated in a third story:

> Mrs Garcia, an elementary school teacher, became interested in teaching language skills to deaf children after her third child, Lucia, who was born deaf, successfully learned to communicate by attending special classes for those with hearing impairment. Mrs Garcia enrolled in a health professions course directed toward training teachers of deaf persons.
>
> During her clinical education, she was surprised and alarmed that some of the mothers requested that she not be assigned to their children. Finally, she approached one of the mothers whose child she had been working with and with whom she felt comfortable 'What's wrong?' she asked. 'Do they think I'm incompetent because I am an older student? Is it my personality? I want so much to help these children, and I can't understand what I'm doing wrong.' The embarrassed mother replied, 'Well, since you asked, I'll give you a direct answer. *I* don't feel this way, but some of the mothers think that you don't understand their children's difficulties because every time they start to tell you something about their children, you immediately interrupt with an experience that *your* child had.'

In short, overidentification leads to an 'I-know-how-you-feel' reaction that can be helpful or can convince the patient (or the family) of the complete opposite! The health professional who is astute enough to discern that he or she may be overidentifying will also be able to see that attempts to become close to the patient by pointing out superficial similarities between their experiences are being interpreted by the patient as the health professional's desire to talk about his or her own problem. The health professional should not be falsely led to believe that a closeness has been established. Rather, he or she should be willing to maintain greater distance until the uniqueness of the other person emerges.

Reference

Janicki, M.P. (1970) 'Attitudes of health professionals toward twelve disabilities', *Perception and Motor Skills*, 3077–8.

8

WOUNDED HEALERS: AWAKENINGS

PATRICK WAKELING

I was in my middle thirties: a senior registrar in adult psychiatry. My wife then worked at home, in our hospital house, looking after our five children, three of whom attended the primary school. The area provided good post-graduate training, but the hospital could not, by any stretch of loyalty, be regarded as 'progressive'. Its lifeblood had long since congealed; its purpose dissipated by the almost ceaseless warring of personalities; its old ideals degraded; its original humanity blunted by excessive chemotherapy and ECT. It was, in a word – as I found to my cost – a 'bin'. What resources of my own did I bring to this discouraging place? Let me say just this. There was a gulf between my aspirations (often unrealistic) and the opportunities for their fulfilment. I do not proffer this as the sole cause of the depression, but rather as a contributing factor. My daily routine occasioned more self-reproach than one of robuster personality would have tolerated. I considered that I was in the midst of unimaginative, slipshod psychiatry and tortured myself because I could not put it right. I am surprised that I lasted as long as I did. But my facility for self-deception sustained an impassive façade not only to the world but to my inner self. Kept it up, that is, until one fine summer's evening I felt the first tremors of the force about to engulf me. During the afternoon I had been puzzled by an anxiety possessing neither object nor explanation. It became worse, so I went to the pub and drank three or four pints of beer. I might as well have drunk water. Retreating from the place in some alarm I returned home and went to bed quite early. Sleep followed easily enough, but the following morning at precisely five o'clock I awoke into a world that had changed, and to a state of mind of which I had no previous experience. There was no doubt at all. I was depressed. I lay there filled by the horror of my condition, like a man who has been told he has cancer. I lay on past the time of rising, bursting in tears like a child when my wife asked me what was the matter.

Abridged from 'Awakenings', in V. Rippere and R. Williams (eds), *Wounded Healers*, John Wiley, Chichester, 1985

Ordinary objects were altered. Tables and chairs, or whatever it might be, now appeared as sinister, devoid of familiarity, drained of the feeling formerly invested in them. I felt the cold acutely. That, and the steady pressure on the top of my head, made me feel ill. I would grip anything within reach as though trying to derive warmth and comfort; or reassuring myself that something, at any rate, was real. I sat motionless for hours, not bothering to turn on the light. Everything invoked and reflected my depression. I was extremely irritable, and totally unable to tolerate the least demands put upon me. At the same time I was fearful of being left alone. Time passed but I was hardly aware of it. So retarded in mind and body had I become as to be incapable of any act of self-destruction. I don't recall – in the first few days, at least – thinking about suicide. In a sense I was dead already: my mind a black mass – celebrating despair; mocking hope – from which I could obtain neither grace nor comfort. I had no appetite for food, no sexual needs. I didn't even bother to get myself a glass of water. I just didn't bother about anything.

I brooded – it could hardly be called thinking – upon my plight as a depressed psychiatrist. There is no lonelier man. After a day or two at home I struggled back to work, which I succeeded in reducing to the barest minimum. I avoided as many of my colleagues as possible. It was like being made of glass: a walking transparent cabinet filled with a shapeless jumble of bruised, bleeding nervous tissue. This wretched showcase bore a label informing anyone I chanced to meet: 'This psychiatrist is depressed because he is inadequate.' I was bitterly ashamed at not being a tower of strength and I feared detection more than anything. After three or four weeks, desperation overcame pathetic pride and I decided to approach a colleague – a man of medical assistant grade whose warmth and kindness exceeded a knowledge of psychiatry (I wished to be helped, not understood, you realize). The irony is intended. As a hospital psychiatrist trying to inspire confidence from senior colleagues for the purposes of good references, one has, indeed, to feel desperate before confessing one's infirmity. God, how I longed then that my depression be magically changed into a decent, straightforward physical ailment! The psychiatric hospital is intolerant of weakness in its staff. Compassion is for patients; for 'them' not 'us'. When the dreaded plague strikes a doctor's house, the rest put up their shutters and circulate the comforting notion that the victim's illness is the direct consequence of the sterling qualities possessed by every member of the caring professions: an excess of virtue, if you like, turning upon its owner like a two-edged sword. But in their secret thoughts the survivors are saying to themselves, 'Always knew there was something rum about him. Not surprising really.' I knew there was no recognized way of getting help. Perhaps some could have braved it out, but disclosures do not always make for 'good' professional relationships, and there are very few junior doctors who would risk endangering their prospects by coming clean to those consultants whose work is built upon the ever-pressing need to defend themselves against precisely the same fate.

So, summoning such courage and initiative as remained to me, I invited my nice colleague to the hospital social club for a drink. After a pint or two I said as casually as I could, 'You know I've been feeling very depressed lately.' To which he replied, just as casually, that he was surprised because I certainly didn't look that way. Although this was immensely reassuring I persisted and rather in the manner of one humouring the whim of an overscrupulous colleague who, presumably, knew more about these things, he wrote out a prescription for antidepressant drugs. This medication brought me no relief. One day I had a row with one of the consultants: an overbearing man for whom I had no respect whatsoever. I was stung by his insensitivity and I gave back as good as I got. But I felt terribly hurt; misunderstood and unappreciated. He revelled in quarrels. I did not. I stormed out of his room and went home immediately, trembling with anger. It was early evening. I told my wife that I felt unusually tired and that I was going to bed. Once in the bedroom I took out the drug bottle and swallowed its contents. My hand shook as I gulped down a fistful or more of capsules. It must have taken a couple of minutes to finish them, but I persevered sustained by the mounting excitement of a unique occasion. What I was doing was unambiguous. No obscurity of purpose this time. I lay on the bed wrapped in a blanket of peace and deep satisfaction. Certain of having done the right thing at last, and undisturbed by any thoughts of my family, I slid comfortably into oblivion.

A white wall and a dazzling light from which there was no relief. Total silence. No memories, except that I knew who I was. Pain and stiffness in my back suggested that I was lying supine. Some force prevented movement. At length I discovered I could move my head. This brought no comfort as I scanned the glaring, featureless monotony of a white hell. For without any effort of mind I knew I was in hell. Now it was clear. I had died, and this was my punishment. I could recall no crime, no 'judgement'. I must lie here for eternity – 'for ever, and ever, and ever, and ever'. The horror of endlessness. If only someone would turn down that accursed light. Suddenly my right arm moved as though independent of my will. My left arm was tied. The fingers fumbled for a knot, but in vain. Then a childhood memory. Trying to find the doorknob in the bedroom. Wandering round and round suffocated by the darkness, wishing, praying that someone would come. My free hand continued like a frightened child blindly to explore. It found my penis. Horribly long, it seemed to extend downward out of reach as though tethered somewhere. Frantic tugging caused intense pain. What shameful deformity was this? The air was unbearably hot. As far as I could tell I was naked, drenched in sweat, but, strangely, suffering no thirst. One misery the less. The futile gropings and stirrings continued. I tried again to retrieve some memory, some slender clue as to what had led to this unhappy state.

'He's awake.' There was no doubt – a human voice. Then a white figure just to my left. It commanded, 'Leave that alone. You've given us enough trouble as it is.' Another voice joined the first. A face bent over me. 'Please turn the light down', I pleaded. No reply. Then, 'You can take the drip down now, but leave the catheter in.' Finally to me, 'We're taking you to the ward now. We had to keep you here in casualty because we need the beds for the people who are really ill. You've taken up a lot of our time.'

Clearly, I had been put in my place in the medical scheme of things, but this troubled me less than the disappointment of not discovering a life after death. That, at least, would have been something. As it was I had to accommodate the banal reality of being a damned nuisance; of keeping the doctors and nurses from their proper task of attending the legitimately ill.

In a surprisingly short time something of my old rationality returned. It had deserted me when the going really got tough, calmly slipping back when the danger was over. But it had forfeited much of my respect and I felt less inclined to listen to its advice. In contrast, the beliefs, the certitudes of childhood had been touchingly loyal, despite my neglect of them. Guilt and the inevitability of punishment had been lying low waiting for their moment. Coming round in the casualty department was an awakening with a vengeance. I was trundled to the ward along an intricate route indicated by the changing patterns of the ceiling. The drugs were not yet completely washed out of me, and I felt a little euphoric for some hours. It seemed merely amusing that one of my consultant colleagues stood by my bed declaring that the massive overdose had to be seen as a serious attempt at suicide; and that if I did not agree to become an 'informal' patient then there would be nothing for it but to put me on a 'section'. Good-humouredly and with condescension I agreed to his terms. I was admitted on the following day to a psychiatric hospital some twenty miles or so away from my own.

The third awakening occurred many times – twelve at least, it is hard now to remember. Always it was like coming round before the brain was ready. I saw people and things but could not recognize them or know their purpose. A foretaste of dementia. I lay there struggling to piece together what was surely the fragment of a dream. Nothing made sense until, in an instant, full awareness supervened and it didn't matter anymore. I would regain normal consciousness with all the relief of a child rushing out into the sunshine, released from the lesson it couldn't understand. I was left with a sense of confusion, with the recollection of the faint residue of a frightening perception. All I can say is that things as they are are frightening simply because they have no meaning. We must exude meaning so that life may become digestible and the world made nourishing. The worst moment of all was that of fighting to remember my identity. I always felt I would never succeed until, just in the nick of time, the nightmare was dispelled. Quite often there was headache. Also, the feel of the temples made damp by saline solution. Then I would be very thirsty and hungry, consuming my tea and biscuits greedily. This was remarked on by the gentle nurse – not one of your brisk, jolly kind, thank goodness – who sat beside me like a mother. I am talking, of course, of electroconvulsive treatment, suggested to me by the consultant, into whose hands I had been received, as the best treatment to have. Poetic justice in this. I, who had passed enough electricity through the brains of my patients to illuminate a city, now submitted to the same nostrum. I, who wearied of pressing the button, and who would have gladly burnt Volta in effigy, was at last brought to the same extremity. My consultant had said, 'Well, old chap, what would you do with someone as depressed as you? You'd give him ECT wouldn't you?'

Apart from the quiet attentions of that particular nurse, the only other satisfaction afforded by the treatment was the intravenous anaesthetic, Pentothal. Almost immediately, it imparted an extraordinarily intense sensation of pleasurable relaxation. Then ten seconds or so later, one's brain crumbling like a sandcastle before the tide, one fell asleep with a deep sigh. A fellow patient reckoned it beat an orgasm any day.

So far, then, I had received medication which had not succeeded, and ECT which rid me of my symptoms, no doubt for all manner of incidental, unacknowledged but important reasons. Something must now be said of my experience as an inpatient, and something too of the doctors whose kindnesses could not be faulted, but whose relationship with me was characterized by a collusion into which, it has to be admitted, I readily entered. First the doctors.

I developed a positive talent for divining the 'needs' of my interlocutors. My intuitively composed history succeeded in relieving their anxieties by enabling them to allocate my symptoms to a category with which they felt most at home, and of which they clearly 'approved'. In this essentially defensive game my doctor was allowed to display superior skill. I had a sharp eye for necessary fiction. I knew from sheer experience that consultants of the usual calibre are reluctant to be led into the dark places of what is tritely called depression. I felt that to tell the whole story would not have been a worth-while investment of time and effort. My editing of the truth was prompted by a deep need for sympathy, for 'understanding'.

My dread of being readily explicable within the terms that apply to others was concealed by claims to be as others are. I was thus allowed to pass through customs with relatively little to declare, travelling on to that friendly land (which half of me yearned to inhabit) of jolly good, salt-of-the-earth chaps who are all (bless them) likely to get depressed from time to time. So I went along with the cliché, which my doctors seemed never tired of reaffirming, of the conscientious doctor who works too hard and who succumbs to an illness, 'which really, you know, is just like any other'.

On admission I was given a side room to myself. At first the privacy was welcome, but I soon longed for the mateyness of the open ward. I was, accordingly, moved, and introduced to psychiatry in action as experienced by the punters. I was now one of 'them'. The whole business was about being a helpless 'patient' – a passive, inert lump of problems, some intractable. The days were endless. We waited around, sitting and lounging for drugs, meals, ECT and doctors' visits. I was fitted neither by training nor inclination to man a lathe in the industrial rehabilitation unit to which a chosen few disappeared each day. The rest suffered a kind of stimulus deprivation in that all normal events had been removed from our lives. Consequently our attention became riveted, once the worst of the symptoms were past, upon any and every trivial occurrence. Otherwise unexceptional people became, as soon as they had stepped into our domain, veritable Falstaffs in the fullness and variety of their idiosyncrasies. There was a hugely obese Irish cleaning woman with a tongue as foul as the NCOs of my national service days. A bloated send-up of a Sean O'Casey character, she waddled about emitting an unbroken stream of obscenities larded with Dublin slang. Then there was the nursing assistant, a dreamy, impractical girl who seemed merely to be tolerating her job because she could think of nothing else to do. She was attractive enough to interest men whose sex lives had been interruped and, conscious of her central position on our sad little stage, she played it for all it was worth.

We all became very anxious about the doctors' visits, hanging about waiting for our particular consultant to show up. One noticed that the doctors always made a beeline for the office and would spend as much time with the nurses as with us. I realized later that I must have displayed all the child-like dependence of the others. The nurses tried their hand at discovering why a psychiatrist who knew about mental illness should, even so, land up in hospital. One staff nurse was particularly anxious on the point, and after having me in the office (always a privileged place to be) for a few amateurish interviews, which in my hunger for attention I was pleased to grant, reached the conclusion that worrying about promotion had brought on my illness. Even the doctors fell into the same trap of confusing their own anxieties and preoccupations with mine. One who couldn't stand children ascribed my depression to having five of my own. Another − a devout Catholic doctor − decided that sexual frustration was what we should be talking about.

The ward was a worth-while experience. It seemed to me that patients did more for one another than did the staff. When I began to feel better I tried to be helpful in my turn. I loved their humour and admired their courage. Shared suffering is a great cohesive force. I remember them with affection and gratitude.

And what of the fourth wakening? It occurred three years or so after discharge from hospital, and was part of another depression, but this time of only moderate severity. It was a metaphorical awakening, in which thought and feeling became better acquainted. My wife played a large part. She was midwife, counsellor, and much else besides. Never, during my three weeks absence from work, was time so well spent. Together we began to make sense of what we both knew of my life and personality. This fruitful process has continued, though it has been very difficult at times.

What else have I learnt? It seems to me that from depression itself one learns nothing. Rather it is from what one makes of depression that benefit derives. Depression is depression. It lays waste and may prove, too, a total waste of time unless one uses the experience, and all its consequences, to build anew. In that sense, it is an experience like any other; yet simultaneously unique in the opportunities it affords.

To begin with I have gained an insight into the predicament of those in the hands of doctors and nurses, which I could not possibly have obtained in any other way. Again, I have been enriched in more personal ways: self-awareness and enhanced creativity among them. These bonuses have accrued, as I have implied, despite the treatment prescribed by the doctors, who were, as I can now see, attempting to fulfil their own personal and/or professional needs. Admittedly, I colluded in this, but I think my instinct was right. Progress has to be on my terms and in my own good time.

Perhaps the most precious outcome of this personal development – of which depression was a vital part – has been the certain knowledge that, for me, depression is a sign of not dealing honestly with my problems. That when I am overwhelmed with difficulties, and wonder how I can possibly find a way through, and experience at the same time a feeling of really struggling with it all, then I know that I am, after all, coping. The paradox consists in using the feeling of not coping to know that I am. Being depressed – severely so, I mean, is to have avoided the challenge; to have thrown in the towel without even having faced up to the contest. It's like saying, 'You take over, I can't do anything. I'm a patient. I'm depressed.' I am sure, too, that for many others, depression may be related to what is called 'growth' (for which, as I have said, it provided unrivalled opportunities) and that better arrangements should be made to give psychiatrists the right kind of help. The psychiatrist's family, too, needs special consideration. I have witnessed enormous suffering, compounded of anguish, insecurity, embarrassment, and downright humiliation, in a colleague's family subjected to the brutally insensitive attentions, and arrangements, of attendant consultants who were, in truth, acting out their own neuroses. On the whole, I consider that I've been relatively fortunate compared to some I've known or heard about. Perhaps the most salutary lesson has been that one must not take one's professional status for granted. What matters most to the patient is what mattered most to me: namely, the personal 'accessibility' of the psychiatrist – those subtle qualities of personality rendering him non-judgemental and a fully paid-up member of the human race. Someone who listens to more than the mere words one falteringly utters. Above all, he must be able to distinguish his problems from those of his client. To be a good psychiatrist requires the same honesty and courage expected of the good patient.

9

THE FACE-TO-FACE INTERACTION AND AFTER THE CONSULTATION

GERRY STIMSON and
BARBARA WEBB

Presenting a problem to the doctor

In discussing the patient's prognosis in the consultation, a report from a working party of the Royal College of General Practitioners (1972: 17) advises the doctor to ask himself certain questions:

> What must I tell this patient? How much of what I learned about him should he know? What words shall I use to convey this information? How much of what I propose to tell him will he understand? How will he react? How much of my advice will he take? What degree of pressure am I entitled to apply?

If we change the second from last of these questions to read, 'How much notice will he take of what I say?' then these could be exactly the questions that the patient poses to himself when seeing the doctor. For the patient considers, both before and during the consultation, *what to say* to the doctor. Under this heading we deal with the patient's interpretation and selection of facts and the ways in which he attempts to put these across to the doctor with the maximum effect.

In perceiving his symptoms, the patient attempts to *interpret* them, and in explaining these symptoms, both to himself and to the doctor, he is defining, categorizing and causally linking them to other factors which he feels may be related. For example, the disorder may be presented in conjunction with another physical condition that the patient believes to be relevant. One woman explained her problem to the doctor in this way: 'I've had a lot of headaches lately – I wondered if it could be anything to do with my blood pressure?' The symptoms may be described in terms of a social context which the patient sees as significant, e.g. the woman patient who told the doctor she believed her anxiety and 'nerves' stemmed from her worries about a delinquent daughter. This interpreting is partly an attempt at self-

Abridged from *Going to See the Doctor*, Routledge & Kegan Paul, London, 1975

diagnosis and partly an attempt to 'put the doctor on the right lines'. What is significant to the patient may not be so for the doctor, who may dismiss the patient's perceptions and interpretations as having little relevance and may probe for other factors that the patient has not mentioned.

As well as having to define or recognize a problem and putting this into words, the patient is also involved in 'figuring out' the doctor. Both parties are 'sizing each other up'. The patient may not agree with the doctor's interpretation of the symptoms, especially when this does not accord with his own preconceived ideas and the doctor has not stated his interpretation in terms sufficiently convincing to persuade the patient to accept it. One young woman, consulting the doctor about her small child whose problem the doctor had interpreted as being unimportant and 'nothing to worry about', persistently reiterated that the symptoms in her child were both unusual and worrying: 'Yes, but it's most unusual for him to keep vomiting up his feed like this. And as I say, he's never been like this before.' In cases such as this, the patient may make further and more obvious attempts to persuade the doctor to acknowledge her own perspective on the problem: 'I said, "Well, what about these dizzy spells I've been having doctor?" And he just sat back and stared at me blankly . . . so to help him I said, "Could it be anything to do with my age?" '

From all the many and varied pieces of information that could be given, the patient has also to be *selective* in verbal presentation. This selection may be largely unconscious – in any communication the speaker is necessarily selective – or it may be consciously planned. The problem in selecting what to say is that of estimating what is relevant and significant and what it is necessary or expedient to verbalize. The patient may offer various facts, suggesting or hinting at a possible causal relationship. The patient may select information according to criteria he thinks the doctor wants or needs to hear (those aspects which are believed will have meaning for a doctor) and what he, the patient, wants to tell the doctor and thinks he should be told.

The doctor, too, is selective in what he decides to tell the patient. The doctor may not inform the patient of the type of drug he is prescribing or of possible side effects of the treatment. Similarly, the patient may withhold from the doctor information that he feels will place him in a disadvantaged position, for example, an admission that he has not followed instructions or that he fears a course of action proposed by the doctor. A woman told the interviewer that she was 'terrified' of her forthcoming operation: 'but don't write that down. Don't tell the doctor I said that, he'd shout at me if he heard me say that.'

Influencing the doctor

The ways in which people present themselves in the surgery may be viewed as strategies influencing the course of the consultation. We do not claim that the patient or the doctor always consciously adopt strategies to influence each other. For both, the strategies are part of a repertoire, to be invoked when the situation permits. The efforts made by each to influence the interaction give the consultation its bargaining quality.

In the following example from a surgery consultation, a patient is trying to persuade the doctor that her problem merits medical attention. The woman patient presents her symptoms to the doctor. He can find no explanation for them in the examination he makes or from the medical history on the patient's record card. As a position of stalemate is reached, the patient herself finally offers a proposed course of action in the light of the doctor's seeming inaction. She persists in offering the symptoms as a matter of concern and succeeds, by proposing a solution of her own, in gaining the doctor's recognition that some action should be taken. The consultation began with the woman describing 'odd pains' and giddiness and complaining that she had put on weight. We begin the dialogue with her speaking while the doctor examines her.

Patient: I've taken tablets. I thought I could fight it off.
Doctor: Mmm. Uh-huh.
Patient: This morning I couldn't even drink my cup of tea so I knew something was wrong.
[*Examination ends.*]
Doctor: Well, that's normal, there's nothing wrong there.
Patient: Well, I don't know what causes it, I'm sure.
Doctor: Your blood pressure's all right, there's nothing the matter there.
Patient: Nothing to worry about? Oh well, there you are then.
Doctor: Are you sure you've put on half a stone?
Patient: Definitely.
[*Pause in dialogue.*]
Patient: Is there something I could stop eating? I can't wear my clothes now.
Doctor: Cut out sugar in your tea and flour products, take them only in moderation. Try that and see how you go on. It'll take some time mind.
Patient [*laughing*]: Oh I know that!
[*Both begin to joke about eating and weight problems.*]

There is rarely open conflict in the consultation. Both parties generally recognize and retain some semblance of formality and exercise restraint to prevent the encounter from completely 'breaking down'. A patient seldom makes accusations to a general practitioner's face about what are considered to be inefficiencies and inadequacies; similarly, a doctor rarely loses his temper with a patient. If it appears that this point is being approached, one actor seems to step down and attempts to avoid the issue or heal the breach. A patient who failed to keep her hospital appointment evoked the doctor's annoyance. During the consultation he said to her: 'Well I'm sorry, Betty. What do you expect me to do? I've done as much as I can . . . What's the use if you don't do anything I say?' Betty remained silent throughout, muttering her apologies just before leaving.

Verbal and non-verbal control strategies are often covert and rarely obvious or explicit. On the part of the patient they appear to operate beneath a façade of compliance and acquiescence. The thoughts of the patient which are not articulated during tense or difficult exchanges such as that above, may form the basis for 'stories' told about doctors when the patient is well away from the surgery.

After the consultation

What happens after the patient has left the doctor's room? Our analysis of the consultation process continues beyond the face-to-face contact between patient and doctor. We see the process as including thoughts and conversations about the consultation, and the use of the treatment that has been prescribed by the doctor.

It is known from quantitative studies of patients' use of prescribed medicines, that a high proportion of patients do not follow the instructions of their doctors when taking prescribed medicines. If the treatment is a drug the patient may decide not to take the prescription to the pharmacist or may have it dispensed and not use the drug. The patient may begin to use the drug and then discontinue, or may use it with a frequency or in a dosage other than that advised by the doctor. Other types of treatment, too, may be used in ways other than those suggested by the doctor.

Given that various processes – making sense of what happened, reappraisal and evaluation – occur after the patient leaves the surgery, it becomes apparent that there is not necessarily any simple link between the doctor's action in prescribing a treatment, and whether or not, or in what way, that treatment is used by the patient. It is indeed, difficult to divorce these processes from the patient's treatment decisions and actions.

An initial orientation towards the use of the treatment is found in the reappraisal and evaluation of the consultation. Patients may feel confused or be unable to make sense of exactly what happened, or be in some doubt over the nature of the treatment prescribed. They may decide to 'play safe' and do nothing, as in the case of an elderly woman who consulted her doctor over two recurrent problems – cystitis and blood pressure. She was given two sets of pills: 'When I got the tablets home, I didn't know which to take – the cystitis tablets for blood pressure, or the other tablets for cystitis when I got it, so I never took any. See what I mean? You get very confused.'

If, on the other hand, the patient is convinced on leaving the consultation that the doctor has not made a correct diagnosis, his prescribed treatment may be rejected. One woman, for example, felt that the doctor had failed to appreciate the 'real' nature of her complaint. She had complained of pain behind the eye, while he had given her ointment for the skin around the eye.

She had then made an appointment on her own initiative to see an 'eye doctor' and explained: 'I haven't used the ointment because I didn't want it to affect what's really wrong with me.'

Where do people get their ideas about the use of medicines? Seeing the patient in the formal setting of the consultation the doctor may be led to believe that he is the main source of people's ideas about medicines. He may be a source of ideas, but he is by no means the only source. On two occasions the researcher was asked for advice: on one occasion as to whether the prescribed pills were 'likely to do any good' and another time whether a proposed operation was 'a good idea – do you think I should have it done?'

Advice may be sought out, or may come almost fortuitously in everyday conversations about health and illness. Members of the family are obviously important in this respect. One woman in a group discussion described what happened after seeing the doctor: 'I'd just got back from the surgery when my mother phoned. I told her what he [the doctor] had given me, tranquillizers, and she said to me: "About these pills, you don't want to be drugged all the time; now when you feel better you stop taking them, all right?" '

Medication may be discussed with friends, as well as the family. Experiences may be compared, or the medication may be suggested as potentially useful to someone else. In one group discussion a woman and her friends described how they compared the tablets the doctor had prescribed for them, in order to 'see if we have the same things'. And another, recalling her last bout of bronchitis: 'The last time I went about bronchitis, he [the doctor] gave me these new pills. "Just come out", he said, and you know, they did work, they were better than the ones I had before. And so, there's this other lady I know also gets it badly, so I told her to tell the doctor to give her these ones.'

People have many sources of knowledge which contribute to their overall perspective and actions with regard to the doctor's advice and instructions. 'I have learnt about diabetes – I have a sister who is a nurse', one male patient stated, and added that he had also 'read up' a good deal about his complaint in medical textbooks. Or the university student who said: 'In my experience I've found that they often don't give you the right treatment. Because I've worked in a chemist, I usually know what it is.'

The pharmacist is also a frequently used source of ideas and influence relating to treatment decisions; patients will ask the pharmacist to suggest some remedy before going to the doctor, or present him with a prescription from the doctor and ask his opinion on it. People live their problems and illnesses socially; they cannot be viewed as isolated individuals responding automatically to the instructions of their doctors.

This brings us to the crucial paradox of general practice: while the patient's ability to control the outcome of the consultation is limited, he or she has considerable ability to control what happens after leaving the doctor's presence. In the consultation, the doctor makes the treatment decision; after the consultation, decision-making lies with the patient.

Reference

Royal College of General Practitioners (1972) *The Future General Practitioner*. London: Royal College of General Practitioners.

10

PREGNANCY AND CHILDBIRTH: A HISTORICAL PERSPECTIVE

ELIZABETH ROBERTS

In this extract from an oral history of working-class women 1890–1940, women talk about their experience of childbirth and the role of midwives.

Confinements remained, for many women, dangerous, painful and unpleasant. The dramatic fall in the infant mortality rate throughout the twentieth century was obviously of enormous significance, but it has tended to obscure the fact that the national maternal death rate actually rose until 1936, despite the training of midwives under the 1902 Midwives Act, and the great extension of hospital provision for women in childbirth after the First World War.

The figures for maternal deaths were sufficiently alarming for the Preston Medical Officer of Health to comment on them throughout the 1930s. He blamed the deaths on the failure of women to seek frequent and adequate ante-natal care.

It is perhaps time to re-examine the role of the traditional untrained midwife. These women had virtually no formal training, although they may have been chosen and instructed by a local doctor. More usually they learned their trade from an older midwife, and quite often the skill was passed down in families. Their lack of formal training did not necessarily mean they were incompetent. (They sometimes also acted as the layer-out of the dead, and generally played an important role in the neighbourhood.) The most usual view of the untrained midwife is 'another legacy of the nineteenth century . . . The Mrs Gamp midwife, dirty and illiterate.' But their patients or women whose mothers had been their patients were almost unanimous in their admiration for the way they performed their job. Mrs Heron's mother had eleven children, all born before 1902: 'Oh, I think we managed. Martha used to come, the midwife, and they used to stop in bed a week in them days. She wasn't certified or anything but she was one of the good old midwives and it was only a few shillings for a confinement. I've

Abridged from 'Pregnancy and childbirth', in *A Woman's Place: an Oral History of Working Class Women 1890–1940*, Basil Blackwell, Oxford, 1984 heard m'mother say that she used to give her sixpence a week until she got it paid off. She was a grand old lass.' (The transcript fails to convey the warmth of the respondent's voice when she discusses Martha.) Mrs Dodds commented: 'She used to have these midwives come and they were such good friends a lot of them.' As her mother had twenty-one children (all born before 1900), she presumably had a remarkable opportunity to assess the merits of her midwives.

It appears that working-class women continued to prefer the old, unqualified midwives for many years after the passing of the 1902 Midwives Act. In 1917, the Lancaster Medical Officer of Health reported that out of 613 babies born in that year, 184 had been delivered by one unqualified midwife. A Preston doctor, a respondent, still had an unqualified woman working in his practice in the 1930s, and there was one elsewhere in the county as late as 1937. Why did they continue so long? In the earlier decades the provision of qualified midwives had been very uneven, and women did not always have a real choice. But there were other reasons too: unqualified midwives were cheaper; they were generally thought to be friendlier, and less 'starchy'; and they were certainly less likely to tell the woman what to do, being more likely to cooperate both with her and her female relatives. It is an example of working-class women rejecting the invasion of their homes and lives by the professional. In view of the movement of the maternal mortality figures, her confidence in the 'old ways' was perhaps not altogether misplaced. Only one respondent criticized the competence of an unqualified midwife.

At the turn of the century, working-class childbirth was almost always an unprofessional event; the midwife was untrained, and the doctor was usually called only if the mother's or child's life was thought to be in danger (and not always then). There was also a fundamental belief that somehow childbirth was a female affair, and women should and could get through it on their own. This traditional stoical attitude is expressed by Mrs Hudson, whose confinement took place in the late 1920s:

So did you have to send for the doctor?
   Yes. She wanted to send for the doctor earlier but I said I would manage. She said that I wouldn't. In the end, I was living with father then, she went downstairs and told father he was going to lose both of us if I didn't let them send for the doctor. Father said, 'You send for the doctor, never mind her!' Afterwards, she asked me why I had held out on her. I told her that none of my sisters had needed a doctor, but she said that that was nothing to do with me. She said, 'Good Lord, look at her!' She was navy-blue was Evelyn when she was born. Anyhow, she didn't take any harm. They 'phoned three doctors and they were all out. She sent for Doctor Harrington and as soon as he came he just turned my head round and said, 'Oh, my God!' I was just beyond anything. I must have been too far gone to take chloroform and I had to have a proper mask on. I had to be stitched up. In them days you didn't move for ten days and I had to lie in bed. She told me that if I was going to be silly she would have to tie my feet together. She made me promise that I wouldn't move. My sister looked after me as she lived at home as well.

Examples of this refusal of professional help can be found up to 1940, but a fairly rapid revolution was taking place in working-class women's attitude to childbirth. Gradually, in the inter-war period, it is possible to discern women's changing attitudes to their own health and their own bodies. The fatalism, the ignorance, the shame, the stoicism and the traditionalism are all still very apparent, but a growing number of women from all levels of the working class began to expect more professional help, whether in the form of a doctor or a qualified midwife; they began to expect analgesics, and a hospital bed 'in case something should go wrong'. Mrs Pearce belonged to the very poorest class, her husband being a casually employed outdoor labourer. At the time of her first confinement, in 1923, she was a weaver. She and her husband could not then afford a home of their own, and the confinement took place in their lodgings with the husband's mother. But even this poor family had both a doctor and a nurse, and chloroform at the confinement, and the couple decided that future confinements must take place in hospital (which they did):

They gave you chloroform at home, did they?
  Yes. Well, it were a breech. They did turn me. She [her mother-in-law] said that she had never seen anything like it in her life. The nurse and doctor had both their sleeves rolled right up here. They were sweating. I was in bed about a fortnight and she looked after me while I was in bed. Because we couldn't afford to pay anybody else. After that he said it was a finisher. He said it was my work that had done a lot of that.
  Was this your husband or the doctor?
  My husband. He said, 'You are going away. I'm not having you messed about like that.' So after that, with the other ones, I went away. My sister was frightened to death of hospitals. I thought, if she had gone through what I did at first, then she would want to go in hospital.

11

HOW THE POOR DIE

GEORGE ORWELL

In 1929 George Orwell found himself in a Paris hospital. He observed some of his fellow patients and their treatment.

About a dozen beds away from me was Numéro 57 – I think that was his number – a cirrhosis-of-the-liver case. Everyone in the ward knew him by sight because he was sometimes the subject of a medical lecture. On two afternoons a week the tall, grave doctor would lecture in the ward to a party of students, and on more than one occasion old Numéro 57 was wheeled in on a sort of trolley into the middle of the ward, where the doctor would roll back his nighshirt, dilate with his fingers a huge flabby protuberance on the man's belly – the diseased liver, I suppose – and explain solemnly that this was a disease attributable to alcoholism, commoner in the wine-drinking countries. As usual he neither spoke to his patient nor gave him a smile, a nod or any kind of recognition. While he talked, very grave and upright, he would hold the wasted body beneath his two hands, sometimes giving it a gentle roll to and fro, in just the attitude of a woman handling a rolling-pin. Not that Numéro 57 minded this kind of thing. Obviously he was an old hospital inmate, a regular exhibit at lectures, his liver long since marked down for a bottle in some pathological museum. Utterly uninterested in what was said about him, he would lie with his colourless eyes gazing at nothing, while the doctor showed him off like a piece of antique china. He was a man of about sixty, astonishingly shrunken. His face, pale as vellum, had shrunken away till it seemed no bigger than a doll's.

One morning my cobbler neighbour woke me up plucking at my pillow before the nurses arrived. 'Numéro 57!' – he flung his arms above his head. There was a light in the ward, enough to see by. I could see old Numéro 57 lying crumpled up on his side, his face sticking out over the side of the bed, and towards me. He had died some time during the night, nobody knew when. When the nurses came they received the news of his death

First published by Secker & Warburg, London, 1931; in *Decline of the English Murder and Other Essays*, Penguin, Harmondsworth, 1981 indifferently and went about their work. After a long time, an hour or more, two other nurses marched in abreast like soldiers, with a great clumping of sabots, and knotted the corpse up in the sheets, but it was not removed till some time later. Meanwhile, in the better light, I had had time for a good look at Numéro 57. Indeed, I lay on my side to look at him. Curiously enough he was the first dead European I had seen. I had seen dead men before, but always Asiatics and usually people who had died violent deaths. Numéro 57's eyes were still open, his mouth also open, his small face contorted into an expression of agony. What most impressed me, however, was the whiteness of his face. It had been pale before, but now it was little darker than the sheets. As I gazed at the tiny, screwed-up face it struck me that this disgusting piece of refuse, waiting to be carted away and dumped on a slab in the dissecting room, was an example of 'natural' death, one of the things you pray for in the Litany. There you are, then, I thought, that's what is waiting for you, twenty, thirty, forty years hence: that is how the lucky ones die, the ones who live to be old. One wants to live, of course, indeed one only stays alive by virtue of the fear of death, but I think now, as I thought then, that it's better to die violently and not too old. People talk about the horrors of war, but what weapon has man invented that even approaches in cruelty some of the commoner diseases? 'Natural' death, almost by definition, means something slow, smelly and painful. Even at that, it makes a difference if you can achieve it in your own home and not in a public institution. This poor old wretch who had just flickered out like a candle-end was not even important enough to have anyone watching by his deathbed. He was merely a number, then a 'subject' for the students' scalpels. And the sordid publicity of dying in such a place! In the Hôpital X the beds were very close together and there were no screens. Fancy, for instance, dying like the little man whose bed was for a while foot to foot with mine, the one who cried out when the bedclothes touched him! I dare say '*Je pisse!*' were his last recorded words. Perhaps the dying don't bother about such things – that at least would be the standard answer: nevertheless dying people are often more or less normal in their minds till within a day or so of the end.

SECTION 2

DIVERSITY AND DISCRIMINATION

The helping services in the UK are based on conceptions of normality which then marginalize people who do not conform. Discussion about diversity involves recognition of the range of experiences and lifestyles in existence. The articles in this section explore some of that diversity and place it in the context of the unfair discrimination which is so much a part of the social fabric that it often passes without comment.

In this context the diversities that need consideration are those which result in unequal life chances. But even to name diversities can be a double-edged sword. Diversities in gender, race and class, for instance, should not be seen simply as divergences from white, male, middle-class 'normality'. Nor are diversities mutually exclusive! People are not solely black, old, physically or mentally impaired, male, female, gay or lesbian. Each of these divisions intersect to form the unique experience of individuals. A focus on older people, black people or women can in itself lead to stereotypes. There is a risk of treating these as homogeneous groupings which then fails to acknowledge the diversities among old people, among black people and among women.

We cannot synthesize the different experiences of discrimination into a single formula for the enhancement of practice and policy. Although there are some similarities, racism, ageism, classism, heterosexism and sexism all work in different ways. The issues which receive attention in this section are those raised by gender, race, age and deafness. You will also find articles in other sections of the Reader which take up aspects of discrimination and diversity. For instance, Vic Finkelstein's article (Section 3) addresses definitions of disability; Anita Binns (Section 3) contributes an account of her personal moves towards self-advocacy; and extracts by George Orwell and Elizabeth Roberts (Section 1) provide reminders of the history of class inequalities in the provision of health and welfare services.

In this section we have included accounts which describe personal experience of discrimination as well as more theoretical perspectives and practice strategies. Different articles examine the role of workers, possibilities for improving training, the development of anti-discriminatory approaches, and focus on shortcomings in current provision and attitudes.

The section starts with three articles which address the application of an appreciation of diversity to practice in social work. Jill Reynolds' article examines feminist debates on explanations of the unequal roles of women and men. Feminists have been divided upon which diversities are most central to people's lives. Some see gender difference as fundamental, while others argue that since class and race interact with gender in complex ways they should be included in any analysis. Reynolds traces the links from different theoretical perspectives to broad strategies for action.

Don Naik also draws attention to different emphases, this time in social work education. He contrasts multi-culturalism with anti-racism and maintains that neither approach is enough on its own. To dwell on cultural diversity ignores questions about control, power and conflict. Anti-racist social work education can remain stuck at the level of ideology if it does not flesh out the practical implications for the curriculum. Jalna Hanmer and Daphne Statham explore the theme of diversity from a women-centred stance. They encourage social workers to recognize more explicitly what they have in common with the women who use their services. They argue that when commonality is out in the open, this gives user and worker a stronger basis for understanding the inevitable diversities of status, power, role, lifestyle, race, culture, sexuality, education, work possibilities, access to community resources, degree of stigma and hope.

Amina Mama does not find cause for optimism in black women's experiences of white-staffed refuges. She also suggests that cutbacks in resources and privatization are responsible for a widening gap between the rhetoric of written anti-discriminatory policies and front-line staff practices in the public sector. Through her examination of responses to violence against black women, Mama argues that at times of cutbacks the underlying racism of service provision is revealed, as black women receive the least satisfactory state responses. Yasmin Alibhai describes disturbing evidence of racism within the occupation of nursing. It is not unusual for black nurses to encounter hurtful rejection from white patients. All too often such experiences are made worse by lack of support from within the nursing hierarchy.

The next three articles deal in different ways with ageing. Sara Arber and Nigel Gilbert find evidence in the 1980 General Household Survey data to question the widespread belief that the burden of caring for infirm older people falls mainly on daughters. They suggest that men make a larger contribution to caring than is generally recognized. Perhaps a fuller appreciation of men's involvement as spouses or sons living with infirm older people can help policy-makers avoid stereotypical assumptions about the roles of women and men in caring.

It is stereotypical assumptions about older people themselves which concern Gladys Elder. She points out that older people are often treated as a homogeneous group and described as though they did not have the same needs or feelings as others. Yet class and privilege allow some people to escape such patronizing attitudes: a wealthy and successful retired judge on a pension, for instance, would not normally be referred to as an OAP. Norma Pitfield's article is a more personal journey undertaken by a woman in her middle years as she comes to terms with the death of her mother and the rebuilding of her own life.

Finally, Maggie Woolley's article draws together the personal and the political. Like Norma Pitfield, she had to face loss: in her case the loss of her ability to hear. She explores the meaning of this loss to herself, as well as the impact of the attitudes of others to her new persona. Woolley is able to link the valuation by society of deafened people with her own valuation of disabled people in general, and recognize the contribution of societal valuation to her own internalized attitude of low esteem. Celebration of difference can be a resource for oppressed groups to resist dehumanizing social definitions. It is not always a resource that those acquiring disability can draw upon but, for Maggie Woolley, her introduction to a Deaf community of people who used sign language was a turning point. She describes the process which enabled her to rejoice in diversity, as well as to understand discrimination.

12

FEMINIST THEORY AND STRATEGY IN SOCIAL WORK

JILL REYNOLDS

Women are everywhere in social work. As front-line workers and volunteers, as carers looking after an older relative or a disabled child, as mothers held responsible for the smooth functioning of family life, and as vulnerable people themselves: the anorexic woman, the pregnant teenager, the depressed housewife, the frail older person in need of care. Social work theory and practice have often paid little or no attention to the blindingly obvious presence of women working with women.

Clearly, feminist thinking must have something to offer to social work endeavours. But which thinking? There are a number of different 'feminisms' and each can lead to different overall strategies. This article explores some feminist perspectives and considers areas of difference and of common ground in their application to social work practice.

Feminist theorizing

Feminist theories have been described as 'perspectives which guide one's search for answers to a central series of questions and dilemmas about sex and gender' (Acker, 1987). Feminist theorists have aimed to address key questions around women's roles. Why are women's roles devalued in comparison with men's, how is this inequality maintained, and how can it be changed? Feminist perspectives cover a wide spectrum of debate; none the less they are often banded together under just three headings: those of liberal feminism, radical feminism and socialist feminism. What feminist theories share is a questioning of notions that a woman's place is primarily in the home; that women should hold the main responsibility for child-rearing; and that women are 'naturally' suited to low-paid and low-status caring work. Feminists working from different perspectives have contrasting explanations for the sources of male power, and the resulting unequal roles of men and women in contemporary Western society. These contrasting explanations lead to different broad strategies for change.

Explanations of women's and men's unequal roles: liberal, radical and socialist feminist perspectives

For *liberal feminists* the different roles of men and women result from the translation of *sex* differences, which are strictly biological, into *gender* differences, which are cultural. Only women are capable of childbirth (sex difference), yet this does not explain assumptions that women should take responsibility for raising children (gender difference). By the same token, both men and women have the capacity to pursue careers for financial reward. It is traditions and attitudes which differentiate the roles of men and women and give rise to inequality. Liberal feminist solutions involve creating more equal opportunities through legislation and changing the process of socialization. Thus Betty Friedan, a pioneer of the 1960s wave of feminism, writing in the liberal feminist tradition suggests:

> a massive attempt must be made by educators and parents – and ministers, magazine editors, manipulators, guidance counsellors – to stop the early marriage movement, stop girls from growing up wanting to be 'just a housewife', stop it by insisting, with the same attention from childhood on that parents and educators give to boys, that girls develop the resources of self, goals that will permit them to find their own identity. (Friedan, 1971: 364)

The implication is that women's liberation can be achieved without major change to the economic and political structures of contemporary capitalist society. It is attitudes and opportunities which need to be changed.

Radical feminists see men's entrenched power and privilege as the main problem. This is summed up by the concept of 'patriarchy': the dominance of men over women. There is little agreement over the exact source of male power or its precise structural form. In her *Intergalactic Wickedary* Mary Daly, a radical feminist, demonstrates the power of words. She defines 'professions' as just one of the 'deadly sins of the fathers':

> The ultimate manifestation of empty male 'pride' (vanity); assumption by males of self-legitimating control in *every* cultural activity deemed prestigious by themselves; the consequent condensation of the process of knowing into inert and mystifying 'bodies of knowledge'. Example: male assumption of control over the sphere of healing, reducing this to the 'field of medicine' – a reversal and caricature of genuine healing. (Daly and Caputi, 1988: 70)

Where the liberal feminist seeks to make men and women more equal, the radical feminist believes that differences between men and women are fundamental and should not be ignored or minimized. Radical feminists seek to turn sex differences to women's advantage by celebrating women's capacity for nurturing and cooperation. Solutions vary from separatist feminist structures to creating more woman-centred space in traditional institutions.

Socialist feminists place their emphasis on understanding women's oppression in the context of a class-based society. They argue that class, race and gender interact in a complex way, and that class oppression stems from capitalism (Eisenstein, 1984). They reject any assumption that all women have the same problems or are oppressed in essentially similar ways. Putting this more positively, Lynne Segal (1987: 67) writes: 'But now, in analysing relations of exploitation or oppression, socialist feminists should, I think, begin by asserting the very different problems of diverse groups of women and stress the contradictory changes which have taken place in women's lives.'

Some limitations of the different perspectives

Each perspective has some limitations, and there is much mutual criticism by holders of different perspectives. Liberal feminists are seen by radical and socialist feminists as elitist: offering opportunity only to a few privileged white women who may make it within existing hierarchical arrangements. Furthermore, socialist feminists suggest that the keenness of liberal feminists to prevent decisions being made on the basis of biological difference leads them to underplay genuine differences between the circumstances and desires of men and women. Socialist feminists stress that equality of opportunity is not the same as equality of outcome. In societies where everybody does not start equal, offering fair treatment does little to redress the disadvantages that many women face from the beginning.

Radical feminists are criticized by socialist feminists for their focus on gender differences as the overriding source of inequality as this ignores the diversity of experiences of women from different race and class backgrounds. Indeed, it can be said that the emphasis within radical feminism on women's strengths comes dangerously near to accepting a physiological and unchanging basis for differences between men and women. Arguments about what is natural can trap women into remaining in roles which they want to leave. Men may be characterized as the enemy, and women as their inevitable victims. If women are victims, then how can they also be agents of change?

Socialist feminists are criticized by radicals for their willingness to make alliances with men which prioritize class over gender and keep women's interests secondary. Radical feminists believe the focus of socialist feminists on capitalism fails to explain power relations between men and women, nor does it adequately describe the countless ways in which men hold power over women through control of their sexuality and the threat of violence.

All three perspectives have been criticized as being dominated by privileged white Western women's concerns. Some black women see racism as a more urgent problem than sexism, while others argue for redefining and reclaiming the meaning of feminism (Bryan et al., 1985). Black feminist perspectives are increasingly treated as a further major theoretical perspective in texts on social work and welfare (Dominelli and McLeod, 1989; Williams, 1989).

Work by black feminists has had some impact on the perspectives outlined above. Black feminists have been particularly critical of the tendency of white radical feminists to assume that they can speak for women of all races. Campaigns around abortion, for instance, do not always acknowledge that for black women the 'right to choose' also means the right to choose to *have* children. Many black women have complained that far from being denied abortion their problem has been pressure to use contraception, have an abortion, be sterilized, regardless of their own preference (Bryan et al., 1985). Perhaps socialist feminists have been readiest to adapt practice to meet criticisms from black feminists, since they see different forms of oppression as interlinked rather than standing in a hierarchical relationship.

In recent years, differences between women have been expressed not so much in political terms as in terms of identity. Women have looked for support and change in their lives from groupings which emphasize being black, or disabled, or lesbian or older. These allegiances have sometimes cut across the more political divisions of liberal, radical and socialist feminism. Thus the tripartite classificaton of feminist theory involves some oversimplification of the complexity of debates, and does not do justice to other feminist approaches (more fully discussed in Williams, 1989). However, it is a useful device to highlight areas of disagreement, and to demonstrate the different emphases for strategy produced by contrasting theoretical perspectives.

Feminism and social work

So how have these three strands of feminist theory informed strategy in social work? Social work is essentially an area where women are in the majority: as social workers, users of services, volunteers, carers, home and residential care assistants. The perspectives offered by feminism would appear to be vital to social services workers and to users. Yet it is only in recent years that publications have emerged linking feminist theory and practice in social work (Wearing, 1986; Hanmer and Statham, 1988; Dominelli and McLeod, 1989). Mainstream social work texts have on the whole ignored the obvious: that social work is a gendered activity. In spite of the neglect of feminist perspectives by social work academics, the influence of these different perspectives can be traced in the strategies of some social work practitioners.

Liberal feminism and social work

The major issues of concern to liberal feminists are socialization and sex stereotyping, equal opportunities and sex discrimination. Strategies to counteract sexual stereotyping in the socialization process have been developed mainly in educational settings, but appear too in day-care provision and residential settings. Examples can be found in the conscious use of positive images of girls and women in a children's home, policies that sexist behaviour in a youth club will be confronted, and in efforts to involve men in activities in family centres.

Application of equal opportunities to social work involves a focus on women's rights to professional advancement on equal terms with men; scrutiny of practices in interviewing and selection which may inhibit women's advancement; provision of nursery services and arrangements for job-sharing to make it easier for women to combine work and family life. Countering sexual discrimination involves a questioning of social work practices which identify women as responsible for family life. More positively, it might mean encouragement of women to reach their full potential, whether this is through individual counselling or group activities.

It is rare these days to find a developed argument for liberal feminism in social work literature, as this perspective has received so much criticism from other feminists. However, the liberal feminists' language of equal opportunities is the most acceptable one to the general public, and to social work management. So those feminists who might prefer larger-scale changes may be prepared to compromise and use the liberal feminist language when this seems likely to be effective. Liberal feminist strategies are framed in a way that can be written in official documents, where references to sexism, patriarchy and oppression might cause alarm. In this sense, although the targets of liberal feminists may be reformist and small-scale, they do represent achievable gains.

Radical feminism and social work

Radical feminism has had its most obvious impact in social work in the creation of women only organizations with a specific focus on issues affecting women. Women's refuges, rape crisis lines and women's centres offering advice on contraception, health issues, abortion and mental health have all helped develop recognition in more mainstream organizations of how women's experience differs from men's. As well as developing particular methods of working, such organizations have also had an important campaigning role.

There are limitations to separatist strategies. Organizations which remain outside mainstream social services provision can never really develop as a viable alternative for all women. On the other hand, if they are co-opted by social services, some feminists fear that their radical potential will be destroyed (Wilson, 1980; Mama, 1989). Recommendations for mainstream service-providers have been mainly along the lines that workers should make links with all-women feminist organizations, and learn from them (Hudson, 1985). There may be a need for two-way learning. Lee Ann Hoff (1990) suggests that workers in women's refuges are often resistant to drawing on theories of crisis intervention or counselling, and could benefit from more formal training in these areas.

Radical feminism has the reputation of being an extremist approach. Yet the high campaigning profile and creation of new organizations which demand attention could be said to have provided a more serious challenge than other feminist strategies to the complacency of traditionally minded social service organizations and the men who tend to head them. For instance, the work done by rape crisis lines and women's refuges in publicizing the sexual abuse suffered (in childhood) by many adult women has been crucial in sensitizing social services staff and others to the extent of child sexual abuse.

The literature which stems from a radical feminist tradition tends to be accessible and lively, and has therefore passed more easily into popular consciousness (for example, the work of Dale Spender and Kate Millett). The visible achievements of radical feminist organizations hold out the promise that change is possible, and that women's problems can be re-framed and approached in ways that do not oppress women.

Socialist feminism and social work

The long-term aim of contemporary socialist feminists in analysing Western capitalist states is to remove exploitation and oppression. A more immediate concern is to clarify the processes involved, and to find ways of working within current structures which allow for the possibility of more fully developed socialism in the future. Many socialist feminist theorists have focused on women's position within the economy and the family, and tried to take account of the concept of patriarchy in explaining women's oppression under capitalism. While there are diverse approaches within a socialist feminist framework, areas of agreement include the idea that men's and women's behaviour should be understood as socially constructed differences rather than biologically determined; that links should be made between personal experience and political understanding; and that women of different race, age and class have different experiences and needs as well as some shared experiences of oppression.

In a social work context these themes emerge in the desire to organize provision in non-sexist and non-hierarchical ways, so that divisions between service-providers and users are minimized, greater control over service provision is given to women users, and the unpaid welfare work of caring done by most women is recognized. Lynne Segal (1987: 244) explains socialist feminist strategy as follows:

New cracks keep appearing in the interlinking structures of men's power and privileges in relation to women. It is in deepening these cracks that feminists can work to strengthen the power of women to participate in creating the type of future we want for ourselves and others.

Strategically, this means feminists fighting for minimum wages, shorter 'working' hours, leave for caretakers and an independent income for those caring for dependents in the home. It means policies for the recruitment, promotion and training of women, particularly for jobs which have excluded women.

Clearly some similarities can be found in the involvement of both liberal and socialist feminists in action for more equal opportunities. Socialist feminists stress the point that oppressions are interlinked. So they are likely to be found working not simply on women's issues, but upon more general implementation of anti-discriminatory practice, perhaps through trade union activity or engagement in low-pay disputes. An example of the possibility of working on a number of issues at the same time is provided by socialist feminists who were involved in developing Islington's child protection policy. They aimed to raise awareness of gender issues, but within the context of a policy intended to be child-centred and anti-discriminatory.

Areas of common ground in feminism

These outlines of different feminist theory and strategy may conjure up images of feminists divided into firmly separated camps, the members of which never speak to each other. Yet many feminist activists do not define themselves as espousing exclusively any of the three perspectives I have described. And since the differences between these strands of feminism are mainly about differences of explanation and overall political strategy, feminists of different persuasions are able to find many areas of agreement in practice and immediate strategy.

For example, all feminists advocate that for some purposes women should work together, without men present, using a 'consciousness raising' approach. In social work contexts this could cover a range of possibilities: groupwork with women offenders; therapy groups; support groups at work; self-help groups. Differences between groups would be more in the rationale for their existence than any distinctive methods. For a liberal feminist the rationale might be that women need to work together to gain confidence in asserting their rights. A radical feminist might emphasize that women need to be free from the distraction that men provide in taking centre stage in discussion, as well as free from a reminder of the threat that men have been to them personally; and to have an opportunity to develop their own ways of working together. A socialist feminist might focus on the importance of women linking their own experiences with the social structure; recognizing commonality and diversity in the experiences of women of different backgrounds, classes, races; and seeking to transform social relations.

Thus Trisha Comley (1989: 70), writing from a socialist feminist perspective, suggests that:

> groupwork with women clients could nurture a forum within which the physical and psychological isolation that many women, confined to the demands of home and family, experience, could be counteracted through the development of collective supportive relationships. At the same time, an opportunity is presented for women to explore ideas about the types of social services that would meet their needs. In both instances, a direct challenge is made to prevailing power relations.

She suggests that the same approach could be taken by social workers in their own agencies: 'Support networks of women social workers . . . offer the possibility of mutual support and collective strength . . . a decisive threat to pre-existing relations grounded in notions of hierarchy and exclusion' (Comley, 1989: 70).

Writing of the need for women social services managers to find strategies for survival, in the more liberal feminist territory of equal opportunities, Ruth Eley (1989: 185) also advocates seeking out other women at work:

> Tapping into a network puts me in touch with others, one of whom is almost certainly going to feel able and willing to fight that particular battle at that time . . . .
>
> There is no doubt that the woman manager will need to be assertive. Women in senior positions are a threat and risk rough treatment or humiliation if they challenge male supremacy and even if they don't. Rather than being a domineering, competitive individualistic approach, assertion can be grounded in concern for others.

So where Comley emphasizes 'threat' as a goal, Eley seeks to soften the effect of women taking on unfamiliar roles. She wants women managers to be effective and not embattled.

With a different emphasis again, Jane Black and Bie Nio Ong (1986) write of their experience in running women's health courses. Their approach is in the more radical feminist tradition that challenges the dominant masculine ideas of the medical profession:

> We make connections between women's roles in society (carer, worker, mother, wife, and so on) and patterns of health and illness among women . . . In group discussions, women can recapture medical knowledge and relate it to their own experiences, self-image and concepts of health and illness . . . By sharing, we can go beyond individual experiences, begin to see the more general patterns of health and illness, and relate these to women's role in society and to how we are oppressed by being kept ignorant as a group. (Black and Ong, 1986: 23)

Here the potential for change is in women recapturing power over their own bodies.

Conclusion

Feminism's impact upon social work practice overall has been marginal to date. Perhaps because more work remains to be done, much of the literature on feminist social work has tended to be eclectic, drawing on a range of perspectives, and exploring the possibilities for action that these suggest (see, for instance, Hudson, 1985; Hanmer and Statham, 1988).

While theory can inspire more imaginative practice, it has also to be rooted in the experience of practice. Sophie Watson (1990) argues that there is no such thing as a coherent set of women's demands existing independently outside the political and bureaucratic arenas. Rather, feminist strategy is developed in practice, and is actually constructed by the response of the state to feminist demands. So once demands are met, women begin to have an expectation that further demands may meet with success.

The interaction of practical results with theory-building provides one set of reasons for feminists to be pragmatic and seize opportunities when they arise. Evangelism provides another: feminists want as many people as possible to listen to their arguments about the position of women rather than react with hostility every time the subject of feminism comes up (Radcliffe Richards, 1980). It is in the interests of the development of feminist practice to have as many women as possible thinking of themselves as feminists. This has led feminist social work academics to stress the breadth of possibilities offered by feminism: the common goals rather than the different purposes.

References

Acker, S. (1987) 'Feminist theory and the study of education', *International Review of Education*, 410–35.

Black, J. and Ong, B. N. (1986) 'Women and health courses: our bodies, our business', in C. Webb (ed.) *Feminist Practice in Women's Health Care*. Chichester: Wiley.

Bryan, D., Dadzie, S. and Scafe, S. (1985) *The Heart of the Race*. London: Virago.

Comley, T. (1989) 'State social work: a socialist–feminist contribution', in C. Hallet (ed.), *Women and Social Service Departments*. London: Harvester Wheatsheaf.

Daly, M. and Caputi, C. (1988) *Websters' First New Intergalactic Wickedary of the English Language*, London: Women's Press.

Dominelli, L. and McLeod, E. (1989) *Feminist Social Work*. Basingstoke: Macmillan.

Eisenstein, H. (1984) *Contemporary Feminist Thought*. London: Unwin.

Eley, R. (1989) 'Women in management in social services departments', in C. Hallet (ed.), *Women and Social Service Departments*. London: Harvester Wheatsheaf.

Friedan, B. (1971) *The Feminine Mystique*. London: Victor Gollancz.

Hanmer, J. and Statham, D. (1988) *Women and Social Work: Towards a Woman-centred Practice*. Basingstoke: Macmillan.

Hoff, L. A. (1990) *Battered Women as Survivors*. London: Routledge.

Hudson, A. (1985) 'Feminism and social work: resistance or dialogue?', *British Journal of Social Work*, 15: 6.

Mama, A. (1989) 'Violence against black women: gender, race and state responses', *Feminist Review*, 32: 31–48.

Radcliffe Richards, J. (1980) *The Sceptical Feminist*. London: Routledge & Kegan Paul.

Segal, L. (1987) *Is the Future Female? Troubled Thoughts on Contemporary Feminism*. London: Virago.

Watson, S. (1990) 'The state of play: an introduction', in S. Watson (ed.), *Playing the State: Australian Feminist Interventions*. London: Verso.

Wearing, B. (1986) 'Feminist theory and social work', in H. Marchant and B. Wearing (eds), *Gender Reclaimed: Women and Social Work*. Sydney: Hale and Iremonger.

Williams, F. (1989) *Social Policy: a Critical Introduction, Issues of Race, Gender and Class*. Cambridge: Polity Press.

Wilson, E. (1980) 'Feminism and social work', in M. Brake and R. Bailey (eds), *Radical Social Work and Practice*. London: Edward Arnold.

13

TOWARDS AN ANTI-RACIST CURRICULUM IN SOCIAL WORK TRAINING

DON NAIK

'The problem of the twentieth century is the problem of the colour-line' said W.E.B. du Bois in 1903. Some ninety years later, the truth of du Bois' statement endures in stark defiance of all our efforts to contradict and destroy it.

Britain is a multi-racial society which has been formed to a large extent by immigration from countries with very different social, political and economic histories, thus making it also a multi-cultural society. There are bound to be substantial differences in the needs and requirements of the different cultural groups in British society and these differences are reflected in the ways in which social services are planned and delivered. Social service delivery and practice is thus directly affected by the differential needs and requirements of a multi-cultural society.

Other forces operating in British society are insidious racism which permeates all strata and sectors of Britain's social structure and which impact on social service planning and its delivery systems. In some instances racism is overt, in others covert. Sometimes it manifests as direct racism and on other occasions as indirect racism. Regardless of whatever form it takes, its effect is to disadvantage blacks. (The term 'black' is used in this article to refer to people of Asian, Afro-Caribbean or other New Commonwealth origin or descent.) These facts have a number of clear implications for social work educationists and social work students.

In the past decade, critics of a mono-cultural social work education system have divided into those who advocate 'multi-cultural' and those who advocate 'anti-racist' social work education. The divisions in the late 1980s resulted from the different emphases placed on cultural teaching and its predominantly eurocentric nature. Theories of cultural pluralism, as

Abridged from Central Council for Education and Training in Social Work, *One Small Step towards Racial Justice: the Teaching of Antiracism in Social Work Programmes*, CCETSW, London, 1991 opposed to structural pluralism, in multi-cultural social work obviate facing uncomfortable questions about control, power and conflict. The 'race' dimension in social work education is fragmentary and incomplete, often superficial and inconsequential, and varies widely from region to region. It is non-existent in many areas, and nowhere is it wholly adequate.

As a result, many social work tutors and lecturers cannot teach an anti-racist content effectively because they have not experienced work with an ethnically diverse population and have not had professional preparation for social work teaching in a multi-racial society. The position is that social work institutions have relied on the spirit of voluntarism and altruism in their staff rather than developing competence through an approved programme of study. This is not the case with other social work subjects, programmes and contexts. In fact, staff will not be expected to teach with such a drawback. These factors have created a demand for anti-racist teaching in both social work and other related disciplines. There is therefore a need for conceptual coherence and deliberately planned strategies to prepare social work tutors to teach within an anti-racist framework.

There has been a conflict between anti-racist and multi-cultural approaches to social work education. Anti-racist education is interested in power, rather than culture, the political and economic, rather than mere social work issues and in changing the social and educational structures, rather than the social worker's sensitivities.

Of late, most educationists have begun to realize that both approaches are one-sided. Multi-cultural social work cannot open up the social work educational system unless it challenges the present dominance of euro-centric patterns. It remains ineffective without an anti-racist thrust. Similarly, anti-racist social work education remains ineffective unless it is given a well-conceived curricular content. It thus runs the risk of forfeiting the autonomy of the teaching institutions if it takes the direction towards overwhelming political objectives.

Advocates of both approaches are also beginning to realize that by engaging in ideological rhetoric, they are failing to get down to the tasks of understanding the complexity of the social work education system, examining the experimental and research evidence, and devising effective ways of evolving an anti-racist social work education system.

Race is one of the most important dimensions in social work education where the crisis actively manifests itself. The current social work educational system is a vehicle for racism and needs to be radically changed. Multi-cultural education is essentially 'social democratic'; it fails to attend to *structural inequalities in society*, and masks the dynamics of race, economics and political power – how and why minority groups, whether they be of ethnic, social class or cultural origins, are disadvantaged in relation to dominant groups in society. What is needed is the teaching of various subjects in social work within a clearly stated anti-racist framework.

The position of black communities settled in Britain, as viewed by the white community, range across the whole spectrum of opinion on race issues. Some whites argue that Britain cannot and should not accept the black communities and urge their repatriation. Others contend that such a step is undesirable and would like to see the black communities fully integrated into British society. However, they differ as to what integration actually means and what is involved. To some, integration implies assimilation, understood in its strict sense of obliterating the cultural identity of the respective black communities and requiring them to adopt British values and practices. Others take integration to mean a pluralist society in which black communities are free to retain their cultural individuality consistent with the demands of law and order.

This notion of a pluralist society raises questions about which areas of life cultural pluralism should be tolerated and even encouraged and which areas of life uniformity should be insisted upon. Almost every manifestation of cultural diversity – from diet, dress and language, to marriage tradition and the socialization of children – has relevance to these issues.

These views, in turn, shape the main features of social work policies and practices. The first model is one of integration and assimilation, influenced by a belief that the black community should be integrated into the Western way of life. Integration is regarded as positively beneficial to the black community as they could be assimilated within the service structure.

The second model is one of cultural diversity in which social work practice would be enhanced by knowledge of the culture of black communities. This model leads to the development of cultural modules designed to inform social work professionals about the family patterns of their black clients. It has unwittingly reinforced the prejudice of practitioners and narrowed their perspectives with cultural stereotypes. It is, in fact, a cultural deficit model based on the process of problem orientation with the 'problem' invariably placed within the culture of the black community.

Recently, awareness of the need to focus on social work policies and practices and to link them to multi-ethnic practice without the damaging effects of cultural stereotyping has developed. Attention has also been given to providing services to black communities without discriminatory effects. Yet the influence of the 'integration and assimilation' model still persists in social service structures and operations resulting in this ideology remaining at the root of the practices and structures of the helping agencies. Clearly, the appropriate model for social work policies and practices is neither 'assimilation' nor 'cultural diversity' but that of a pluralistic society based on 'race equality'.

Pluralism means the acceptance of the black person as a full member of British society equally entitled to the liberties and privileges enjoyed by the rest of the community. Such a concept requires three prerequisites:

1 The black person should enjoy full equality in legal, social, economic and political matters.
2 The black person's distinctive cultural identity should be respected and provision should be made to meet his/her basic demands.

3   Nothing should be done to devalue the black person's humanity or to undermine his or her self-respect or to make the black person feel he or she is less than a full human being living at the community's sufferance.

Given this conceptual model, what is the role of the social worker? Is he or she an agent of control and conformity to social standards and if so, whose standards? Is the task to bring about social change? Should social workers manipulate the norms? What should the value system practised by the social worker be within a pluralist society?

At a general level, it can be argued that because the transcultural, socioeconomic and political dimensions are missing from the main theoretical subjects of psychology, sociology, social policy and social work methodology that these subjects lack relevance to a pluralistic society. It could be further argued that teaching and practice in social work are geared to the concept of a uni-racial rather than a multi-racial society. The uni-racial society concept suggests that Britain is a white society upon which certain marginal groups have been appended, with the consequences that there is a predominant norm (value system) based on 'whiteness' in which other cultural characteristics can be tolerated or accommodated as long as they do not threaten white values, norms and mores.

At the other end of the spectrum, the pluralist view of society, recognizes the existence of opposing interests and a different distribution of power and resources by which interests can be protected and enhanced. The structural origin of such group conflicts manifests itself in social roles which are endowed with expectations of domination or subjection.

It appears that social work has embraced the theory of integration as its ideology, based on the concept of a uni-racial model of society. The black community regards British society as made of different racial groups. The black community thus interprets events within the framework of a conflict and coercion theory and the social work educationist and the practitioners interpret the same events within a consensus theory.

This divergence implies that the two (the practitioner and their subject) adhere to different sets of premisses. This two-party model implies different ways of viewing and relating to social work. One practical manifestation of social work's perspective is the exclusion of conflict strategy from the professionals' knowledge base and techniques. Practitioners who engage in or actively encourage the use of conflict are denounced as performing illegitimate professional roles.

In the main, black people are excluded from key decision-making processes of public and private institutions and organizations. Evidence suggests that many of these bodies treat black people less favourably on racial grounds, because institutional racism is an integral feature of organizational structures and individual attitudes. It follows that the organizational arrangements in social work agencies and the educational institutions, which determine how jobs are offered, to whom services are provided, facilities made available and resources allocated have to be radically re-appraised.

The present system (Ouseley, 1980) comprising managers, tutors on social work courses and administrators who run these institutions are not only powerful but their attitudes, actions and practice ultimately distort the student composition of the course structures and its underlying ideology.

English language (Ohri, 1982) is also used as a powerful means to obscure primary issues, particularly in relation to racism. For example, white racism is not highlighted as a primary issue; instead, the emphasis is placed on the phenomenon of racism and emphasis is laid on the victims of racism as a phenomenon for study rather than the structural dynamics of a funda-mentally racist society. The result is that racism is reduced to racial disadvantage and the question raised is how to address that inherent disadvantage as opposed to how to change the system using the strategy of anti-racism.

Curriculum issues

Objectives of social work teaching can be defined in terms of the behavioural and content aspects. What are the ways of thinking, feeling and acting that the student needs to learn to become a social worker? What knowledge content will the student be expected to understand? The content and behavioural aspects are so closely related that they must be defined almost as one process in developing the curriculum (Tyler, 1960).

In the behavioural model the process starts by the selection of objectives, goes on to the identification of learning experience to achieve those objectives and terminates with an evaluation of how successful the learning experiences have been. For evaluation to be possible, the objectives must be behavioural, that is, precisely stated, observable and assessable. Learning experiences are interpreted as a purely instrumental function, and it is assumed that those which will lead to the achievement of stated objectives can be ascertained. The difficulty for social work educationists is how to translate teaching in terms of race-related issues and their impact on social work practice.

Social work teaching requires a balance between how blacks view their place in British society and cope with its imperatives (experiential rather than empirical) on the one hand and research-related material, on the other hand. It must also be acknowledged that research related to black experiences uses methodological and conceptual tools which are not rooted in, and formed by, a living contact with their subject matter. Until research can offer coherent and vigorous theoretical accounts of black experiences in Britain, which is theorized by black people, the experiences of the black com-munities and black students on social work courses will have to be used in a positive teaching form, rather than be dismissed as lacking in empirical evidence.

The main components of the curriculum should include multi-cultural conceptual and philosophical understanding; sociocultural sensitivity to ethnic communities; cultural knowledge; learning to analyse students' own and clients' ethnic attitudes and values, culturally relevant diagnosis and assessment techniques; appropriate strategies for combating racism, developing different methodological skills for implementing anti-racist social work in the community (Baker, 1983). Specific knowledge, skills and attitudes essential for effective anti-racist practices must stem from personal, professional and community needs and perspectives.

An essential aspect of anti-racist social work, one closely related to theory, is philosophy. That is, the values, beliefs and assumptions which constitute the ideology of anti-racist practice. Social work courses should include comparative analysis of the different ideologies of multi-culturalism so that social workers can: (a) become familiar with different ideological positions in conceptualizing anti-racist social work; (b) understand how and why ideology influences practice; and (c) establish a basis from which they can forge their own personal philosophy of anti-racist practices. On the whole, the anti-racist social work curriculum needs to be both international in its choice of content and global in its perspective.

A common approach in teaching is to take immediate surface mani-festations of a problem at face value and to look at how prejudices arise through an attitudinal or social-psychological perspective. A more effective approach is to examine the structures which generate particular kinds of discriminatory attitudes between people from different ethnic populations and prejudicial actions, beliefs and opinions.

This will allow tutors and students to question the deep structural factors which not only perpetuate racial practices and institutional racism but also re-enact them in a pervasive and entrenched form. Teaching strategies which engage students' obvious apprehensions about race are also important.

Anti-racist social work education can only become clearer if the issues of institutionalized racism and the problems between dominant and sub-ordinate groups are identified. Those who adhere to multi-culturalism do not tend to come to grips with the substantive issues raised by this concept. They also tend to develop those perspectives which only deal mechanistically with issues of racism while ignoring institutionalized inequalities.

Social work education requires an analysis of the multi-cultural and anti-racist aspects of the total curriculum thereby making social work teaching and its practice relevant to the present day multi-ethnic society. For the future it should aim towards social work education for a non-racial society.

The alternative is to risk the charge that social work training and social workers today are irrelevant to black people. This charge is justified if all they can bring with them is the knowledge, skills and attitudes belonging to the operating procedure of a mono-racial social work education system, designed to maintain the structural inequalities of institutional racism.

References

Baker, G.C. (1983) *Planning and Organising for Multicultural Education*. Reading, MA: Addison-Wesley.

Ohri, A. (1982) *Community Work and Racism*. London: Routledge & Kegal Paul.

Ouseley, H. (1980) *The System*. London: The Runnymede Trust/South London Equal Rights Consultancy.

Tyler, R.W. (1960) *Building the Social Work Curriculum. Report of the National Curriculum Workshop*. New York: Council on Social Work Education.

14

COMMONALITIES AND DIVERSITIES BETWEEN WOMEN CLIENTS AND WOMEN SOCIAL WORKERS

JALNA HANMER and DAPHNE STATHAM

We are not accustomed or trained to think about commonalities and diversities between ourselves and our clients as a rich resource for practice. To be useful for practice, commonality and diversity have to be re-recognized and re-conceptualized. This is necessary because commonalities can be confused with sameness, and diversities can be confused with traditionally drawn boundaries between clients and workers.

Generic issues

As we all know, client groups are the elderly, children and young people, the mentally and physically handicapped, ethnic minorities, the delinquent and criminal. Attention is focused on certain aspects of problems while ignoring other areas of commonalities between the individuals contained within these classifications. For example, most clients are working class and poor, but these are not the commonalities around which social work practice and services are organized (Jones, 1983). Similarly, gender is excluded as a means of categorizing the people who use social services.

There is no particular logic in excluding from social work classifications the categories adults, women, men, the poor and unemployed, except that client groups are those categories for which the state has accepted overtly some responsibility for their care and control. These responsibilities are formalized through the statutes relating to social services and probation. Yet they do not necessarily make sense as a way of categorizing people to those

Abridged from *Women and Social Work: Towards a Woman Centred Practice*, British Association of Social Workers/Macmillan, Basingstoke, 1988 outside social work. For instance, physical handicap is a meaningless grouping to an anthropologist (Oliver, 1983), and community groups are more likely to find common cause around such issues as poverty, housing, unemployment, racism, women or neighbourhood.

The idea of gender as a significant dimension in social work is not a new one. Kadushin as long ago as 1976 stated that gender issues are embedded in the profession and service delivery. Even using existing client categories, specific problems, such as drug use or offending behaviour by women, involve returning to the position of women in society (Gottlieb, 1980; Garvin and Reed, 1983).

Commonalities

Women social workers and clients share commonalities. They group around being female, their relationships with men, children, living within the nuclear family, employment possibilities and working conditions, and more general cultural expectations and pressures on women. These commonalities offer both a resource and a strength for practice. We suggest that it is only through a recognition of commonalities that a true assessment of the situation facing women clients and a client-centred practice can emerge.

In social work there is no stress on commonality between social workers and clients. We come across commonalities more by accident than as part of our formal training and education. We can feel surprise, shock, shame and denial. To recognize commonalities is thought to raise the danger of overidentification, of overemotional involvement, thereby producing an inability to respond to the clients' problems 'objectively'. This can negate important commonalities like gender, class, age, race, sexuality, culture and other differentiating characteristics between people.

The capacity to become self-aware is valued in social work. Understanding ourselves, our values and attitudes and the impact our style of work has on others is regarded as an important part of training and professional development. Recognizing and understanding gendered experience, however, is largely ignored as an important element in developing self-awareness.

Discussions on self-disclosure are equally gender-blind. While the merits and demerits of self-disclosure are frequently discussed in the literature on counselling and interviewing (Sutton, 1979), gender, like being black or age, is not something we can choose when or where to disclose. It is not a matter of working at the client's pace or, for that matter, our own. It is visible from first contact.

In making the commonalities we share as women conscious visible parts of our practice, we learn that we need not, and indeed must not, be ashamed or surprised by them but incorporate them into our work. One way to bring commonalities into the open in our thinking and planning is to make them explicit in some way, for instance, beginning with the individual or collective drawing up a list. We can then build on it and revise it as our lives change and develop thereby making the recognition of commonalities a conscious part of our practice.

For men the task is different. They need to find ways of drawing into their conscious practice what they see as commonalities between women in an effort to move towards a more sophisticated understanding of gender. A move is required from stereotypical assumptions and responses such as: 'typical woman', 'just like a woman', 'can't trust a woman', towards a deeper understanding and perception of the lives and experiences of women clients and colleagues. It then becomes possible for male social workers to examine the impact of their behaviour towards colleagues. Equally important for male workers whose work is primarily with women is to translate these understandings into practice. Men can also begin to identify attitudes and behaviour towards male clients and colleagues whose work or family situations involve them in tasks usually carried out by women. Men need to learn to be comfortable with gender deviance and diversity amongst themselves.

Diversities

Diversities exist between the same categories of women: between clients; between women workers; between women generally. Diversities, however, are frequently not readily apparent except in stereotypical ways. The task of identification requires conscious deliberation and gives rise to questions such as: are power relations basic to diversity? Who decides what is a diversity between women? What is the significance of diversities? For example, how do race or class or gender or the expression of sexuality interact? Are these diversities natural qualities or socially determined attributes? All are important questions to which there are no easy or simple answers. They need debate and discussion; there will be disagreement and conflict. Over time we may change our minds because of new experience or knowledge, but it is important to make these opinions part of our conscious assessment and plans.

Employment

Professional status brings social workers as opposed to women clients a higher earning capacity and equal pay with men, greater access to education and training, better conditions of work, and a job which allows greater flexibility to plan and organize work. Adequate pay gives social workers access to decent housing, transport and opens up options for women generally.

Unlike social workers, most women clients will be in workplaces where there is occupational segregation of men and women. In a survey of women's employment carried out in 1981, 63 per cent of women worked in jobs done only by women at their place of work (Martin and Roberts, 1984).

In the same survey, 81 per cent of the women's husbands worked only alongside men, where the pay and often the conditions of employment were better.

Black and white women

The recognition of diversities is particularly acute when black clients meet white social workers and black social workers meet white clients. Combining gender differences with race intensifies diversity; for example, white women clients with black men social workers or black women clients with white men social workers (Bhavnani, 1987). Black social workers also experience a status contradiction from being black and holding power as a social worker (Harrison, 1987).

The day-to-day lives of poor black and poor white women within the family, combining paid work with domestic labour and caring for children and dependent adults are commonalities. However, racism means that black women have to live with a sharper sense of the contradiction that the family is both oppressive to them and at the same time a source of support. For black women, the family is a refuge from racism. For a number of black people immigration controls mean separation from their children and husbands, wives and fiancé(e)s. The aim is to unite the members of the family (Cohen, 1980; Cohen and Siddiqi, 1985; Women, Immigration and Nationality Group, 1985).

Recognizing commonalities means understanding that there are areas in which black women's struggles and issues are different from those of white women. In action a black woman may decide to prioritize being black. In terms of her experience, however, being black and a woman is hard to separate (Bhavnani, 1987). Black women are acutely conscious of the discriminatory way black men are treated at their places of work, on the streets, and by the criminal justice system. Both in the UK (Home Office, 1986) and in the USA (Burden and Gottlieb, 1987) the construction of black men as abusers, aggressive criminals and rapists feeds into the power of white people and, in our view, particularly that of white men.

Feeling powerful – feeling powerless

Women clients and social workers do not meet as equals, and in focusing on commonalities we must not forget the power differences between social worker and client. But this is not a simple dichotomy, although the powerful statutory social worker versus the powerless women clients is a theme in many discussions. A second way in which a power–powerlessness dichotomy is organized is to experience oneself, a woman social worker, as powerless and the agency as powerful. Although we all feel like this at times, in relation both to clients and organizational structures, a crude division of powerful–powerless is an oversimplification. This is so both in a general sense when thinking in categories, i.e. clients and social workers, social workers and organizations, and when considering the relationships of specific clients with specific social workers or individual social workers with individual line managers.

Awareness of differences arises out of direct experience and sharing what we learn with and from each other. There is a danger that in a predominantly white, heterosexual, able-bodied and middle-class workforce certain differences are given more attention than others. Income, relationships with men and education are emphasized rather than disability, race, ethnic minority memberships, lesbianism or age.

We suggest that how *this* particular woman's situation and problems differ from one's own should become a part of assessment. Differences in status, power, role, lifestyle, race, culture, sexuality, education, work possibilities, access to community resources, degree of stigma and hope are elements in the differentiation of social worker from client. But how is the recognition of diversities aided by the recognition of similarities?

Recognizing diversity through commonality

Recognizing commonalities affects the approach of the social worker. While it may appear paradoxical, recognizing commonalities gives the social worker the psychological distance necessary to see the client in her setting. The worker is given both the personal space and the theoretical perspective to enable her to recognize how the forces of society in general and of personal relationships in particular affect the client's emotional and practical responses.

Without a process of recognizing first commonalities and then differences, the danger of stereotyping women clients as the 'not coping' and social workers as the 'coping' is far greater. This process of psychological distancing results in objectifying the woman client; seeing her in terms of social roles rather than as a person in her own right. The recognition of the woman's own strength, powers and her ability to solve problems, is inhibited. There can be a lack of contact rather than a reflective response.

The greater insight that comes from the recognition of diversities in the context of commonality is rooted in genuine contact with and perception of the other person. Social workers who are open to this process and knowledge are less likely to impose either their own stereotypes or their personal solutions onto women clients. They will be able to make an assessment focused on the woman and on women clients, and will be more likely to facilitate groups for women who have common life experiences. The empowerment they offer woman clients individually and collectively extends to themselves. They are less likely to despair within themselves; to see themselves silently and secretly as the only social worker who is 'not coping' among all their amazonian colleagues. They possess the potential to break through the definition of reality for women workers and clients which is portrayed by the cartoon showing women in little box-like flats in a tower block surrounded by dirty dishes and children asking 'Why can't I cope?', while the social worker in the nearby single-rise office surrounded by mounds of paper asks 'Why can't I cope?' This powerlessness can be broken by practice which makes the recognition of commonalities its cornerstone.

Recognizing commonalities encourages empathy and avoids responses that arise from victim blaming. Empathy facilitates the acknowledgement of the lack of choices for women. It inhibits the 'you ought' response however covert. For example, recognizing that difficulties in relationships with men are a part of many lives focuses attention and practice on how the client can gain more support from other women. The acknowledgement of shared health issues focuses attention on how to help the client reduce and deal with stress. Recognizing that women are oppressed as women creates reality in the social worker's approach.

References

Bhavnani, Reena (1987) Personal communication.

Burden, Dianne S. and Gottlieb, Naomi (eds) (1987) *The Woman Client: Providing Human Services in a Changing World*. New York and London: Tavistock.

Cohen, Steve (1980) *You Don't Have to be a Lawyer to Help Someone being Threatened with Immediate Arrest, Detention or Expulsion under the Immigration Act*. Manchester: Manchester Law Centre Immigration Handbook No. 4.

Cohen, Steve and Siddiqi, Nadia (1985) *What Would You Do if your Fiancée Went to the Moon?* Report of a working visit to Pakistan to investigate the cases of several Manchester residents whose fiancés/husbands have been refused entry into Britain. Manchester: The Manchester Wives and Fiancées Campaign, Manchester City Council.

Garvin, Charles and Reed, Beth Glover (1983) 'Gender issues in social group work: an overview', *Social Work with Groups*, 6 (3/4): 5–18.

Gottlieb, Naomi (ed.) (1980) *Alternative Social Services for Women*. New York: Columbia University Press.

Harrison, Mary (1987) Personal communication.

Home Office (1986) 'The ethnic origins of prisoners: the prison population on 30 June 1985 and persons received July 1984 – March 1985', *Statistical Bulletin*. London: HMSO.

Jones, Chris (1983) *State Social Work and the Working Class*. London: Macmillan.

Kadushin, Alfred (1976) 'Men in a women's profession', *Social Work*, 21: 440–7.

Martin, Jean and Roberts, Ceridwen (1984) 'Women's employment in the 1980s', *Employment Gazette*, May.

Oliver, Michael (1983) *Social Work with Disabled People*. London: Macmillan.

Sutton, Carol (1979) *Psychology for Social Workers and Counsellors: an Introduction*. London: Routledge & Kegan Paul.

Women, Immigration and Nationality Group (1985) *Women, Immigration and Nationality*. London: Pluto.

15

VIOLENCE AGAINST BLACK WOMEN: GENDER, RACE AND STATE RESPONSES

AMINA MAMA

Amina Mama examines responses to Black women, who have suffered domestic violence, in the context of rationing of resources. Such rationing may still be accompanied by proclamations of anti-discriminatory intent. Mama argues that welfare has never been evenly distributed in Britain, and that stereotypes of Black women place them at the back of the queue when resources are in short supply. Mama reviews local authority responses and the controls that are placed upon support to women's refuges. She notes that when there has been support and recognition of Black women's specific needs this has been on the basis of cultural difference rather than an acknowledgement of the effects of racism.

The women's refuge movement in Britain arose in the 1970s to meet the desperate situation of women seeking to escape from violent assaults in their homes, most commonly at the hands of their spouses. As a spontaneous initiative, the refuge movement was closely related to the women's movement, and operated mainly on the basis of the feminist ethos of the times: the principles that Women's Aid took up were those of sisterhood, collectivism and self-help. The network of refuges that sprang up in various parts of the country mainly retained these basic principles, and most of them affiliated to the Women's Aid Federation (WAFE) when it was formed in the mid-seventies (Binney et al., 1981).

The welfare state and the erosion of privilege

A race and gender analysis of British welfare service delivery indicates that welfare has never actually been a citizen's right in Britain, but rather a

Abridged from *Feminist Review*, 32, 1989, pp. 31–48

privilege delivered differentially to different groups by custodians of public resources.

Sections of the British left, for example those within Labour local authorities (LAs), are becoming increasingly vociferous about the erosion of rights. Yet the history of the development of welfare, and the circumscription of access to it, demonstrates that from the state's viewpoint these have been privileges directed to groups identified and defined as deserving. Municipal housing, for example, was developed initially to accommodate (white) war heroes returning from the trenches after the First Great European War rather than to accommodate poor or homeless families, or even Black war heroes.

With Britain grudgingly becoming more involved with the rest of Western Europe (albeit on the limited terrain acceptable to the Conservative government), the state of British welfare provision, which some would argue is shoddy and backward anyway, is being thrown into relief.

The disjuncture between paper policies and front-line staff practices is widening under the depletion of resources through cutbacks and privatization. In boroughs where dedicated women officers have struggled to develop a policy for rehousing the victims of domestic violence, resources are often not available to ensure its implementation. More than ever, declaring policies is being reduced to a rhetorical display motivated by what it is politic to appear to be doing. The same applies in the developing area of policies concerning the housing of victims of race attacks and to many of the other equal opportunities strategies developed in Labour LAs in recent years. As a result, it is now more evident than ever before just how difficult it is to effect changes in the practice of state institutions. It is not too much of an exaggeration to suggest a scenario in which town hall corridors echo with declarations of intent, even as their powers and resources are being stripped away from them, while queues build up of particular groups of people suffering the multiple degradation and oppression of long-term homelessness. This contradiction has taken material form in the reinforced structures now separating so-called front-line staff from the public in some boroughs. In Lambeth and Brent Homeless Persons Units, workers have been on strike demanding this top security protection from the increasingly desperate, and so increasingly threatening, public.

Progressive forces have been slow to respond to the recent deluge of changes, and reactions of outrage have been largely impotent in political terms. This is mainly because the British left has assumed that certain basic humanistic values would prevail, even in the corridors of power. This assumption renders them unable to comprehend the new and changing character of the British state in the late eighties. A consideration of service delivery to Black citizens demonstrates, beyond doubt, that the assumption of humanism is a fallacy. For example, if services had been delivered by right, Black people would not have had to wage a constant struggle against racism in the schools, hospitals, DHSS offices and housing departments, since delivery would have been egalitarian in the first place. The fact is that the welfare state has never existed universally for the public: it has always discriminated against certain groups of people and behaved punitively and coercively at the same time (Lawrence and Mama, 1988). In the most proudly Conservative boroughs, officials pride themselves on keeping their service delivery departments as empty as possible. But they are empty because people do not even get to the form-filling stage, as they are told that since they will get nothing they should not even apply, and that their application will not be registered in any case (Mama, 1989).

Neither equal opportunities policies nor the institution of various appeals mechanisms and tribunals have succeeded in ameliorating a situation in which front-line workers continue to enact their particular sense of civic duty *en masse.* So it is out of a sense of civic duty that they are racist, and this is in keeping with the contradictory but dominant discourses around race, empire and welfare, which position Black citizens as aliens, as rapidly breeding hordes, lazy scroungers, inherently violent criminals, or merely people with anti-social culinary habits and dirty lifestyles. These stereotypes enable the indirect manifestation of racism through ill-defined notions of deservability and respectability. Front-line officers heroically guard public resources from certain sections of the public; it is their duty to do so through the exercise of their perceptual and discretionary powers, and on the whole, they perform it well.

Autonomous resistance and state responses: refuges for women and Black women

In the present context, alternative action takes on a particular urgency. Autonomous initiatives that already exist (housing cooperatives, women's refuges) can be seen to hold the keys to survival strategies for the foreseeable future. The contradictory nature of public services regarding the needs of all women is most clearly seen in the gaps and omissions from policies and provisions. The reluctance of the state to respond to the crime of wife battering is one example. Women's refuges, set up at the initiative of small groups of women all over the country, are still the only agencies that offer anything like an appropriate service for abused women.

Take the cases of women subjected to violence in their homes. Women's refuges sprang up in the late 1970s in a community-initiated response to the refusal of agencies to respond to the most immediate emergency needs of women subjected to violent assaults by their sexual/emotional partners. This collective action brought the matter on to the agenda. It has been responded to in different ways by different organs of the state.

Initially, refuge provision was largely run by middle-class and white women, with very little involvement and uptake by other groups of women. The policy of employing women who had experienced violence themselves and stayed in refuges, initially as volunteers, not only guaranteed the reproduction of the collectivist self-help ethos, but also a gradually increasing involvement of working-class and Black women. Refuges are diverse in character, however, and many (particularly suburban and country refuges) remain exclusively white-staffed and run. Black women who are referred to these have been known to leave, unable to cope with the consequences of this in their already vulnerable state. Racism and insensitivity have thus sometimes combined and so returned them to the men they had sought to escape.

Local authority responses

Local authorities have responded in various ways to the existence of refuges. Some have been deliberately obstructive, or have simply ignored the existence of refuge provision and not informed women about Women's Aid. Others, out of a shortsighted vision of refuges as hostels that are substantially cheaper than bed and breakfast hotels, have abused refuges by filling them up with women who did not require the specialist provision which Women's Aid provides (i.e. a women-only environment in which women are encouraged to make their own decisions, and which provides emotional support and advice), by obliging women demanding housing to stay at the refuge before they would be considered. For example, Women's Aid was forced to stop accepting referrals from the Royal Borough of Kensington and Chelsea because of this practice. Other LAs have supported and made appropriate use of refuges, for the most part referring women who would benefit from their specialist support, and developing a working relationship between the housing department and refuge workers. Greenwich Women's Aid, for example, get on well with the housing department, but its staff are all white and few Black women stay there for any length of time. Lambeth Housing have established an annual quota reserved for homeless women referred from the refuge. A working relationship or agreement between housing department and refuge workers is important to facilitate the rehousing of women and the proper use of refuge facilities.

While the refuge movement has been an autonomous initiative its formal status is built on a contradiction. Most refuges have charitable status, but they have also had to obtain houses and sometimes workers' salaries from LAs. Many obtained some funding from the Greater London Council, and the London Borough Grants Scheme took over the GLC's obligations for the most part. The latter are currently reviewing their funding of refuges. The management of refuges has remained voluntary, and therefore free of state control, but this, too, is a constant struggle with, in some cases, council officers on management committees, ostensibly to help and facilitate liaison with the relevant LA.

The power struggle that is occurring is about control. It highlights the contradiction between the need for resources and funding, and the politically important struggle for autonomy waged by both white and Black women. It also illustrates the point that few resources – even if they are public resources paid for by people's taxes – come without demands for state control in one guise or another. What is being witnessed is a state encroachment into refuge management, even though it may be through supportive and well-intentioned liaising officers. This encroachment is most evident in refuges for Black women, and the race implications of this deserve particular attention. It is important that this power struggle is recognized as such, and the implications worked through. For example, it is questionable whether local authorities are in any position to be expanding the terrain over which they exercise their power in the voluntary sector. It does seem that well-intentioned officers would be better channelling their energies towards holding back the present erosion by central government of resources over which they have been in control rather than moving into new terrain. LA-controlled refuges would represent an attack on the autonomy which has been the force behind the refuge movement, and refuges are in danger of becoming another form of welfare if they compromise this autonomy too readily. Coming under increasing LA control may also drag refuges further into the mire of erosion and cutbacks that many LAs are suffering under the present central government.

In many (usually Labour-controlled) boroughs, the local state has introduced policies or codes of practice around the needs of battered women which cannot be detailed here. Policy development and practical implementation in this area, like the initiatives of the women's movement, are currently being seriously undermined by the central state, most obviously through the attack on public housing. Women have fought hard battles to gain the most from municipal housing, but now stand to lose all this because they depend on it more than men.

Central government responses

The development of refuges, and the agitation around violence against women from the women's movement, has produced contradictory responses from central government. On the one hand, a parliamentary committee was set up to investigate violence in marriage (Select Committee, 1975). Their recommendations concerning greater resources for refuge provision have, however, been ignored by the government. For example, they recommended one refuge place for every 10,000 of the population but there is still only one refuge for every 25,000 of the population (WAFE figures). On the other hand, in the past two years large sums of public money have been invested into Victim Support Schemes (VSS), which are a voluntary network. Domestic violence is the sole specialism of the women's refuge network which already exists and has accumulated substantial experience over the years. The resourcing of VSS over Women's Aid, despite their reluctance to relate consistently towards battered women, suggests that the issue is that of control and power: refuges are autonomous women's organizations with their own feminist ethos, policies and practices. Refuges also differ from most Victim Support Schemes in other ways: they do not often get involved in crime-reporting, for example.

Central government policies have had a negative impact on the success of the refuge movement over the recent period. The housing crisis brought about by the assault on local authority and public housing has meant that the refuge system has not simply remained congested due to acknowledged shortfall; but has become blocked because of the slowness of rehousing. Initially intended to be emergency temporary accommodation to support women while they obtained their own homes, refuges now find themselves housing women and their children for as long as two or even three years. The deleterious effects of this on women and children do not need spelling out. Refuges are generally overcrowded multi-occupancy dwellings, often in serious disrepair (because they are under-resourced). The increasing difficulty of getting women rehoused has the devastating effect of keeping the system entirely clogged up, so that there is no space for women seeking to escape from violence. The London Office of Women's Aid currently turns away more than half of their requests for accommodation because there is no place available. This has the effect of circumventing the most immediate aims of the refuge movement – to provide emergency support for women who have been assaulted by their partners. It also forces us to take on the broader problem of women's housing.

Refuges for Black women: vagaries of race in funding

In recent months it has become clear that, in some cases, the struggle for refuges to remain autonomous is not always being won. In Ealing there has been a battle over the council not including women from the community in the management of an Asian refuge that the council has agreed to resource and then apparently decided to manage. In Waltham Forest the Women's Unit has established a refuge for Asian women. While this may well result in a much-needed service, the strategic and political import of such a development does need to be considered.

From a perspective informed by both race and gender, the fact that both these examples are refuges for Asian women cannot be dismissed as incidental. This suggests a readiness to ignore the principles of autonomy and self-help adhered to by Women's Aid and fought for by Black women's organizations when it comes to domestic violence against Asian women. It is important to question whether this willingness to intervene is based and capitalizes on perceptions of the passivity of Asian women, as well as the racial assumptions about the prevalence of domestic violence in the Asian community in particular.

Black women initially organized separate refuges in response to the problem of ethnocentrism and racism within the refuge movement. It has been argued that although the wider society is mixed and Black women have to confront racism on a daily basis, they should not be forced to confront it when they are already in a vulnerable and traumatized state as a result of having been abused by their sexual/emotional partners or husbands, and the establishment of refuges for Black and ethnic minority women has, until now, been a community-based response. Further, Black and ethnic minority refuges point to ways in which Black women creatively apply themselves to addressing our own needs and to help ourselves when empowered to do so.

There is a further question to be addressed in the racial politics of the state responses to refuges: that is, why were no refuges for women of Caribbean or African origin resourced when the six Asian refuges were? This suggests an interplay of gender and ethnicity in state responses to Black women. I would argue that this indicates that the state has found it more acceptable to ʻund refuges for Black women on the ticket of 'special needs', as in cultural difference, rather than on the basis of racism creating special needs. The argument goes that since most women of African descent in Britain speak English and can eat chips, they do not need special provision on the basis of language differences and exotic diets. Special provision has not, in other words, been granted on the basis of racism. Yet racism in all the institutions that Black women have to deal with means that they do require extra support and advocacy from refuge workers, not least because they currently tend to be in the refuge for longer periods of time awaiting rehousing. This suggests a denial and suppression of the non-ethnic aspects of racism – when it is not about the language and ethnic differences that the state readily acknowledges – but about skin colour.

The one Black refuge which opened in 1988 did so through a Black Housing Association (UJIMA), rather than a Black women's group, and is open to all Black women, not just women of South East Asian origin.

For those who were willing to provide facilities for refuges (the more progressive Labour boroughs), this was less contentious when it was done so on the ticket of 'culture' than when it was demanded because of racism. Funding for Black refuges, when it has come from the state, has been to Asian women on, as I have argued, the basis of 'ethnic characteristics': language, diet, religion. The acknowledgement of cultural differences does not contradict racist discourses. Furthermore, racial stereotypes of Asian women differ significantly from those of Afro-Caribbean and African women. If the former are passive, exotic, quiet and inspire paternalism, then the latter are aggressive, promiscuous, violent-like-their-men and more threatening than mysteriously silent. In other words, even within its more supportive (Labourite) responses to feminist initiatives, the machinations of the state, in terms of who they will fund and not fund to start refuges, indicate an exercise of power which ensures the reproduction of a particular racial politic. This is what happened when the more progressive elements of the local state (as manifest in the late GLC and some Labour local authorities) recognized the demand and funded refuges, but only according to their own ethnicized racial criteria.

References

Binney, V., Harkell, G. and Nixon, J. (1981) *Leaving Violent Men – A Study of Refuges and Housing for Battered Women*. London Women's Aid Federation.

Lawrence, E. and Mama, A. (1988) 'The reproduction of inequality in housing', public Lecture delivered to The Runnymede Trust, London, 22 November 1988.

Mama, A. (1989) 'The silent struggle'. London Race and Housing Research Report.

Select Committee on Violence in Marriage (1975) *Report*. London: HMSO.

16

BLACK NIGHTINGALES

YASMIN ALIBHAI

In a small flat in Camberwell, three black women sit on a settee. They look as crushed as the cushions around them. Three generations of women from the same family, all of them nurses. Wide-eyed six-year-old Naomi, moving from lap to lap, represents the fourth generation. She is, her mother firmly says, never going to get a nurse's uniform to play in. Nursing, a profession that inspired them once, has left all three embittered and unfulfilled.

May came to Britain in 1949 to train as a nurse, with many others from the Caribbean who were actively recruited to satisfy the burgeoning labour needs of the National Health Service. She left after 20 years of stoic tolerance. Audrey, her daughter, is a district nurse and her grand-daughter, Rose, works in the labour ward of a large London hospital. And as they talk about their disenchantment with the service, Rose's despair pumps out at furious speed. 'You have no idea how much it hurts. For hours, this young white woman in labour kept on screaming racial abuse at me. She shouted and said not to touch her baby with my filthy hands. I tell you I nearly dropped the baby then.' She claims that she got no tangible support from her colleagues when this happened.

Audrey, who works as a district nurse, has been denied access into homes, accused of stealing and even been physically attacked by an old age pensioner who was angry that they had sent him 'black dirt' instead of the nice (white) nurse who used to come. Audrey initially told her line manager but, she claims: 'There was no serious concern. And because it happens so often they think it is your fault. So you cry, or you get hard and don't care any more.'

These kinds of experiences are widespread, not random aberrations. And on the whole nothing is done to protect black nurses from them. Their deep feelings of anger and rejection are captured in the words of Mary Seacole, the black nurse who went out to the Crimea in 1857: 'Did they shrink from

From *New Statesman and Society*, 7 October 1988, pp. 26–7

accepting my aid because it flowed from a somewhat duskier skin than theirs?'

And if black nurses had had more positive professional experiences – in terms of promotion, recognition and encouragement – then patient racism might have mattered less. But most health authorities, unions and professional bodies have also operated in discriminatory ways towards ethnic minority nurses and continue to do so. Teresa Jerome, a former senior nurse, believes: 'The whole thing was set up with the idea of exploitation and if the British don't choose to remember anything else they owe us, they could at least thank us for their wonderful NHS.'

Like May, she too put up with overt and covert racism mainly because she needed the work and in the vain hope that the future would be better. 'What I feel most angry about is not how I was treated, but that they should have expected my children and their children to put up with the same kind of nonsense.'

It seems that the children have decided not even to try: fewer of them are applying to get into nurse training. And as more and more black nurses leave the profession, both because of the general labour needs of the service, and the fact that these nurses are essential to provide appropriate care to a multi-racial society, their loss will soon be felt. It is ironic that this is happening at a time when the government has launched a £4 million campaign to recruit more nurses. As Carol Baxter in her recent book *Black Nurses, an Endangered Species*, says: 'The endurance of black nurses has been tested more cruelly and far longer by persistent and systematic racism in the NHS, and the long-running haemorrhage of their commitment and skill which the NHS can ill afford to lose will not be staunched until positive measures are taken to eliminate racism in this the most avowedly caring of professions.'

These measures will not be forthcoming until some of the strong mythologies that flavour the public view of nursing are dispelled. It is seen as a caring profession, which has been beleaguered for some time, a combination which makes it particularly defensive to criticism and blind to certain realities. People always feel slightly guilty (unlike when they are bashing social workers) when they criticize nurses – who themselves have been exploited by the imagery that surrounds them as being angels of mercy, giving devotion without expectations. For black nurses these expectations have been even higher ('Perhaps', says Rose, 'because we are still seen as those nurturing slaves on plantations') and their sense of disappointment is acute.

There are also structural impediments which prevent this problem from being dealt with head on. Nursing is a rigidly hierarchical profession with little scope for dissent. The comeback if you do rock the boat can be terrifying. The fear of this is clear from the fact that not one of the nurses I interviewed, many of them in senior positions, wanted to be identified.

On the whole, the approach in the health service is overwhelmingly colour blind, and managers reject allegations of racism by claiming all the evidence is anecdotal, exaggerated and impressionistic. They can make this claim, because the DHSS has not so far instituted a central ethnic monitoring system which would give a clear national picture. A number of recent reports, however, looking at specific areas, show clear trends, and that race discrimination is prevalent throughout the service.

17

MEN: THE FORGOTTEN CARERS

SARA ARBER and NIGEL GILBERT

The financial, psychological and social burdens of caring for the infirm elderly have been widely explored. However, many studies, such as Nissel and Bonnerjea's pioneering work (1982), have focused specifically on married daughters as carers, leaving the impression that it is they who are most likely to take on caring responsibilities.

Who cares for the infirm elderly is of increasing importance. The number of people aged 75–84 has risen by 38 per cent over the past fifteen years and the number of very old elderly people, aged over 85, has risen by 46 per cent (OPCS, 1987: Table 7). These major changes, together with government policies to shift care into the community, have well-recognized implications for those who provide care for the elderly living at home. From the 1980 General Household Survey (OPCS, 1982), we estimate that 10.7 per cent of elderly people living at home find it difficult or impossible to manage basic daily activities such as walking outside or bathing and washing all over. In varying degrees, they need help from others and, in practice, this usually means help from their family. The proportion needing help with these basic activities is 6 per cent of those aged 65–74, 15 per cent of those aged 75–84, and 41 per cent of those aged 85 and over.

The idea that the burden of caring falls mainly on daughters, coupled with the belief that men are unable to care for themselves, is widespread and deeply rooted in social policy on community care (Land, 1978). The result is that it is commonly assumed as almost self-evident that:

- men are very unlikely to be the primary carers of infirm elderly people;
- elderly men receive much more support from statutory and voluntary services than equally disabled elderly women; and
- when men do perform a caring role, they are more likely to obtain support than women carers.

In fact, our research on a nationally representative sample of elderly people living at home shows that each of these assumptions is far from the truth.

Abridged from *Sociology*, 23 (1), 1989, pp. 111–18

Men and caring

The few studies which have systematically examined the gender balance of carers have shown that between a quarter and two-fifths of carers are men (EOC, 1980; Briggs, 1983; Levin et al., 1983; Charlesworth et al., 1984). However, these studies used small samples, often from specific localities, that may have been unrepresentative of the wider population.

More reliable data can be obtained from the replies to a section of the 1980 General Household Survey which asked people aged over 65 living in private households about their ability to carry out various domestic and self-care tasks and about their receipt of statutory health and welfare services. The extent of help needed by the 4,553 elderly people in the sample was measured using a series of questions about their ability to perform daily tasks. Six tasks formed a linear scale of increasing difficulty for most people: cutting one's toenails, getting up or down stairs, walking outside, bathing or washing all over, getting around the house, and getting in and out of bed. Elderly people who said they could do a task easily were given a score of zero for that task, those who could do it only with difficulty were given a score of one, and those who could not manage the task at all except with help scored two: 10.7 per cent of people aged 65 and over had a total score of six or more on this scale and were defined as 'severely disabled'. They were unable to walk outside without help and most could not manage a bath nor wash all over unaided (Arber et al., 1988).

Table 1 shows that 38 per cent of 'severely disabled' elderly people live

Table 1 *Living arrangements of severely disabled elderly people and proportions living with male carers*

Type of household in which elderly disabled live	% of all severely disabled elderly	% with male co-resident carers	No. for whom information on disability is available
Alone	38.3	–	1,483
With spouse			
Couple only	31.3	51	1,998
Couple and adult children	5.8	28–84	260
With siblings or other elderly	7.3	9–33	178
With unmarried child	9.0	38–45	277
With married child (and some lone parents)	8.1	–[1]	178
	100 (467)	35–44	4,374

[1] The wife is assumed to be the carer in all households, including an elderly infirm person and a younger married couple.
Source: derived from the General Household Survey, 1980

alone. The 1980 GHS only provides a broad indication of who helps such elderly people and does not distinguish their gender. For example, 'sons and/or daughters' are the main source of informal support for elderly people living alone (Evandrou et al., 1986). Because of this lack of information on carers' gender, this article focuses on the two-thirds of frail elderly who share their home with others.

We have assumed that in these households, the primary carers of the elderly person is another member of the same household. Although this assumption is not always valid, earlier analyses of the 1980 GHS (Evandrou et al., 1986) show that it is generally the case. For example, over 90 per cent of married persons were helped with domestic and personal self-care tasks by their spouse and, where an unmarried elderly person was living with younger household members, under 5 per cent received any help with activities of daily living from people living outside the household.

Table 1 shows that 31 per cent of 'severely disabled' elderly people live in households as couples with just their spouse. These couples are almost exactly equally divided between those in which the wife is caring for the husband and those in which the husband is caring for the wife. Another 6 per cent have a spouse and one or more younger unmarried adults, usually their children, living with them. It is difficult to identify from the GHS the gender of the carer among these latter families, because it is not clear whether it is the spouse of the infirm person or the younger person who is the main carer. However, it is possible to define a range: the proportion of male carers lies between 28 per cent (if a woman is assumed to be the carer in all the uncertain cases) and 84 per cent (if a man is always assumed to be the carer).

Seven per cent of severely disabled elderly people are living with other elderly people who are, in most cases, their brothers or sisters. Only from 9 to 33 per cent of carers in these households are men. A minority (17 per cent) of severely disabled elderly people live only with members of the younger generation, generally their adult children. In just over half of these households, the younger people are unmarried and among these, there are nearly as many men as women carers, a fact which has often been overlooked.

Only 8 per cent of the elderly in need of daily support are living with a younger married couple, generally their married daughter and her husband. We assume that in these households very few, if any, of the husbands are the primary carers for the disabled elderly person. Thus, the gender balance of co-resident caring for the elderly differs according to four types of kin relationship: (a) caring as part of a marital relationship – men and women are equally likely to care for an elderly spouse; (b) a filial relationship involving an unmarried carer – slightly fewer unmarried sons than unmarried daughters care for an elderly parent; (c) a sibling relationship – elderly sisters are much more likely to be carers than brothers; and (d) a filial relationship involving a married carer – we assume that men are unlikely to be carers.

The contribution of men carers

Overall, therefore, although a majority of the carers of severely disabled elderly people are women, over one-third of co-resident carers are men. Why, then, is there an overwhelming impression that carers are female and silence about the contribution of male carers? An explanation can be found in the life histories of the relationship between the carers and the cared for.

Three-quarters of the men are caring for spouses with whom they have probably lived for most of their lives. Love may be the major motivating factor, as suggested by three out of the four men caring for their wives in Ungerson's study (1987). The majority of the other male carers are unmarried men caring for an elderly parent and are most likely never to have moved out of the parental home since they were children or to have returned following a divorce. In all these households, there is likely to be a strong bond between the carer and the cared for.

The relationship between the carer and the cared for will have gradually changed from reciprocity to dependency. The carer has 'little choice' but to care and the transition to caring is often seen as 'natural' – it would be unthinkable to do otherwise than care for the spouse or parent with whom one has been living for many years. In contrast, the married women who care for elderly parents in their own home are much less likely to have been living with their parents for most of their lives (Arber and Gilbert, 1989). The elderly person will often have 'moved in' to the household because of their infirmity and dependency. Caring will be motivated by kinship obligations, which in turn are influenced by norms about gender obligations and feelings of duty (Finch, 1987). This is the major source of gender inequalities in caring: married women are much more likely to be the carers when an elderly person moves into another household. The responsibility for caring is more likely to be the result of a conscious decision than the result of 'drifting into care'.

Help for male carers

One reason which has been put forward to explain why men carers have been so 'invisible' to policy-makers and researchers is that it is presumed that men carers get much more support from the voluntary and statutory services and therefore do not suffer the burdens of caring in the same way as women. However, the evidence from the GHS does not bear this out. Table 2 shows that unmarried male carers living with an elderly severely disabled person (usually sons caring for an elderly parent) are marginally less likely to get home help support than unmarried women (usually daughters). Nor does the gender of a younger unmarried carer have any important influence on the elderly person's likelihood of getting Meals-on-Wheels or being visited by the district nurse in the last month.

Home helps are very infrequently provided for households in which an elderly infirm person is living with a younger married couple. An elderly

Table 2 *Receipt of services by the elderly living in different types of households*

Type of household in which elderly people live	Likelihood[1] of receipt of		
	Home helps	Meals on Wheels	District nursing
Alone			
Man	5.66	15.27	1.91
Woman	5.21	5.22	1.68
With Spouse			
Couple, both elderly	1.00	1.00	1.00
Couple, one elderly, one younger	0.24	0.00	0.56
Couple and adult children	0.00	0.00	0.90
With siblings or other elderly	1.29	2.69	2.84
With unmarried			
male adult child	0.74	1.48	1.43
female adult child	0.80	1.37	1.28
With married child (and some lone parents)	0.30	0.36	0.72

[1] Odds ratio of receipt of the service within the past month, controlling for level of disability.
Source: derived from the General Household Survey, 1980

person living alone is eighteen times more likely to have a home help than an elderly person with an equivalent level of disability living with a younger married woman. The likelihood that these households will obtain Meals-on-Wheels is about a quarter of the likelihood for households in which an unmarried person is the carer. The picture is similar for visits by the district nurse, where the likelihood is about half that for households with unmarried carers, suggesting that some of the tasks which are done by the district nurse where an unmarried adult is the carer are being left to the married daughter. Overall, it looks as though the variation in the provision of these services is not due to discrimination against women *per se*, but discrimination against households in which non-elderly married women predominate as carers.

It has been argued that men do not 'really' care for elderly people because they receive considerably more support from informal carers living outside the household. Data from the 1980 GHS show that men carers in most types of household receive somewhat more help than women (Arber and Gilbert, 1989). However, the difference is very small for elderly married couples. For example, 9 per cent of husbands receive help with bathing their wife from informal carers compared to 1 per cent where the wife is caring for her husband. Where a younger unmarried man is caring for an elderly parent, slightly more support is given by 'sons/daughters' living outside the household than where an unmarried daughter is the carer, but even unmarried sons provided nearly three-quarters of the shopping for their frail elderly parent. The least help from informal carers is provided where the elderly person lives with a younger married couple. Since men who care receive only slightly more help from informal carers than women, they cannot simply be dismissed as not being 'real' carers.

Conclusion

Once one has controlled for the level of disability, the major source of variation in the amount of support services received by elderly infirm men and women seems to be not the gender of the recipients nor the gender of the carer, but the kind of household in which they live and, in particular, whether there are others in the household who could take on the burden of caring. Thus infirm elderly people living alone get much more support from formal services than those living with others. Elderly people living with their elderly spouse or with other elderly people get more support from formal services than those in households in which there are younger unmarried members. In all these households, the amount of support does not depend much on the gender of the carer.

Married daughters caring for elderly infirm parents receive considerably less support than unmarried carers, male or female. For these women, caring for an elderly person can conflict with the needs of their children as well as restricting their opportunities for employment and other activities. These burdens may be particularly onerous to married carers because of their relative lack of statutory and voluntary support, together with the fact that in most cases the elderly infirm person will have joined the household as someone needing care.

References

Arber, S. and Gilbert, G.N. (1989) 'Transitions in caring: gender, life course and the care of the elderly', in W. Bytheway (ed.), *Becoming and Being Old: Sociological Approaches to Later Life*. London: Sage.

Arber, S. Gilbert, G.N. and Evandrou, M. (1988) 'Gender, household composition and receipt of domiciliary services by elderly disabled people', *Journal of Social Policy*, 17: 153–75.

Briggs, A. (1983) *Who Cares?* Chatham, Kent: Association of Carers.

Charlesworth, A., Wilkin, D. and Durie, A. (1984) *Carers and Services: a Comparison of Men and Women Caring for Dependent Elderly People*. Manchester: Equal Opportunities Commission.

EOC (1980) *The Experience of Caring for Elderly and Handicapped Dependents*. Manchester: Equal Opportunities Commission.

Evandrou, M., Arber, S., Dale, A. and Gilbert, G.N. (1986) 'Who cares for the elderly? Family care provision and receipt of statutory service', in C. Phillipson, M. Bernard and P. Strang (eds), *Dependency and Interdependency in Old Age*. London: Croom Helm.

Finch, J. (1987) 'Family obligations and the life course', in A. Bryman, B. Bytheway, P. Allatt and T. Keil (eds), *Rethinking the Life Cycle*. London: Macmillan.

Land, H. (1978) 'Who cares for the family? *Journal of Social Policy*, 7: 357–84.

Levin, E., Sinclair, I. and Gorbach, P. (1983) *The Supporters of Confused Elderly Persons at Home*. London: National Institute of Social Work.

Nissel, M. and Bonnerjea, L. (1982) *Family Care of the Handicapped Elderly: Who Pays?* London: Policy Studies Institute.

OPCS (1982) General Household Survey 1980. London: HMSO.

OPCS (1987) *Population Trends*. London: HMSO.

Ungerson, C. (1983) 'Women and caring: skills, tasks and taboos', in E. Gamarnikow et al. (eds), *The Public and the Private*. London: Heinemann.

Ungerson, C. (1987) *Policy is Personal: Sex, Gender and Informal Care*. London: Tavistock.

18

THE ALIENATED: GROWING OLD TODAY

GLADYS ELDER

Mr M is nearly 80. His ground floor flat is in bad condition. He is very confused, does not know who the landlord is. Council gave notice to quit, verbally, because he is blind. One week's notice only. Woman friend helped him and kept him company. Council refused permission for them to live together so they married before moving into a housing estate. She died soon afterwards. Mr M is now very lonely. Volunteers visited him at Christmas. Council complain his rent is in arrears. It was later discovered this was because he couldn't go out to pay it. (from a Task Force report)

Franz Kafka's novel *Metamorphosis* is, I think, the most terrifying tale every written. It begins: 'As Gregor Samsa awoke one morning from uneasy dreams, he found himself transformed in his bed into a gigantic insect.' His family's reaction is first one of revulsion, then kindness, finally contempt, merging into total neglect; not only had he become a revolting object – he could no longer fulfil his function as breadwinner for the family.

The parallel is clear in society's treatment of the aged. It refuses them the necessary minimum, thus condemning them to extreme poverty, to slums – such as in the case quoted above – ill health, loneliness and despair, asserting that they have neither the same needs, nor the same rights as others in the community. In Britain today when the cost of living is still spiralling rapidly, the pension increases offered to the aged almost immediately become farcical, the cost of living having already risen beyond the level of each new increase. Those who have won rate and rent rebates are more than likely to have these rebates decreased, thus all but cancelling out whatever advantage might have been gained by the original pension increase.

Simone de Beauvoir (1972), the French author, asks 'Are the old really human beings?' They are treated as outcasts, she says, and not considered

From *The Alienated: Growing Old Today*, Writers and Readers Publishing Cooperative, London, 1977 'real people' – apparently they have neither 'the same needs or the same feelings as others'. She points out that there is an enormous difference between the wealthy and successful elderly, and those of us from the working class who have retired, often living on inadequate pensions, trying vainly to catch up with the soaring cost of living. 'The class struggle,' she writes, 'governs the manner in which old age takes hold of a man: there is a great gulf between . . . the wretchedly pensioned ex-worker and an Onassis.' Says John Galbraith (1975):

> People are poverty-stricken when their income, even if adequate for survival, falls radically behind that of the community. They cannot have what the community regards as the minimum of decency, thus they cannot wholly escape the judgement of the larger consumer that they are indecent. They are degraded for, in the literal sense, they live outside the grades . . . which the community regards as acceptable.

In another context, Dr Alex Comfort (1965) writes:

> Poverty is a great robber of self-esteem; failing health and the infirmities of old age in no way boost the morale, nor does society's attitude help to sustain a sense of identity. And once the mirror-image, so laboriously fashioned throughout a lifetime, is shattered, how many are able to acquire a fresh identity? This is especially difficult when self-evaluation has always had to battle against society's attitudes towards those given a low status in the social hierarchy.

Wearing, like the Star of David worn by the Jews in Hitler's Germany, the label OAP, the mass of pensioners are treated as children, lumped together regardless of their right to as much dignity and respect as any retired professional man or woman. Would anyone, for instance, dare to apply the designation 'OAP' to a retired judge living on a state pension? It has a wholly working-class connotation, with overtones suggesting that OAPs are the recipients of philanthropy – the Welfare State grandiosely distributing alms to the maimed and old. For pensioners have taken the place of the indigent poor of the past, while groups like 'Help the Aged' appeal for funds and thus salve a thousand consciences. As for the powerful media, the advertising industry has long since divided the nation into six social categories; the very bottom one (labelled E) covers state widows, pensioners, casual or low-grade workers – a position not unlike the untouchables of India. And how does a pensioner on a low income manage to exist? Why, like those indigent poor of the past, by hunting round for centres where cheap lunches are served (soup kitchens); buying secondhand clothing from jumble sales; by having to struggle, with the help of the more fortunate members of the community, for special benefits and reduced transport fares: in short, by pleading need, showing their sores and sacrificing their pride.

I was first amused and then angered to read Dr Joan Gomez, who has this to say about the aged in her *Dictionary of Symptoms*: 'Unfilled leisure-time is psychologically dangerous; it causes teenagers to make nuisances of themselves, and older people to make miseries of themselves.' The same source supplies this example of patronizing disparagement:

> Make friends, but do not hanker after those in full flurry of activity . . . If you are past seventy, the middle-aged may have minds too agile for you. Your own contemporaries tend to self-centredness, though they are worth cultivating. You will find the greatest expanse of common ground with children.

In just such a manner have minorities everywhere been stigmatized as being mentally inferior at one time or another. Suddenly, come seventy – metamorphosis! Does it perhaps depend on class and status? The average age of politicians, members of the judiciary and religious hierarchies is, after all, pretty high – imagine the reaction of some of our high court judges if they were seriously told to run off and play with the children!

References

de Beauvoir, Simone (1972) *Old Age.* London: Weidenfeld & Nicolson.
Comfort, Alex (1965) *The Process of Ageing.* London: Weidenfeld & Nicolson.
Galbraith, J.K. (1975) *The Affluent Society.* Harmondsworth: Penguin.
Gomez, Joan (1967) *Dictionary of Symptoms.* Fontwell, West Sussex: Centaur Press.

19

MAKING GARDENS FROM WILDERNESSES: THE LIVES OF OLDER WOMEN

NORMA PITFIELD

I guess I was in love with my mother from childhood to her death. An only child, born when she was 35, I was forever fixed on her as the arbiter of my character, or rather my morality. A loving, indeed a dedicated mother, I believe now that she saw herself as the setter of standards and myself as the ever potential breaker of those. When, in 1954, I became an unmarried mother it was, in a sense, a triumph of her belief in my ability to disappoint her.

From that time onward the guilt I felt toward her fuelled a constant struggle to prove myself worthy in her eyes. The passionate love I also had for her, my awareness of her frustrated intellect and creativeness, kept her always in the forefront of my mind. Thus I spent a substantial proportion of my time with her, and when I wasn't with her I was worrying about her and struggling with anger and resentment.

Always dogged by bad health, her last decade was distressingly and increasingly painful. In spite of that she lived fully. There was a gallantry of spirit about her which attracted many people, and she was proud of her independence. She was buried on her eighty-first birthday. She had, with my father, come to live with me, very reluctantly, five months previously. I nursed her night and day over those last terrible months. She was the first person I had seen die, indeed the first person I had seen dead. Our intimacy over that time was complete. Although she resented her reliance upon me, she valued the fact that she could depend upon me. She fought desperately to live on, day by day, hour by hour, refusing to let go. Her way of dying stretched me to breaking point since it taxed my physical and emotional stamina to the ultimate. I fumed against her refusal to let go and release me from this final test. Yet I felt impelled to support her manner of death.

From 'Making gardens from wildernesses', in S. Hemmings (ed.), *A Wealth of Experience: The Lives of Older Women*, Pandora, London, 1985

Scrupulously I performed every intimate personal service with passionate care, even though all my life I have found such tasks anathema. I would help her try to evacuate, devise ways to help her urinate, clear up vomit over and over again, then later rush to the bathroom to heave and heave.

Her death brought immense relief, but the guilt of feeling that relief added an intolerable dimension to my inconsolable grief. All this coincided with the onset of my menopause and of complex personal relationship problems. At that time I had also taken on a new and very responsible job. The job should have been a culmination of my working career giving, as it did, the opportunity to develop and put into practice my ideology about teaching my subject: art and design. Sadly, my taking up the post coincided with all the changes and financial cuts in my particular field, teacher education.

I started the job in a very debilitated state, shocked, bereaved and physically at sixes and sevens. Everything was new, students, staff, the content of the course. I discovered there was some resentment at my appointment: the course had moved premises and nothing was ready. But the students were a delight, and despite everything the staff began generously to accept me. Later to my surprise I found that the students had little inkling of the strain of all the problems, and in retrospect I feel proud that, in spite of the constant panic I was experiencing inside my head, I was able to function professionally well enough.

While I was trying to cope at work my father was needing a lot of care at home. I was conscious of the strain his presence was inflicting on the people I lived with, even though I found a kind and efficient woman to care for him during the day. Looking back I see how amenable my father was until his sudden death eighteen months after my mother's. He had always been loving and supportive to me.

For some years I had spent holidays on the East Suffolk coast, an area I love. I had taken my parents there, my father just before his death. Remembering him saying how he wished I could have my own place there, I suddenly determined that I would buy a cottage from the proceeds of the sale of my parents' home. The search for somewhere suitable lifted me out of the depressive state the anxiety about my job and the problems at home were provoking. Having found the cottage I set to work on making it as peaceful and comfortable a haven as I could for my family, friends – but mainly for myself. I enjoy physical work. I also enjoy creating efficient and visually pleasing living space. In spite of menopausal problems, I tackled the difficult, neglected garden and in quite a short space of time it looked well and, with the cottage, provided a comfortable and pleasing place to rest and work.

After this bout of energetic activity the depression returned in full force and threatened to overwhelm me. At the worst times I believed myself to be a fraud, likely at any time to be discovered as an inadequate sham at home and at work. I had been given a commission to write a book. The cottage seemed to provide the ideal quiet retreat for this purpose on my weekend visits. As the date for completion, the end of the summer vacation, drew near, I settled in and tried to get down to finish the work. But the depression was at its worst and my thoughts suicidal.

I felt that the book's potential failure would at last reveal the truth, my fraudulence, poverty of ideas, incompetence, unworthiness! One dreadful morning I rushed into the garden in the pouring rain, frenetically hacking down bushes and thorns on a steep and slippery bank in an effort to prevent myself from some terrible deed of self-destruction. I paced the garden for hours, day after day, trying in a way that was *physically* painful to focus my mind and evolve some plan of self-salvation. Grimly I imposed a regime of writing, gardening, writing, playing my piano, writing, drawing in the evenings, and then writing into the early hours. Sticking to the plan in an utterly joyless way the deadline was met and I flew to New York to meet some friends as pre-arranged. I remember spending the flight trying to suppress my conviction that, while in America, all those miles away from home, I would fall seriously ill, or go mad.

Neither happened. Instead, I returned to work, edited and re-edited the book, and tried to cope with ever-increasing difficulties at work. Cuts in staff and facilities were made. I was involved in endless complex meetings and the preparation of detailed documentation arguing for my course and submitted time and time again to various supervising committees. All this involved constant rewriting late at night on top of a heavy teaching and administrative schedule. Each committee meeting was a nightmare. I was having to articulate in detail reasons for the way the course was taught and run, indeed for its very existence, a huge responsibility towards many people. While my immediate colleagues and I felt confidence in what we were doing, I had always known that my immediate superiors would have preferred a more traditional approach. Now I discerned open hostility and, as I saw it, of lack of professional support for the innovatory nature of our work. At one meeting I was publicly insulted by one man's rudeness, based on his own well-known prejudices and ignorance about art education. No one challenged him, though afterwards in private there were commiserations. To me this signalled that my work world was collapsing and I went home convinced that I could take no more.

From that time, as I wept and fumed, I believe I began to recover from the years of depression. For as long as I could remember, my work had been where I felt I functioned well. Divorced as it was from my mother's sphere of influence, I had enjoyed my competence free from guilt and doubt. With my mother's death and the onset of the menopause, due to either, both, who knows, the eroding canker of uncertainty started to eat into that aspect of my life. It also coincided with the unhappy state of affairs in higher education. I have seen many professional colleagues go under, giving up work, becoming seriously ill, suffering mental breakdowns, even prematurely dying. My own health often faltered under the pressure, with the return of the persistent asthma I'd suffered in my twenties.

As it turned out, I was extremely fortunate. Premature retirement or voluntary redundancy was on offer on good terms. Originally I'd refused to entertain the idea. I'd always been convinced that I would want to teach forever. Moreover, to get a pension at my early age seemed immoral. Now I thought again. Life without a job or work imposed from outside seemed, to my surprise, a definite possibility. Having my cottage had proved to me I could function alone, at least for a considerable proportion of the time. It had also confirmed my love of living in the country.

All the possibilities were discussed at length with my partner, who generously backed me fully in my decision to leave work. Within a year we sold our beloved home and acquired a very much more modest London base, sold the cottage and bought for me a house in a small country town large enough for me to run the occasional residential art course.

I have lived in that house for five months now and experience once again a pleasure in my ability to create a place where people love to come to stay. Another garden is in the process of being created. I am learning new art skills and practising old ones. For years any political involvement had been fraught with problems of time and energy. At 52 I find I am able to join campaigns again and work for them in a consistent and reliable way. When I was younger I was very active in the peace movement. Now I've joined again, and I'm helping in CLAM (Coastal League Against Missiles), which is affiliated to CND. I've been to Greenham Common and I support and admire the stand being made there. And I've rejoined the Labour Party.

I am genuinely enjoying meeting new people, establishing new friendships and actively enjoying old ones. For the first time since before the menopause I feel confident to sustain and cherish friends. This is not to say that for all those years I have been friendless – far from it. My contacts through the women's movement have given me loving support through so many traumas. The difference is that for a long time I construed such support as compassion and pity. Now I have the time and confidence to think about friends dispassionately *and* passionately, free from any turmoil of guilt or doubt. I feel justified in planning and using my time according to my own decisions and energies.

I have truly started again, a new kind of life.

Eight years ago when my mother died, to my surprise and disappointment, there was no sense of the liberation I'd expected. On the contrary, I too believed I had begun to die. Everything for a time conspired to reinforce this conviction: ill health, evidence of physical ageing, the running down of sexual responses in myself and from others. Older women are very conditioned to feeling self-disgust and the physical symptoms of the menopause can be construed to reinforce this. I suffered not only heavy bleeding, severe headaches, hot flushes, uncertainty of mood but also water retention which caused swelling of hands, feet, abdomen and face. My otherwise kindly doctor could only offer HRT (hormone replacement therapy) of which I was afraid. All the reading I did on the menopause, especially by women, advocated keeping fit, slim, active.

Unable to manage any of this I felt, like many others I'm sure, even more of a failure. Later I developed severe neuralgia and arthritis, very frightening, and extremely painful. But these illnesses took me to an acupuncturist. I gained relief and, through his confidence in me, the strength to try self-help in the form of careful diet, exercise and visualization. I also sought psychotherapy which provided the opportunity to think and talk about my mental and emotional bad, and good, habits. Gradually mourning for my youthful body gave way to pride in my older one. When I joined the Older Feminist Network, the beauty and strength of older women became more and more apparent and admirable.

Even though those eight years since my mother's death have been so difficult, I now see them as very productive. They saw some of my best and most informed teaching. A book was written. I made and exhibited drawings. I made a garden out of a wilderness. I acquired many friendships which I know to be lasting. Not only that: stretching ahead is the exciting prospect of a new way of being.

Many things have been left out of this account, most significantly the complexities and richness of my closest personal relationships. But this story is about an equally important aspect of life – the experience of oneself. We all live partially in reaction to the needs, experiences and demands of others, many of us completely so, especially women. Getting to know and appreciate oneself I now see as an important priority and an exciting and stimulating adventure and I count myself lucky to have the opportunity to embark on a new life as an older woman in a positive frame of mind.

The menopause and the depressive state that often seems to accompany it for so many women could be seen as a change of life in the best sense. It so often marks changes other than the physical. The death of parents, the departure of children, could be the end of an era of succouring and serving on a day-to-day basis. My work too had this nurturing dimension. Now I know I did my best for those others. I can rue my failures and rejoice in my successes, but I no longer dwell upon them.

20

ACQUIRED HEARING LOSS: ACQUIRED OPPRESSION

MAGGIE WOOLLEY

In this article Maggie Woolley discusses the importance of the 'loss' of hearing for a deafened person, and the confidence she regained through finding the Deaf community.

The experience of loss is central to the experience of the newly deafened adult and yet the opportunity fully to express initial fear, anger, distress and grief is rarely fully realized. Continuing sense of loss therefore remains as a barrier to adjustment, and the deafened person is impeded in 'giving up the tragedy' of deafness. While still a hearing person, the deafened person learned to have able-bodied attitudes towards disability which deaf and disabled movements now identify as key disabling factors in their oppression. But the newly deafened person continues to function from these oppressive attitudes and sees them daily reinforced by society now that she also has a disability. Initial strategies involve denying disability, pretending to hear and avoidance of situations in which the disability will be exposed. The deafened person looks to medicine for a cure to problems which are seen as stemming from faults in the ear. When the cure is not forthcoming, the deafened person experiences a further loss – that of hope. Rehabilitation medicine in the form of hearing aids, lip-reading, hearing therapy and other therapies offer help with mechanical aspects of communication and relating to the sound environment but the professional's patient relationship is characterized by one of dependency in which he assumes to control and know best about 'priorities', 'problems' and provision of 'solutions'. The fundamental experience of loss and tragedy remains and the deafened person still struggles with despair, powerlessness, loss of self-confidence and positive self-image. The deafened person blames her deafness and hates being deaf with self-contempt, therefore, lurking at the periphery of her consciousness. Society in turn blames the victim of deafness.

Abridged from J.G. Kyle (ed.), *Adjustment to Acquired Hearing Loss*, Centre for Deaf Studies, School of Education, Bristol, 1987

Have we anything to learn from the past ten years in which the movements of disabled people and the Deaf community have rejected medical models of who they are; located disabling factors in the attitudes and power structures of society; created new identities based on proud self-definitions and celebration of their difference, and tried to build confidence so that they can intervene more effectively in creating new and more appropriate services which are under their direction? Does adjustment to acquired hearing loss also involve adjustment to, or rather liberation from oppression which is social, psychological and political? Does an agenda for the future require a liberation movement of deafened people?

I was diagnosed deaf at the age of eighteen in 1967. Twelve years later I finally sat down and cried about it. I've never enjoyed such a jolly good cry in my life. It was marvellous. My whole body shook and I seemed to be going down deep inside me trying to get rid of every ounce of pain in great sobs and tears. I must tell you that this happened in a counselling session where I was quite free to express such emotion without being thought mad' or without upsetting anyone else or without anyone leaping forth to stop me crying. After some time I stopped, blew my nose, calmed down, giggled for a bit and then felt very happy. The world seemed to be a great place to be in and I was glad to be so powerfully alive. I was finally dealing with feelings of *loss* in the most natural way known to human beings. I was physically expressing grief, fear, anger and a whole range of emotion that had been locked inside me for twelve years. I was dealing with *loss* in a totally safe environment.

I am not a psychiatrist. I'm not well read in the psychology of loss and bereavement but I do know that a key word here is that of loss. My own experience and that of other deafened people I know tells me that an understanding of *loss* is essential to anyone around the newly deafened person and especially to the professional. Family and friends may be too upset by the deafened person's loss to cope with the physical expressions of grief I have described above, but professional counsellors may be better equipped to provide the necessary safe environment. If loss can be fully expressed, then the necessary grieving period can be relatively short and the deafened person can more rapidly adjust to the changes in her life. She can meet them as a much stronger and more confident person than if she were still suppressing the initial trauma.

We *acquire* a hearing loss we didn't ask for and most certainly didn't deserve. It may be the result of an accident, disease or even human error or cruelty. (I am thinking here of deafness caused by medical error or deafness caused by noise levels in industry or acts or war.) A deafened person may have to deal with feelings of injustice and powerlessness which relate to the way in which she was deafened. She may even have the right to take her deafness into a court of law.

In my case, I inherited a form of deafness which is always acquired rather than present at birth. I could hardly turn round and blame my parents for falling in love and creating me. As a hearing child I enjoyed a very happy childhood with a deafened father and hearing mother. I don't remember any family relationship problems which stemmed from my father's disability. We all knew how to talk so he would understand and he was always included in everything we did. We automatically helped him to understand other people and thought nothing of it. Indeed, as a very young child I discovered that I was the only person who had a deaf father and I was so proud of the fact. It made my father, and more importantly me, a very special person. I had a daddy *who couldn't hear a thing* but *who could read lips*. My father never talked about losing his hearing. To me he had always been deaf. As I grew older I realized that his deafness meant it was harder for him to get work or to get the jobs he deserved and we were all angry about that in my family. But on the whole his deafness was no big deal. He was just this man we all loved a lot.

So while I had a wonderful understanding of the deafened person's communication needs, I didn't really know what it felt like to be deafened. After I was diagnosed deaf, I assumed that my father and I could talk about it and that he would be someone I could share my feelings with. But when I told him he said the news had broken his heart. I felt that I had broken my parents' hearts. There was no way I could show them how distressed I was about being deaf. I had to help them feel that there was no cause for worry. I was just the same happy daughter they had always had. So I talked to my parents about everything else except being deaf. Family and friends were also upset. My teachers at drama college were upset. It was as if I had to help others with their distress rather than expect help with mine. After all, it was my deafness that was causing the upset. Everyone in the world was upset except my ear, nose and throat specialist! As the only person I could talk to without breaking people's hearts, he became the only person I did talk to – for ten minutes twice a year!

On one occasion I rehearsed a question for my ENT specialist and plucked up the courage to say 'I'm worried about what deafness is doing to me. It's not that I can't hear but what this is doing to my life.' He looked up and said 'Oh you mustn't worry; that will only make things worse. Eventually you will come to terms with it.' Now I don't know what you make of that response but the worries of the deafened patient are not the concerns of the ENT specialist after all. One can't blame him for dismissing my distress in such a way. Indeed, what he said turned out to be the most influential thing that anyone had said up to that time. After I left him, I walked about in the Glasgow rain for hours. I was so angry and my mind chattered over and over. 'I can't come to terms with living like this. I can't come to terms with a world in which I hardly know what anyone is saying. I can't come to terms with being left out of everything. I can't come to terms with this weight of hopelessness and being expected to deal with these problems all alone. The day I come to terms with it will be the day life isn't worth living. If my family and I as a child knew what it took to relate to a deafened person, then the rest of the world can. It isn't that I have to come to terms with this disability but that the very terms themselves have to be changed. The terms on which I am disabled have to be changed.' I am now thirty-eight years old and I still have not changed my mind about this.

Despite all the loss and pain of acquiring something they didn't ask for, deafened people have a strength hidden within them that holds far more appropriate analyses of their disability and solutions than any person in the medical profession they are likely to encounter. And deafened people have this knowledge without knowing any more about the insides of the ear than they do about life on Mars. But there is no one around who can really listen to them. Even lip-reading teachers and hearing therapists are functioning from established and rigid solutions which require the deaf person and not the rest of the world to do most of the adjusting; which require the deaf person to adjust to hearing people's rules in a society which is constructed without much thought for the deaf. The deafened person is also at a disadvantage with her knowledge because of communication barriers and her own loss of self-confidence. She is new to deafness and there seem to be so many people around who claim to know so much more than she does. They are articulate and can use a wide range of very sophisticated language and are able to mystify her with their expertise. All the deafened people I know went home from encounters with professionals to look words up in dictionaries and read up about deafness in medical books. So here we are at this stage in our loss feeling like everyone knows better about deafness than we do. Not only that but everyone who can hear seems to know better about *everything* than we do. We have become so dependent on professionals and other hearing people.

Now we are really learning what disability is about for those who have been disabled or deaf for all their lives. As hearing able-bodied people we learned how to see disabled and deaf people as dependent and pretty useless members of society. As deafened people we have carried this prejudice towards disabled people into our own deafness. We are also experiencing feelings of powerlessness, and how we are made to be dependent. So those attitudes are being reinforced everyday.

We want 'the hearing person I once was' back again because she had control of her life. We think that all this is happening because we can't hear; because of some tiny fault in our ears. But we aren't faulty people. If we could get our hearing back, then 'all the problems would go away'. So we shop around for cures for a bit until finally giving up, except perhaps, to monitor cochlea implant experiments. I put it to you that all this wasn't happening because of the fault in our ears or because we can't hear, but because society does not value the deafened person and because we who were once hearing, like the rest, also learned not to value the deafened person. We are oppressed from without by a society which does not value us and therefore does not give priority to our needs and we are oppressed from within because we have internalized those same attitudes towards ourselves. Read any book on deafened people and the lack of self-confidence and the poor self-image of the deafened person is discussed. But, without exception, all see this as being a product of inability to hear, of faults in the ears and not of a society which does not value us. We are stuck with these pathological models and medical definitions of who we are, when in reality we are not sick or ill people. We are people who are socially, psychologically and politically oppressed.

When I was twenty-three I was in a restaurant with three hearing people and unable to follow their conservation. I looked across to the people at the next table. They were laughing and very happy. They were also very deaf. I could see this because they were using Sign Language. Hey!!, people like that could go out and buy meals, chat to the waiter and get him understanding them even though they didn't speak. People like that could do all this without a hearing person to help them or without being terrified they'd lip-read things wrongly. People like that could go out for a meal and enjoy themselves and have no problems understanding each other. And they didn't even care if people like me stared at them because they were different. People like that could be happy. People like that were deaf. So was I. I could be happy being deaf.

Born deaf people in the Deaf community weren't upset that I was deaf. They welcomed me. I made so many friends. I learned Sign Language and with interpreters could go to conferences, meetings and ultimately stand on a platform myself. They gave me back my confidence. I went back to teaching and eventually I went into my original chosen profession as an actress and TV presenter. Deaf people gave me not only their world but access to the whole world. Born with far greater odds against them than I was, they gave me a completely new insight into being deaf which no other person had been able to give me before. I learned that their oppression was different from mine. It wasn't that they had lost their hearing but that their linguistic rights were being denied. With Sign Language banned in deaf education since 1880 and actively suppressed throughout the Western world, deaf people had known the most inhumane cruelty through being deprived from an early age of the only language which could help them acquire spoken languages. I, on the other hand, had spoken English as my native language. My problem was one of access to spoken English. Their language of signs gave me access to spoken English, but more than that their analysis and ideology helped me to see that deaf people were not alone. We share fundamentals of oppression with the deaf and many other oppressed groups in the world.

I don't know whether we need or can have a movement of deafened people. Perhaps we will achieve change for ourselves in the deaf and disabled movements. In Britain, quite a few deafened people are identifying themselves as deaf or disabled in this way. But our own experience and particular needs must not be lost in these campaigns. Five years ago I discovered that my young daughter will also acquire the family deafness. Thousands of people are still losing their hearing today. They need a positive identity and ability to deal with loss and to meet the oppression which perhaps only we can encourage.

Finally, I have drawn on personal experience here which lays me open to accusations that my experience has been different from most and is therefore inadmissible as evidence for acquired hearing loss as acquired oppression. The true experience of every person who acquires a hearing loss is a valid and important experience. Our experience is always unique and yet when we begin to talk openly about it, we find others begin to rejoice in those parts of our experience which have also been their own. My experience is no more invalid than the experience of any deafened person. From the celebration of our difference and shared experience, great movements and a better world can evolve. There is no good reason why my deafened daughter should suffer as we have done. There is no good reason why any of us should deserve anything less than total respect.

SECTION 3

EMPOWERMENT AND POWER

It is fashionable to think of practitioners acting to 'empower' users of services. The implication of this is that some people have more power than others, and that they should be encouraged to share their power with those who have less.

In considering this, it is important to unravel certain assumptions about power, and where it resides. As Roger Gomm in the first article in this section puts it, 'power itself is a very tricky idea'. It is true that helping relationships and expert services usually place the helper or provider in a powerful position in relation to the person on the receiving end. But does this mean that the helper has power to give away? And, if it does, in itself a questionable assumption, how best can the helper assist the people they help to acquire power? Is power something that is finite, that can be subdivided and reapportioned if the correct formula is adopted? Or is empowerment only something you can find for yourself? Several articles in other sections of the Reader are relevant to issues of empowerment and power: you might like to consider what Jan Williams (Section 1), Hanmer and Statham and Amina Mama (Section 2) and Tara Mistry (Section 4) have to say that relates to the empowerment and power theme.

In this section articles about disability are well represented. This is not accidental. Some of the most powerful critiques of the way services reflect and perpetuate unequal power relationships have come from writers like Vic Finkelstein who are active in the disability movement; and these critiques have given rise to some interesting experiments in empowerment such as that described here by Christopher Brown and Charles Ringma. But perhaps the most powerful light on empowerment is shed by Anita Binns who describes her own personal development towards an increasing sense of her own power to shape her own life, and influence other people.

The first article sets the scene. Roger Gomm takes a sceptical view of empowerment, arguing that it has different meanings to different people, and that it can be used and abused in the name of enlightenment and progress. He suggests that people only empower others to the extent it serves their own ends. It is a sober beginning.

The following four articles take up differing positions on Roger Gomm's continuum of the meanings of empowerment. Vic Finkelstein argues that disabled people are disempowered because other people, most notably health care professionals working within a medical model, define disability as residing within the individual's personal impairments. If this is turned around, disability can be seen as a reflection of the powerlessness of disabled people – the product of a disabling society. Nora Ellen Groce is an oral historian. Her book *Everyone Here Spoke Sign Language* describes a community, Martha's Vineyard in the States, where hereditary deafness was common. As a result, sign language was widely spoken and deafness was relatively insignificant. The history of Martha's Vineyard reiterates the point made by Vic Finkelstein that disability is a social construct. It may sound strange but, according to this historian, deaf people on Martha's Vineyard were not disabled!

David Ward and Audrey Mullender place the meaning of empowerment firmly in the radical social work tradition. It is the job of the social worker to enable service users to recognize their oppression and, through cooperation, to break out of it. However, empowerment is not easy. The next article by Christopher Brown and Charles Ringma describes an experiment in empowering consumers; the power relationship is apparently reversed when the consumer becomes the employer, but the outcomes of this are not necessarily straightforward.

The language of empowerment may be new, but the ideas it expresses are not. The extract we have chosen from David Wills' *The Barns Experiment* describes an experiment in power-sharing in a home for adolescent boys. Writing in the mid-1940s, Wills' account is illustrative of a particular style of democratization within institutions also espoused by A.S. Neill at Summerhill. It is interesting to reflect on the 'progress' of empowerment: such experiments would seem equally radical in the 1990s.

The next two articles are based on personal accounts by disabled people. Maggie Potts and Rebecca Fido worked on an oral history project with residents of a long-stay mental handicap hospital, the 'colony'. They use people's own words as far as possible. The extract we have chosen illustrates both the power of the institution to regulate the lives of its inmates, and something of the inmates' resistance to the regime. Anita Binns' story is an account of learning to see herself as a powerful person. No one *gave* Anita 'empowerment', but in developing a sense of her own power she turned her own life around, and had an impact on the lives of others.

The final article in this section 'Rules, Roles and Relationships', by Sheelagh Strawbridge takes us several steps back from immediate day-to-day settings, and allows us to reflect on the sources of power. She asks how far people do have the power to challenge cultural norms, to write their own scripts, to 'be themselves'. While denying the extreme individualistic position that we can be arbiters of our own destiny, she gives us grounds for optimism that within limits we do have room to negotiate our roles and relationships, to empower ourselves and others.

21

ISSUES OF POWER IN HEALTH AND WELFARE

ROGER GOMM

In health, welfare and education services, 'empowerment' is a buzz word. It litters mission statements. It is a rallying cry for health and welfare charities. The time of empowerment has come and the word has taken its place among other descriptors of good things, such as 'natural', 'additive free', 'community', 'freedom', 'quality', 'truth' and 'justice'.

What can we do with a term which on the right of politics can mean privatizing public services, and on the far left can mean abolishing private services; which can mean all things to all men, and something different again to some women? In a rational world it would make sense to wipe the slate clean and start again, with this and other words which impede clear thinking. If what it designates has any merit, we should use other words instead.

However, no one is going to give up using such a nice word for the time being and no one has the power to make them. And this in a sense is what it's all about. Some people do have more power to decide the meanings of words under some circumstances, but other people contest them. Contested definitions are an index of deeper conflicts. Many people are empowered to use language; no one has the absolute power to determine what the language finally means, and we should be glad about that. A world in which a word had but one unambiguous meaning, would be a world of rigid totalitarian control. Thus, we will have to take things as they are, and try to tease out what different meanings are poured into this term 'empowerment', and try to understand the broader systems of meaning to which they belong.

Power and responsibility

Empowerment suggests that some people have power and have too much of it, other people have too little, and those who have too little should get more. However, power itself is a very tricky idea. Finding out where the power is involves at least two manoeuvres. First, we ask ourselves: who is in a position to influence or control the lives of whom? Secondly, we ask ourselves: in whose interests is this influence or control exerted?

It is the second rather than the first question which most people find important. On the whole, people do not find objectionable the idea that someone else has power, so long as the power is exerted to the benefit of the less powerful, and so long as they are convinced that this is the best way of serving their interests. If I am knocked down by an articulated lorry I am quite prepared to allow the accident and emergency services to take charge of my life for the time being. But if they make a mess of me, and amputate my left leg rather than my right, I will want to be empowered to sue them for redress.

Discussions of power, then, are rarely just about the factual issue of who controls whom. They are nearly always also about the moral issues of whose interests alleged patterns of power serve best, and who should be blamed for the disadvantages and damages of life. As with all moral issues there are possibilities for infinite disagreement.

Power and worker–user relationships

I will simplify things down to four possible views on power and focus them on health, welfare and education services. Once these views have been outlined, we can read off four different ways in which the term 'empowerment' can be used as a logical predicate.

An oppressive or a liberating relationship

Here services are seen as components of a much wider system of oppression which enables the powerful and rich to go on exploiting the powerless and poor. Health, welfare and education services play their role in this by maintaining the oppressed at a minimum level of efficiency so that they can be useful to the powerful, and by misleading people about the sources of their problems. They help to spread ideas that, despite appearances, the world is a fair place, and that those who have problems have no one to blame but themselves, or their parents, or germs or accidents, or anything other than the real causes of their problems which are the advantages enjoyed by the powerful. And if health, welfare and education fail to convince, then there is always imprisonment, probation and drug therapy.

In the classic version of this model, the oppressors are capitalists and the oppressed are the working class (George and Wilding, 1976), which often includes nearly everyone. For some feminists the oppressive system is patriarchy, the oppressors are men and the oppressed are women (Firestone, 1972), and for anti-racists, the oppressive system is racism or imperialism, the oppressed are black and the oppressors are white (Sivanandan, 1982, or any issue of *Race and Class*). There are various combinations of these three

(Ward and Mullender, in Section 3; Mama, in Section 2), and there are gay versions (Evans, 1990, or any issue of *Gay Times*) and age versions (Bytheway and Johnson, 1990), differently abled versions (Oliver, 1984) and mental health versions (Cooper, 1972; Pilgrim and Rogers, 1989).

Health, welfare and education workers are also numbered among the oppressed. They are oppressed oppressors. Those who do not recognize this are just as much duped by the system as are the users of services. For those who do recognize this, the only proper course of action is to ally themselves with users and challenge the system: to become liberators rather than oppressors.

A helping relationship

In this view, workers with expertise identify the users' needs, and satisfy them, or help users satisfy them themselves in a way that they could not do unaided. Workers will quite frequently claim to know what users need better than the users themselves. This 'expertise gap' is an essential feature of worker–user relationships if they are to be successful for the user (Williams in Section 1). So long as workers are competent, and abide by codes of good practice, disparities of power between workers and users are in the interests of the users. The proper judges of competence and good practice are self-regulatory bodies, like the General Nursing Council, the Bar Council, ethics committees and professional associations. If there are things wrong with services then it is practitioners who will know how to put them right (Wright, 1990). Legitimate power equals expertise. The illegitimate use of power equals professional malpractice.

A disabling relationship

Workers and agencies are seen as exploiting users for their own benefit. The users' problems provide secure and relatively well-paid jobs for workers, and for this reason the secrets of the occupation are closely guarded, the value of the service is hyped up, the numbers and kinds of people who can join the occupational group are strictly limited and the boundaries of 'our kind of work' are fiercely defended (Freidson, 1970; Dalley, in Section 1). Workers claim the right to define what users need, and what users need is what the workers need them to need. This kind of practice 'disables' lay persons because it denies them the facilities and the knowledge to do things for themselves. The claim to expertise is the basis of power, but it may be a hollow claim. This view is closely associated with Ivan Illich (1977).

A brokerage relationship

Here, workers are seen as brokers between users and services, and sometimes, as in community social work, between different social groups. Users can have all kinds of problems, some rooted in their personalities, some caused by inequitable social arrangements. What users need is less important than the practical issue of what it is possible for users to get. Practice is the art of compromise, balancing the interests of one user against another or the interests of the worker and the agency against the interests of the user: playing one service off against another. The world in which this takes place is made up of many social groups, some more powerful than others, all jockeying for the best position and all competing for scarce resources. Workers are not very powerful; they have to negotiate with their clients (Stimson and Webb, 1975), but skilled workers can use strategies to get the best deal going for their clients.

Empowerment

We can now work out some different meanings for the word 'empowerment'. In the liberation model the sources of problems are the advantages enjoyed by the powerful. They, or the system which serves them, take the blame, whether for crime, ill health, homelessness, unemployment, poverty or despair. The powerful are not going to give up their power willingly. Power will have to be wrested from them. The first stage of empowerment means spreading the word: convincing the oppressed that they are indeed oppressed and that their disadvantages are foisted upon them.

Words such as 'conscientization', 'consciousness raising' and 'demystification' are frequently used in this context, all with the implication that people are misled and have to be led to the truth. The proper practice for this is not individual tuition but groupwork in which the oppressed can explore their situation together, reach a new understanding, and develop solidarity with one another (Ward and Mullender, in Section 3 of this volume). Workers do not so much give up power over users, as stand side by side with users to challenge and contest the power of capital (Ward and Mullender, in Section 3), patriarchy (Hanmer and Statham, in Section 2; Mistry, in Section 4) or white racism (Mama, in Section 2).

In health and welfare practice, empowerment rarely goes beyond this stage, but the hope of those involved is that groups will coalesce into movements, new and liberating understandings will spread among the oppressed, and they will engage in political action and transform society. Empowerment in locations such as the territories occupied by Israel, or in Central America, does of course include gaining access to armaments and fighting real wars.

Practitioners in Britain who take this line often encounter considerable consumer resistance. Relatively few people seem to want to believe that they are dupes of a corrupt and oppressive system. Even among those who do believe it, few have much faith that anything can be done about it. Some of the oppressed seem willing to stay in the struggle until they have achieved some gains, but then drop out. The anti-racist literature is full of complaints about black groups who have won the right and the resources to express themselves as Hindus or Moslems or Afro-Caribbeans, but have dropped out of the struggle to free all black people from oppression (Bourne, 1980). For the convinced liberator, however, all this serves to confirm just how misled and oppressed these people are.

The women's movement and gay movement have made great strides in changing the understandings of many women, some men, and probably most gay people. Anti-racists have forced agencies to review their practices and become less discriminatory. But in the liberatory model these are not necessarily seen as victories. When governments give grants to black community groups or implement equal opportunities policies, or companies try to increase the number of senior female executives, this may be seen as a 'buy-out': an accommodation made by the powerful to prevent more radical and meaningful change (Gibbon, 1990).

We can contrast this picture with that of the 'helping relationship' model. Power is not really an issue for people who hold this view. The sources of problems experienced by users are generally seen as no one's fault in particular, or quite explicitly as the fault of the client. Users have a deficit. Workers empower users by making good the deficit. They teach them to read. They teach them English. They give them 'confidence'. They help sort out their emotional or health problems. If they are successful they put the user in a position where they have the same kind of power as ordinary folk; enough to get a job, make a normal family life, vote in an election, write a letter to an MP, and stop being a problem to other people. 'Empowerment' was employed in exactly this way by the bodies which used to run YTS schemes (Williams, 1983; Cohen, 1984), and by the government-funded Adult and Basic Skills Unit (ALBSU). It is not the kind of empowerment which changes relationships between workers and users or the nature of society, and indeed it may make a good society run even better by correcting the faults of deficient people. Consumer resistance is unlikely to be seen as self-empowerment. It is more likely to be described as 'non-compliance' or a lack of insight (Potts and Fido, 1991, see Section 3). Policies in the name of empowerment here often do mean the acquisition of important skills, self-confidence and considerable improvements in people's lives, but it is misleading to refer to this in terms of changing power relationships.

Where power is seen in terms of a professional conspiracy disabling users, empowerment means cutting professionals down to size and making them responsive and accountable to users. There are two versions here, depending on whether the services offered are seen as genuinely valuable, or as a sham. Where they are seen as a sham, as Ivan Illich sees them, then empowerment means people gaining the skills to do without them, and the courage to do things for themselves. Empowerment means enablement. In this vein we can see many self-help and self-health groups, which draw upon their own resources to bypass the formal structures of health, welfare and education. There is 'Education Otherwise', for example, which helps parents to educate their own children (Meighan and Brown, 1980), and in the USA and UK (MacKeith, 1976) there are self-health groups using simple home remedies or alternative therapies rather than the national medical system. One of the problems with self-help groups is that it doesn't take very long before experts emerge, who might be said to disable and disempower the other members. The building society movement in this country started with small informal groups of workers pooling their savings to build houses for themselves to bypass money-lenders. Look at it now! (Gosden, 1973; Stoker, 1985).

Where the services offered are seen as potentially valuable, but over-controlled by professionals and bureaucrats then the trick of empowerment is to make them more responsive to users' demands. In this sense much of Conservative health, welfare and education policy in the 1980s could be seen as empowering; for example, the sale of council houses, local school and college management, systems of financing services whereby money follows the user (be the users students or patients); citizen charters (Taylor, 1991/2) and ombudspersons to add power to the complainant's elbow. Competition and surveys of consumer satisfaction can be used as disciplinary devices to keep workers on their toes. Putting representatives of users onto managerial committees or onto watchdog bodies dilutes the power of occupations.

All this could be represented as the empowerment of users. It would probably be more accurate to represent it as the disempowerment of the immediate providers of services, and the further empowerment of central government which has more and more narrowly defined the kinds and quantity of public services which users can be empowered to demand. Understandably, such programmes often cause considerable dissatisfaction and resistance among workers (Hughes, 1977; Brown and Ringma, in Section 3).

Where practice is a kind of brokerage what users seem to lack most is competitive edge. Empowerment means helping the less competitive to compete more effectively. This may mean establishing and servicing lobby groups, and running consultation exercises. It may mean marketing positive images of previously stigmatized client groups. The most impressive manifestations are advocacy and self-advocacy systems, whereby users are helped to participate fully in the decisions being taken about them and about the organization of services provided for them (Atkinson and Williams, 1990; Werthheimer, 1990; Winn, 1990).

It is very laudable to spend public money on schemes to help (say) people with learning difficulties to express their demands more clearly and to make decisions about their own lives themselves rather than have these taken on their behalf. It certainly can improve the quality of their lives (Brown and Ringma, in Section 3). But look where this has got us. It has got us to a paradox. It was not people with learning difficulties who made the decision to spend public money in this way. Someone made it on their behalf. Someone is deciding who deserves to be empowered. And that is a very powerful thing to do.

The paradox of empowerment

This paradox runs through the entire literature on empowerment. To empower oneself, to seize power, is a perfectly logical idea, and we don't need the word 'empowerment' to express it. To empower someone else implies something which is granted by someone more powerful to someone who is less powerful: a gift of power, made from a position of power. The paradox is easily resolved, however. Those people who say they are in the business of empowering rarely seem to be giving up their own power: they are usually giving up someone else's, and they may actually be increasing their own.

It is hardly surprising that people should only be prepared to increase the power of others on their own terms, but it would be more honest and clear-thinking to admit this. The term 'empowerment' designates many excellent practices, and some dubious ones, but exactly what they are, and who is doing what to whom, is hidden by its usage.

References

Atkinson, D. and Williams, F. (1990) *Know Me as I Am*. Sevenoaks: Hodder & Stoughton.

Bourne, J. (1980) 'Cheerleaders and ombudsmen; the sociology of race relations in Britain', *Race and Class*, 21 (4): 331–52.

Bytheway, R. and Johnson, J. (1990) 'On defining ageism', *Critical Social Policy*, 29: 5–26.

Cohen, P. (1984) 'Against the new vocationalism', in I. Bates, J. Clarke, P. Cohen, D. Finn, R. Moore and P. Willis (eds), *Schooling for the Dole*. London: Macmillan.

Cooper, D. (1972) *The Death of the Family*. Harmondsworth: Penguin.

Evans, D. (1990) 'Section 28, law, myth and paradox', *Critical Social Policy*, 27: 73–95.

Firestone, S. (1972) *The Dialectics of Sex*. London: Paladin.

Freidson, E. (1970) *The Profession of Medicine: a Study in the Sociology of Applied Knowledge*. New York: Dodd Mead.

George, V. and Wilding, P. (1976) *Ideology and Social Welfare*. London: Routledge & Kegan Paul.

Gibbon, P. (1990) 'Equal opportunity policy and race equality', *Critical Social Policy*, 28: 5–24.

Gosden, P. (1973) *Self-help: Voluntary Associations in Nineteenth Century Britain*. London: Batsford.

Hughes, (1977) *The Sociological Eye*. Chicago: Aldine Press.

Illich, I. (1977) *The Disabling Professions*. London: Marion Boyars.

MacKeith, N. (ed.) (1976) *Women's Health Handbook: a Self-help Guide*. Leeds: Women's Health Handbook.

Meighan, R. and Brown, C. (1980) 'Locations of learning and ideologies of education: some issues raised by a study of "Education Otherwise" ', in L. Barton, R. Meighan and S. Walker (eds), *Schooling, Ideology and the Curriculum*. London: Falmer Press.

Oliver, M. (1984) 'The politics of disability', *Critical Social Policy*, 11: 21–32.

Pilgrim, D. and Rogers, A. (1989) 'Radical mental health policy', *Critical Social Policy*, 25: 4–17.

Potts, M. and Fido, R. (1991) *A Fit Person to be Removed*. Plymouth: Northcote Press.

Sivanandan, A. (1982) 'From resistance to rebellion: Asian and Afro-Caribbean struggles in Britain', *Race and Class*, 23: 111–52.

Stimson, G. and Webb, B. (1975) *Going to See the Doctor*. London: Routledge & Kegan Paul.

Stoker, G. (1985) 'The building societies and the Conservative housing strategy into the late 1980s', *Critical Social Policy*, 12: 63–8.

Taylor, D. (1991/2) 'The big idea for the nineties? The rise of the Citizens' Charter', *Critical Social Policy*, 33 (Winter): 87–94.

Werthheimer, A. (1990) *Self-advocacy Skills Training*. London: Kings Fund.

Williams, F. (1983) 'The Youth Training Scheme and education', *Critical Social Policy*, 2 (3): 89–95.

Winn, L. (1990) *Power to the People: a Key to Responsive Services in Health and Residential Care*. London: Kings Fund.

Wright, S. (1990) *My Patient, My Nurse*. London: Scutari.

22

FROM CURING OR CARING TO DEFINING DISABLED PEOPLE

VIC FINKELSTEIN

Let us look at the dominant meaning associated with the word 'disability'. In the first instance, it is usually a helper (often a medical worker) who attaches the label 'disabled' to an individual with a physical or mental impairment because that individual appears not to be functioning 'normally'. The young child, for example, may appear to have difficulty chewing food and, compared with children of the same age, show little sign of developing speech. The doctor may then be approached to assess whether the child's functioning is indeed different from the majority of children of the same age and sex. At this initial contact the main focus of concern is usually the fact that a limb, organ or mechanism of the body is impaired when compared to the norms established in medical practice. The young child who can only manage to walk slowly and with apparent difficulty, the accident victim who, having recovered from a coma, cannot speak, the older person who has failing eyesight and is now having increasing difficulty preparing meals, are all examples of people in whom helpers may first identify the presence of disability.

The common feature contributing to the initial decision to label someone as disabled is the presence of a permanent impairment that causes difficulty in performing the activities of daily living. In each case a diagnosis will be made and the person classified as having a specific type of disability. Disability, therefore, seems to be consciously seen in the mind of the helper as a facet, or personal possession, of an individual. The main objective of the doctor is to treat the individual with a view to curing the impairment and returning them to a state where they can function according to the norm expected for their age, sex and class. Successful treatment means a return to normality and elimination of the personal disability problem.

The emphasis our society places on being and behaving as normally as possible can condition work colleagues, helpers (voluntary or professional)

From the Open University pack, *Disability: Changing Practice*, Open University, Milton Keynes, 1990 and planners to think very narrowly about the meaning of 'normality' and the kind of lives that disabled people can lead. Given that the disabled person's impairment is permanent and therefore cannot be 'cured', the degree of normality achieved can assume great significance in the minds of those who plan helping services. The logic seems to be that the closer the person gets to functioning in a normal way, the more they are thought capable of living in normal society; the further they are from normal functioning, the greater the degree of care expected.

There are two ways in which this medical emphasis on 'normality' is reinforced: at the practical level and at the psychological level. At the practical level, since the social and physical environment has been designed for people who do not have impairments, it is perhaps not surprising that disabled people have difficulty in functioning in them. The deaf person, for example, cannot participate in a television game show because the use of sign language interpreters has not been considered a design standard for developing such shows. If a slow walker cannot use a pedestrian shopping precinct because of long distances, they may be forced to rely on personal care services to do the shopping. In this context the choice for disabled people is either to try to succeed in behaving as 'normally' as possible or face the prospect of indefinite medical and paramedical 'care in the community'.

At the psychological level, because the key objective of medical intervention is 'normality', it seems natural to encourage disabled people as far as possible to assimilate the standards of normal role models. Since disabled people have some form of permanent impairment they already differ from this idealized expectation of bodily perfection according to age and sex. They may not look or behave 'normally' and there can only be a limited possibility of carrying out activities of daily living according to such ideal standards when a person has such an impairment.

Even when the objective is to be as 'normal as possible' the inaccessibility of the world designed for people with able bodies constantly reinforces the message that disabled people have failed the ultimate goal of normality. Those who work with disabled people and who start with the assumption that being 'normal' is equally important to all people, thus have a powerful incentive to put pressure on disabled people to see their own bodies as limiting their ability to carry out activities of daily living. In this context the choice for disabled people is either to assimilate the values of normal society or else to suffer indefinite feelings of inadequacy.

Once the emphasis shifts from seeking a medical cure for the disability to caring for the disabled person, there is great incentive to encourage 'patients' to assimilate medical assumptions based upon idealized standards of the perfect body. This makes the idea of dependency upon 'community care services' easier to accept as a natural consequence of disability. The 'cure or care' approach, therefore, associates the term 'disability' with the following characteristics:

- It is personal – disabled people need personal help in overcoming the problems they face (hence impairment, disability and handicap are defined in personal terms).
- It is abnormal – these problems result from an individual's abnormality of body or mind (hence an emphasis on assessing individual functioning for access to the services).
- There is an inability to function in normal activities of daily living – the abnormality of body or mind is interpreted as preventing the individual from doing something that is normal for their peers (hence the emphasis on caring services).

Redefining disability – an interactive approach

We have seen that the medical profession's way of defining disability is a consequence of the emphasis it naturally places upon expectations of normal body functions and its presumption that all people have the same desire to be normal. This attitude arises out of the curative approach to illness and, when applied to disability, means that interventions are required to seek a cure or failing this, to enable the development of humane caring. Once a 'cure or care' interpretation of disability is made, it will tend to colour all interpretations of what is possible for disabled living in the community. Planning services will depend upon information gathered from the various branches of the medical profession and this in turn will ensure that such services are targeted on the individual rather than on making the social and physical environment more accessible to that individual.

A very good example of how medical definitions individualize the social aspects of disability is provided by the Social Survey Division of the Office of Population Censuses and Surveys in its report *The Prevalence of Disability among Adults* (OPCS, 1988). In this report we are told that the survey was conducted 'for the purposes of planning benefits and services'. The introduction goes on to say 'The survey focuses on disability [note: not the barriers that disabled people face!], a restriction or lack of ability to perform normal activities, which has resulted from the impairment of a structure or function of the body or mind' (OPCS, 1988: xi). This definition is based upon one constructed by members of the medical profession for the World Health Organization. It has been severely criticized by research academics and organizations of disabled people because it locates disability in the body of an individual: 'The problem with this [WHO classification of impairment, disability and handicap] is that these schemes, while acknowledging there are social dimensions to disability, do not see disability as arising from social causes' (Oliver, 1986: 11). The report is consistent in applying the medical concept of disability in gathering statistical data about the situation of disabled people. For example, we are told that 'In some areas of disability the order of severity of particular limitations is obvious: not being able to walk is clearly more limiting than being able to walk only 50 yards' (OPCS, 1988: 50).

If one accepts that disability is directly related to impairment, what may seem obvious can in fact turn out to be based upon false assumptions. For example, the Open University campus is spread over a large area and anyone who cannot walk would already be using a wheelchair to move from building to building (in this case an electric wheelchair). The person who can manage to walk 50 yards may not have a wheelchair and consequently have great difficulty moving between buildings beyond this distance. In such a situation the ambulant person would be more limited in functioning as an employee on the Open University campus than the non-walking wheelchair user! Clearly, in this example not having an electric wheelchair is the decisive limiting factor to mobility, not the body imperfections of the individuals involved. It is difficult to see how gathering data about which or how many people can walk, how far they can walk etc. can help in more effective planning for disabled people. It is therefore unclear how the OPCS focus on the individual can have any national planning implications apart from enabling the government to make more accurate estimates of its benefit payments.

Some disabled people have reacted to the dominant medical interpretation of disability and argued that it is the social and physical environment which forces individuals to rely on help rather than the degree of an individual's impairment:

> Because the social and physical environment has been designed by people with able bodies . . . it is no surprise that those who are not of normal mind and body cannot manage and are forced to rely on personal care services. For example, since public transport (an able bodied mobility aid) cannot be used by people with mobility impairments, they are effectively prevented from doing their own shopping. In the circumstances they have no alternative but to rely on others to care for them. (Finkelstein, 1988: 10)

Interpreting the meaning of disability from this social perspective involves a major shift in the focus of attention. In this interpretation disability is seen as the consequence of things like public attitudes and environmental architecture rather than the consequence of personal inadequacies. Looking at mobility, for example, could we say that a person's inability to move from home to a place of work (hence to obtain employment and avoid dependency upon state benefits) is the consequence of inaccessible public transport rather than their inability to walk? From this point of view, gathering data which focuses on social and environmental barriers (such as the number of accessible buses or number of people who can communicate through British Sign Language) might be more helpful in planning interventions which would facilitate the greater involvement of disabled people in their communities.

References

Finkelstein, V. (1988) 'Planning services with disabled people', paper presented to the United Nations training workshop on the UN Disability Database, Hungary, November.

Oliver, M. (1986) 'Re-defining disability: a challenge to research', paper presented to the Social Science Research Group Annual Workshop in London.

OPCS (1988) *The Prevalence of Disability among Adults*. OPCS Surveys of Disability in Great Britain, Report 1. London: HMSO.

23

A COMMUNITY'S ADAPTATION TO DEAFNESS

NORA ELLEN GROCE

In her book, Everyone Here Spoke Sign Language, *Nora Ellen Groce recounted the history of Martha's Vineyard, an island community in the USA, where hereditary deafness was common. In this short extract, she argues that deafness was no handicap in the Vineyard.*

How does a community with a pattern of hereditary deafness adjust to that disorder? In modern Western societies 'handicapped' individuals have been expected to adapt to the ways of the non-handicapped. But the perception of a handicap, and of its associated physical and social limitations, may be tempered by the community in which it is found. The treatment of the deaf people of Martha's Vineyard is an interesting example of one community's response.

Unlike individuals similarly handicapped on the mainland, deaf Vineyarders were included in all of the community's work and play situations. They were free to marry either hearing or deaf persons. According to tax records, they generally earned an average or above-average income (indeed, several were wealthy), and they were active in church affairs. Enough can be gleaned from the records, furthermore, to indicate that this situation existed not only in the late nineteenth century but for more than three centuries. This implies that the social attitude was fully accepting of deaf individuals and that it was firmly in place from the time that the first deaf man settled in Tisbury in the 1690s.

Attitudes toward deafness

Vineyarders had no clear understanding of why deafness appeared in their families or how it was passed from one generation to the next. Deafness was seen as something that just 'sometimes happened'; anyone could have a

From 'The island adaptation to deafness', in *Everyone Here Spoke Sign Language*, Harvard University Press, Cambridge, Massachusetts, 1985 deaf child. The Vineyarders' social response to this was a simple acceptance of the inability to hear. This is clearly shown in the responses of my informants to questions about how hearing members of the community treated deaf members. The following replies are representative:

> You'd never hardly know they were deaf and dumb. People up there got so used to them that they didn't take hardly any notice of them.

> It was taken pretty much for granted. It was as if somebody had brown eyes and somebody else had blue. Well, not quite so much – but as if, ah, somebody was lame and somebody had trouble with his wrist.

> They were just like anybody else. I wouldn't be overly kind because they, they'd be sensitive to that. I'd just treat them the way I treated anybody.

The community's attitude can be judged also from the fact that until I asked a direct question on the subject, most of my informants had never even considered anything unusual about the manner in which their deaf townsmen were integrated into the society. They were truly puzzled by an outsider's interest in the subject. Almost all informants believed that every small town in New England probably had a similar number of deaf people and adapted to them in much the same way. Many were genuinely surprised when I told them that the incidence of deafness on the island was unusually high.

Those few who had wondered about the rate of deafness or the attitude toward islanders who were deaf had either stumbled across one of the nineteenth-century articles on Vineyard deafness or had spent some time off the island: 'I used to wonder why there was so much deafness, because when I went away to school in Boston, there wasn't anybody around who was deaf. I never saw anybody who was deaf, and I wondered why there wasn't.' Another man recalled:

> The only time that I ever thought about it was when I read an article in the Boston paper. I thought it was so funny that they should write about it in the paper . . . It struck me funny that they should have an article, because to me, you know, it was something very ordinary and I used to think, wasn't it funny that a Boston paper would be interested in it.

I found no disagreement on this subject. Although people's recollections of the 'good old days' usually gloss over or ignore the rougher, less appealing aspects of community life, that does not seem to have been the case here. The oral histories I collected hardly lead one to conclude that everyone lived in harmony and was always thoughtful and kind to neighbours and relatives. I heard numerous accounts of feuds, dissension and strife. Even an occasional murder slipped in. Stories about those who were mentally retarded or mentally ill make it clear that the Vineyard attitude toward these groups a century ago differed little from what is found today in our own society.

Vineyarders did not try to give me an idealized version of how the deaf people were treated; the inability to hear simply did not affect a person's status in the community.

The feelings of the deaf islanders about being unable to hear are less easily known, since none of them are still alive. Those who remember the deaf islanders do not recall them saying much about the subject. One woman remembered that her 'old maid aunt' regretted being unable to hear. 'She rebelled very much because of her inability to hear. Every once in a while she would, she'd say [in signs] "I hear no, shake-fist-at-God." ' Another woman recalled that her deaf mother would get 'terribly frustrated' at times. But this, the woman believed, was because her mother was the last deaf person up-island, and by that time there were few people left who could communicate with her in sign language.

Most people remembered the deaf as being far more positive about their inability to hear. 'I know that I asked him once, I never forgot it, because, well, because it was typical of him. I said, "Have you ever felt you missed anything important in life because you couldn't speak and hear?" And he said, "No, I have never had to listen to anything unpleasant." '

24

EMPOWERMENT AND OPPRESSION: AN INDISSOLUBLE PAIRING FOR CONTEMPORARY SOCIAL WORK

DAVID WARD and AUDREY MULLENDER

Rather as happened with the concept of 'community' in the 1970s, 'empowerment' has become the current bandwagon term in social work and is being used to justify what are, in fact, varying ideological and political positions. Because it creates a vogue image and an aura of moral superiority, it affords protection against criticism. Yet the term lacks specificity and glosses over significant differences. It acts as a 'social aerosol', covering up the disturbing smell of conflict and conceptual division.

Broadly, empowerment is associated at one end of a continuum with the New Right's welfare consumerism (Tonkin, 1988: 16; Department of Health (DoH), 1989) and, at the other, with the user movement which demands a voice in controlling standards and services themselves (Kearney and Keenan, 1988: 3; Brandon and Brandon, 1987, 1988; Brandon, 1989: 36). One is 'the essential expression of individualism' (Heginbotham, 1988: 24); the other rests on a collective voicing of universal need.

Croft and Beresford (1989: 5–6) point out that the user movement itself is part of a wider philosophy:

> It's also concerned with how we are treated and regarded more generally and with having greater say and control over the whole of our lives. Whatever our age, ethnicity, gender or sexuality we are entitled to be ourselves, be accepted for what we are and not devalued or subject to oppression.

This takes empowerment beyond the manner in which services are provided or help is offered to those in need or in trouble, into a number of

Abridged from *Critical Social Policy*, 32, 1991, pp. 21–30

reformulations: of the way we see the users of welfare services; of their own self-image; of the source of these old and new perceptions in the power relationships within our society; and of the nature of oppression.

Taking a stand on empowerment: confronting oppression

So what does it mean to empower someone? It has become clear that, by itself, the term cannot provide an adequate foundation for practice. The language of empowerment trips too lightly off the tongue and is too easily used merely as a synonym for 'enabling' (Mitchell, 1989: 14). Unless it is accompanied by a commitment to challenging and combating injustice and oppression, which shows itself in actions as well as words, this professional Newspeak allows anyone to rewrite accounts of their practice without fundamentally changing the way it is experienced by service users.

As Mitchell has stated for social work, there is only one way out of this danger for all related forms of intervention:

> British society is saturated in oppression . . . An empowering social work practice derived from such an understanding addresses itself to the powerlessness and loss which results from the material and ideological oppression of black people by white people; working class people by middle class people, women by men; children and old people by 'adults'; disabled people by 'able' people; and gay people by 'straight' people. This social work practice recognizes oppression not simply in the behaviours, values and attitudes of individuals and groups, but in institutions, structures, and common sense assumptions. (Mitchell, 1989: 14)

We begin here to move into a wider arena of change. Oppression, unlike such terms as 'poverty', 'deprivation' and 'disadvantage', is not ambiguous as to the exploitative nature of economic and social relationships (Kidd and Kumar, 1981: 5). Consequently, empowerment, if connected with a notion of oppression couched in these terms, *can* become a distinctive under-pinning for practice, and one which does not become colonized or domesticated in the service of the status quo.

Defining our terms: oppression

'Oppression' can be understood both as a state of affairs in which life chances are constructed, and as the process by which this state of affairs is created and maintained. As a *state of affairs*, oppression is the presumption in favour of men, white people, and other dominant groups, which skews all social relationships and is encoded in their very structure (Fine et al., 1985: 34). It is not simply the sum of individual attitudes, though it is revealed at the micro level in the nature of personal relations and at the macro level by 'the assignment of privilege in social hierarchies' (Fine et al., 1985: 35). It grossly impairs the lives of all those whose experiences are constant reminders of their oppressed status, and leaves them only the choice of adopting the values of the oppressor or of fighting back. So pervasive and powerful is the oppression, however, that, not infrequently, the former happens by default. The role of consciousness raising then becomes crucial in awakening people to their enslavement and in freeing them to choose active opposition in its stead.

Oppression is also the *process* which creates, maintains and emerges out of this state of affairs: 'Oppression is the process by which groups or individuals with ascribed or achieved power (the oppressors) unjustly limit the lives, experiences and/or opportunities of groups or individuals with less power (the oppressed)' (NCVS, 1989). This definition continues with the assertion that 'Oppression is supported and perpetuated by society's institutions.' In a sophisticated society, it is likely to take on a variety of subtle forms — moderating and containing conflict and defining what is to be seen as 'normal' and 'acceptable' through, for example, the workings of the law, the media and the educational system.

What is more, the various forms of oppression are entwined together and must be understood and confronted together. To do otherwise, is to allow one oppressed group to be played off against another in an invidious hierarchy which subverts into fruitless comparisons the energy which should be used in challenging the maintenance of injustice. The fight cannot purely be waged against racism or any other single '-ism'. It well suits the vested interests of those who benefit from oppression to see the effectiveness of those who would oppose it diluted and neutralized by competing claims to the position of 'most oppressed'. We must be on our guard for attempts to lead the debate in that direction: 'It is important to stress the importance of refusing to collude with the establishment of a hierarchy of more or less "worthy" oppressions. Such a hierarchy enables those in power to pitch one set of political rights and demands against others' (Hudson, 1989: 25).

Power

According to Lukes (1974), such ploys are a classic manifestation of power. Power is the capacity not only to impose one's will, if necessary against the will of other parties, but also to set the terms of the argument, including at the national and international level. A good example of this has been the repackaging of public ills under the guise of private troubles (Wright Mills, 1970) by three consecutive Conservative governments. Thus, social explanations of offending have given way to stress on personal culpability in criminal justice policies; changes in benefits have signalled to individuals that they must ultimately be prepared to provide for themselves or to beg for charity as 'deserving cases'; and the welfare of the poorest and weakest sections of the population has been attacked in hard financial terms, thus threatening to leave people so preoccupied by the suffering of their own families that they have neither the strength nor the motivation to band together in opposition.

The same attempt to individualize all arguments lies behind the official preference for 'consumerism' over user movements. Though its effect is gross, the exercise of power, as Lukes argues, may be hidden and subtle, not least in the way it is embedded in our expectations and perceptions. Thus, empowerment as we define it is committed in its politics. It recognizes that the response to what may appear personal has to be highly political.

Action for change

An understanding of oppression and power, then, is what draws empowerment away from the meaninglessness which otherwise afflicts and devalues the term. Practitioners require more clarification than this, however, to enable them to move from the inaction of endless conceptualization into facilitating real change among groups of service users, without requiring superhuman skills or inexhaustible resources.

Those forms of progressive practice which actively confront oppression and the power that holds it in place include attempts to develop anti-sexist and anti-racist social work. Feminists have developed forms of consciousness raising as a means both to conceptualize and to tackle individual and organizational sexism. Black activists have reached their own conclusions about ways to promote change, and there have also been pockets of activity among white workers who accept the responsibility for making fundamental shifts in confronting their own and others' racism.

Until now, however, the impact of such developments has been limited by two major factors. First, they have tended to be confined to fairly narrow areas, remaining on the edges of mainstream professional practice. Secondly, they have been colonized by those who win reflected glory from adopting the terminology without the pain of confronting their own oppressive attitudes at a level deep enough to root them out.

Feminist practice

Both limitations can be clearly observed in accounts by feminist writers. Hudson (1985: 635–6) argued that feminist perspectives had the potential to contribute far more to social work (and, one might add, other professional) practice than the 'incremental and patchy' picture she saw around her. Since then, two major explorations of the issues surrounding women and social work have appeared (Hanmer and Statham, 1988; Dominelli and McLeod, 1989), but practice continues to progress at a regrettably slow rate. Even now, there remains much work to be done in conceptualizing the detailed implications of gender-informed approaches for empowering intervention (Wise, 1986: ii). After all, the canvas is vast and the traditions to be challenged daunting in their scope and smugness. As a woman student riposted to a male class-mate who enquired where the counter-arguments were to a feminist line being presented by the tutor: 'Just read the whole of the rest of social work literature!'

Even where there is a gloss of accepting anti-sexism as an essential prerequisite of empowerment, there may be a failure to dig deeply enough into the old assumptions: 'Radical social work writers have largely "added in" feminist perspectives into what are usually explicitly Marxist paradigms' (Hudson, 1985: 639). If we are to rethink practice from a feminist perspective, we have to recognize that patriarchy is as polluting as capitalism. By developing 'a theory of power rather than of the state' (Rojek et al., 1988: 99), patriarchy, racism and other forms of oppression can be revealed as significant factors.

Anti-racist practice

The history of anti-racism is certainly one of active struggle and not just of analysis through raised consciousness. Sivanandan (1982) documents how struggle and direct action have been a constant theme for black people, providing a link between earlier anti-colonial struggles in the Empire with those still continuing in Britain today, but gradually resolving itself into 'a more holistic, albeit shifting, pattern of black unity and black struggle' (1982: 116). Because this struggle confronts, as Dominelli (1989: 13) puts it, the 'razor-sharp' edge of oppression in the form of racism, it contributes to consciousness raising a new clarity of analysis, and a commitment to real and concrete action for change.

It has been marginalized by many factors, however. For black women, there has been the frustration of being left out of account by those white feminists who fail to see the importance of a combined struggle:

> Black feminists have focused in particular on the way white feminists' presumptions about the 'intrinsic oppression' of the family have denied both the impact of racism on black families and the role of the family as a bulwark against a racist world . . . Racism and sexism . . . have different historical roots; their consequences are also generally dissimilar. (Hudson, 1989: 74–5)

Black women have been left to fight alone and have had to make their own connections (Bryan et al., 1985). Foster-Carter (1987: 53) shows how black women have fought back, organizing themselves without support from existing movements, not borrowing theories and practices but making the struggle relevant to their own experiences. She acknowledges the interlocking dimensions of their oppression – racial oppression, sexual domination and class – but emphasizes how 'a common experience as second class citizens in contemporary Britain' (1987: 47), an experience which is specifically black and structured by racism, provided the basis for solidarity and collective action. Workers – even, sometimes, black workers because of their socialization into white agencies – have to learn to recognize and work with these strengths.

For Foster-Carter (1987), Cashmore and Troyna (1982), and other writers (for example, CCCS, 1982; Gilroy, 1987), the manifestation of raised black consciousness is to be found in the direct action which not only black women but others, too, have taken to minimize the pernicious impact of racism on their lives. The nature of the action has worked according to the differing circumstances in which they have found themselves. The industrial campaigns to which Foster-Carter refers (Grunwick, for example), on the surface could not be in a greater contrast to the Rastafarian movement that Cashmore and Troyna describe. However, both represent disenchantment and resistance to a mainstream society (Cashmore and Troyna, 1982: 19).

The challenge to the white majority and particularly to white professionals is to join the fight against racism without altering its terms. Only the black experience of oppression can give the lead. The best that can be said of white activists may be: 'They are colonised too, just like us. The only difference is we see the bars and chains' (Cashmore and Troyna, 1982: 28). For white anti-racist advocates, the imperative is to try to understand the urgency of the struggle, and why, for black colleagues and service users, there can never be any rest from it. In this way, we can inject enhanced meaning into the statement that the personal is political, demonstrating incontrovertibly that individual woes reflect wider social status.

A combined way forward

In summary, then, there is an urgent need to fill the vacuum of empowering activity in the mainstream of professional practice, on the basis of principles of anti-oppressive working. An approach is needed which can readily be adopted by all those who share these aims and who have a genuine desire to work in a way which supports the activists' struggles. The current norms, of effectively ignoring them on the one hand or, on the other, subverting them by a failure to understand their true philosophy and impact – illustrated by any social worker who refers a woman to a refuge as if it were just another residential alternative rather than a place which actively aims to change her life – is simply not good enough.

Workers who begin to talk about empowering people must be clear about what they then have the responsibility and the skills to deliver. Nothing would be more inexcusable than raising commitments and expectations which then founder because the worker does not know how to deliver his or her contribution.

Self-directed groupwork

An approach to practice which we have described in detail elsewhere (Mullender and Ward, 1985, 1989, 1991) – self-directed groupwork – attempts to fill this vacuum. This approach has been developed by and with the users of mainstream welfare agencies and, at the same time, is rooted in anti-oppressive values. The principles which underpin anti-racist, feminist and related struggles are also embedded in self-directed work. Practitioners who use the model are challenged to combine their own efforts with those of oppressed groups without colonizing them. This is achieved by placing the reins in the hands of service users organized together in groups and by offering them help in achieving their own goals, in place of the customary 'we know best' of traditional practice. Both user-led *analysis* and user-led *action* work better in such groups, grounded as they are in collective strength.

Taking analysis first, Longres and McLeod (1980) argue that consciousness raising is best achieved within groups because it is only there that the full implications of social experiences may become apparent. In groups, personal troubles can be translated into common concerns. The experience of being with other people in the same boat can engender strength and new hope where apathy reigned beforehand: a sense of personal responsibility, internalized as self-blame, can find productive new outlets. It is for these reasons that it seems to us that groupwork lies at the heart of empowerment.

In summary, our proposition is that groupwork based on clearly anti-oppressive values can be immensely powerful because it is affiliated to a purpose which explicitly rejects the 'splintering' of the public and private, of person and society. We believe that 'to bring together clients with common needs and problems to engage in collective action on their own behalf' (Brake and Bailey, 1980: 25) still represents the essence of empowerment, and that the methodology of self-directed groupwork can more clearly indicate how this may be achieved.

References

Brake, M. and Bailey, R. (eds) (1980) *Radical Social Work and Practice*. London: Edward Arnold.
Brandon, A. and Brandon, D. (1987) *Consumers as Colleagues*. London: MIND.
Brandon, D. (1989) 'Better to light a candle than curse the darkness', *Social Work Today*, 9 November: 36.
Brandon, D. and Brandon, A. (1988) *Putting People First: A Handbook on the Practical Application of Ordinary Living Principles*. London: Good Impressions Publishing.
Bryan, B., Dadzie, S. and Scafe, S. (1985) *The Heart of the Race: Black Women's Lives in Britain*. London: Virago.
Cashmore, E. and Troyna, B. (eds) (1982) *Black Youth in Crisis*. London: Allen and Unwin.
CCCS (Centre for Contemporary Cultural Studies) (1982) *The Empire Strikes Back: Race and Racism in 1970s Britain*. London: Hutchinson.
Croft, S. and Beresford, P. (1989) 'User-involvement, citizenship and social policy', *Critical Social Policy*, 26: 5–18.
Department of Health (DoH) (1989) *Caring for People: Community Care in the Next Decade and Beyond*. Cm 849. London. HMSO.
Dominelli, L. (1989) 'White racism, poor practice', *Social Work Today*, 12 January, 12–13.
Dominelli, L. and McLeod, E. (1989) *Feminist Social Work*. Basingstoke: Macmillan.
Fine, B., Harris, L., Mayo, M., Weir, A. and Wilson, E. (1985) *Class Politics: An Answer to its Critics*. London: Leftover Pamphlets.

Foster-Carter, O. (1987) 'Ethnicity: the fourth burden of black women – political action', *Criticial Social Policy*, 20: 46–56.

Gilroy, P. (1987) *There Ain't No Black in the Union Jack*. London: Hutchinson.

Hanmer, J. and Statham, D. (1988) *Women and Social Work: Towards a Woman-centred Practice*. London: Macmillan.

Heginbotham, C. (1988) 'Consumerism in care', *Community Care*, 21 April: 24–5.

Hudson, A. (1985) 'Feminism and social work: resistance or dialogue?', *British Journal of Social Work*, 15: 635–55.

Hudson, A. (1989) 'Changing perspectives: feminism, gender and social work', in M. Langan and P. Lee (eds), *Radical Social Work Today*. London: Unwin Hyman. pp. 70–96.

Kearney, D. and Keenan, E. (1988) '"Empowerment" – does anyone know what it means?', *Lynx*, 34: 3–5.

Kidd, R. and Kumar, K. (1981) 'Co-opting Freire; a critical analysis of pseudo-Freirean adult education', *International Foundation for Development Alternatives Dossier*, 24: 25–40.

Longres, J. F. and McLeod, E. (1980) 'Consciousness raising and social work practice', *Social Casework*, May: 267–76.

Lukes, S. (1974) *Power: A Radical View*. London: Macmillan.

Mitchell, G. (1989) 'Empowerment and opportunity', *Social Work Today*, 16 March: 14.

Mullender, A. and Ward, D. (1985) 'Towards an alternative model of social groupwork', *British Journal of Social Work*, 15: 155–72.

Mullender, A. and Ward, D. (1989) 'Challenging familiar assumptions: preparing for and initiating a self-directed group', *Groupwork*, 2: 5–26.

Mullender, A. and Ward, D. (1991) *Self-directed Groupwork: Users Taking Action for Empowerment*. London: Whiting and Birch.

NCVS (Nottingham Council for Voluntary Service) (1989) *A Working Definition of Oppression*. Nottingham: NCVS.

Rojek, C., Peacock, G. and Collins, S. (1988) *Social Work and Received Ideas*. London: Routledge.

Sivanandan, A. (1982) 'From resistance to rebellion: Asian and Afro-Caribbean struggles in Britain', *Race and Class*, 23: 111–52.

Tonkin, B. (1988) 'What the boys in the backroom will have', *Community Care*, 7 April: 14–16.

Wise, S. (1986) *Doing Feminist Social Work: An Annotated Bibliography and Introductory Essay*. Manchester: University of Manchester, Department of Sociology.

Wright Mills, C. (1970) *The Sociological Imagination*. Harmondsworth: Penguin.

25

NEW DISABILITY SERVICES: THE CRITICAL ROLE OF STAFF IN A CONSUMER-DIRECTED EMPOWERMENT MODEL

CHRISTOPHER BROWN and CHARLES RINGMA

In this article the authors report on the results of their evaluation of a new consumer-directed empowerment model of community living for physically disabled people. A house was set up for four disabled people, one woman and three men. These consumers were involved in every stage of the project, including the selection and management of staff. In this extract the authors discuss the role of staff.

The staff role was to meet the basic care needs of consumers and to facilitate growth towards greater independence and community integration. The expectation was generated that as the consumers acquired these new skills, the level of staffing hours would be reduced.

The role of carer and trainer, however, proved to be problematical. Staff were asked to facilitate the four consumers in assuming responsibilities for household management and to stimulate the development of new living skills and recreational and social interests. Yet, consistent with consumer control, staff were to offer suggestions and advice without deciding for the consumers. The house, moreover, was home for the consumers and not a training centre.

Difficulties occurred when it became unclear whether the consumer had maximized the acquisition of particular new skills, or was unwilling to take further risks, or felt pushed beyond normal comfort levels. This took place with regard to cooking and household responsibilities, personal care needs

Abridged from *Disability, Handicap and Society*, 4 (3), 1989, pp. 251–4 and the development of further social skills. One pertinent example of these difficulties was the attempt to withdraw staff from the house for periods of time before some of the consumers could cope with being left alone. This process was further complicated by the fact that consumers in the same household will develop new skills at different rates of progress. Moreover, the ever-pressing role of providing basic care may conflict with the more difficult and time-consuming role of trainer.

For the above difficulties to be overcome it is essential that consultation and communication be maintained and that trust is developed. Consumers must be able to express their expectations and needs, as well as their fears. They need to set the pace in their growth towards greater independence. Staff need to facilitate that process without pushing them beyond their risk and comfort levels.

Assistant v. friend

Within this personal setting, staff have the opportunity to work closely with consumers. Some staff and consumers will work well together when trust and respect develops. The nature of the tasks and the climate in which they are performed increases the likelihood of emotional involvement between staff and consumers. Staff become involved in the journey of the household members towards independence. Loyalty and commitment to them is evident. In some cases, genuine affection may develop.

It is not intended, however, that staff become the focus of the consumers' social world. While staff do bring variety into the life of the household members, it is important that consumers develop and maintain their own social networks in the community. In this way, dependency on staff relationships for social needs is minimized.

However, when a mutual working relationship does develop, perception of staff as friends does occur among the household members. To some degree, staff may reciprocate. This becomes complicated if staff are unable to pursue commitments and expectations of friendship outside working hours. Staff are employed to be assistants, not friends. If friendships develop, this is over and above the requirements of the role.

In this context, sexuality can be a problem. A staff member may be requested to fulfil the sexual needs of a household member. In this project a male consumer developed a romantic crush on one of the female staff members. At this point, client control and the perceived role as personal assistant become problematical. The nature of the staff–consumer relationship in this case would require negotiation between the parties concerned. Expression of affection occurs in the personal setting where a friendly atmosphere is created. Such expression ought not to be partial or at the expense of quality of care to the other members of the residence. But clearly this becomes difficult where a more exclusive relationship is expected between a consumer and a staff member.

This aspect of the consumer–staff interaction requires further clarification. While staff roles are more clearly defined in institutional settings, they are less so in this environment. While friendships can occur in both institutional and consumer-directed settings, the context of the latter is more difficult because it is less formal and more intimate. Further clarification on staff roles will need to be achieved. While assistant and friend seems to be fairly compatible, friend and trainer may be more difficult. The fact that the consumers are also seen as the employers complicates the roles even further.

Employee–employer relationship

Staff in this service model are employed to perform tasks (including training) in an employee capacity. While the funding agency (the Catholic Social Welfare Secretariat) formally pays staff, the household members are seen as the employers. Consumers also participated in staff selection, organization of staff rosters and tasks and, if necessary, staff dismissal.

Staff are thus responsible to the people they care for rather than to an administrative structure. In an institution, staff are employed to provide services as determined by the institution. In this project, members of the residence have been empowered to recruit staff to perform the services they require. Thus, while in an institutional setting staff may be seen as trainers, carers and friends, they do not see the residents as employers, as is the case in this project. This further complicates the staff–consumer relationship.

While it is possible to envisage employing staff to be trainers, carers and personal assistants, it is harder to employ someone as friend. This does not mean that staff–consumer interaction cannot be friendly and amicable or that friendships will not develop. Rather, the employer/employee dimension is the basic reference point from which staff and consumers can evaluate their involvement.

In an institutional setting, boundaries are often very clear. Responsibilities and functions of staff are understood or specifically conveyed. Residents comply with the institutional procedures and routines. When staff–resident relations become difficult, both parties can retreat to the traditional roles and thereby maintain the balance.

In this project, staff and household members have negotiated new ground for themselves in operating with consumers as the employer. Consumers need to develop skills in declaring their needs and in directing staff while recognizing their dependence on staff to provide basic care. For staff, it has been necessary to clarify expectations with the consumers and to understand what is required of them. As household members have authority to terminate services of unsatisfactory staff, staff have to overcome the sense of always being on trial.

Working for four employers in the same house can cause conflict. Differing requirements and competing demands for services cause difficulties in determining priorities. The individual focus of the model generates the expectation that staff will provide individual and tailored attention. This is difficult in a group-living situation. In practice, the most demanding or most assertive person may be the influential factor in determining staff service priorities.

Ideally, the household as a group would determine the priorities and direct staff accordingly. Again, the individual emphasis in the project with staff servicing specific consumers to fulfil specific tasks has been at the expense of addressing the group dynamics of a corporate-living situation. In such a situation, group decision-making and negotiation are important tools for the consumer. Furthermore, it must be clarified whether a staff person is employed by the household or by individuals within it. The resolution of this issue was not satisfactorily achieved in the project.

Empowerment v. disempowerment

The consumers acknowledge that they have been empowered to exercise choice in many basic daily activities of household and staff management. They also exercise freedom in lifestyle development. It is in these areas that they have previously felt powerless. However, household members also acknowledge that they will always need staff support to live in the community. This is only different in degree from the way we all need others to provide us with a range of services. Empowerment is therefore not independent of relationships with those who provide care and with the wider community in which they live.

In this consumer-directed model, decision-making and power have been given to the consumers. The recognition that they are still dependent on a level of staff support places some power in the hands of staff. For example, a staff member may favour a particular client or begrudgingly perform tasks for another. In the extreme, staff could deliberately delay attending to a consumer's request or withhold services. Such abuse of staff power has not been observed in this project.

On the other hand, consumer empowerment could mean disempowerment of staff. This is particularly the case in the exercise of the training role. Trainers normally exercise initiative and have the power of status and knowledge with regard to those they are training. In this model training was consumer-initiated. Therefore, the training aspect needs careful negotiation with each person. Staff want to contribute to the consumers' development and independence. By undermining the training role, by not doing tasks they are capable of doing, or by being 'authoritarian', they presume on the goodwill and commitment of staff.

Considerations such as these highlight the need for careful negotiation of the role. Development of trust and a recognition of the respective contributions of staff and consumers in the provision of care is required.

Conflict resolution

Negotiating an appropriate staff role in this model requires further attention. Role conflict for staff can cause undue stress. An area of difficulty affecting the staff–consumer interaction is conflict between household members. The model does *not* give staff a mandate to intervene in such conflict situations. Rather the staff task is to encourage the consumers to develop skills for conflict resolution. At the very least, staff can suggest that household members 'get together to sort things out'. To initiate and facilitate resolution of conflict is not seen as an appropriate role for staff. Staff are available to provide advice and assistance if the consumers so choose.

However, group living implies group conflict and some issues would be more appropriately addressed in the group context. For example, household management issues, clarifying individual responsibilities, communication of plans and generally keeping one another informed have been sources of conflict between consumers. Staff in their training role could help the household members to develop skills in conflict resolution.

Conflict has also arisen between staff and consumers. Mutual adjustment to the staffing model and negotiating appropriate assistance have been minor hurdles. When staff are unable to work with a particular consumer or vice versa, consumers need to decide whether the services of that person will be retained. (In the broader agency model, that person could be deployed elsewhere.) Staff and consumers have recourse to the programme director in determining the outcome of such conflict. Inappropriate response to consumer direction was the reason for the dismissal of one staff member. Household members found this a difficult and challenging task. The programme director was consulted regarding procedure and was present when they informed the staff member concerned of the decision.

Overcoming the potential pitfalls mentioned above has been challenging and demanding for both staff and the four consumers. Nevertheless, staff have provided a quality of service which consumers assert is empowering and enhances quality of life. Further clarification of the staff–consumer interaction is necessary. The training role and how it can be successfully integrated into a client-controlled service model requires clearer definition. Examination of the employer/employee dimension as a reference point could produce productive and constructive outcomes.

26

THE BARNS EXPERIMENT

W. DAVID WILLS

The Barns was an evacuation hostel initiated by the Society of Friends (Quakers) during the Second World War. The boys who attended it were, in the author's words, 'all difficult boys, hating school, punished often but not wisely, fearful, suspicious, aggressive, untruthful, uncared for and in the main unloved . . . they strove hard to compel us to furnish them with the only kind of security they knew, the security of outward compulsion; and we were determined to give them security on a different level – the security that comes from a knowledge of being loved.'

W. David Wills was in charge of the hostel: in this extract he describes something of the process of handing over authority for discipline and organization to the boys. As an experiment in what in modern terms might be called 'empowerment' it has some interesting messages.

There are three grades of authority at Barns. There is the authority of the adults, which is absolute on matters of health, and which includes the delegated authority of outside agencies, such as the Education Authority; there is the 'influence' which I deliberately bring to bear (as infrequently as possible), usually in connection with something concerning our relations with the outside world – less often to prevent a boy being victimized; and then there is the authority of the House meeting (now known as the General Meeting), which covers everything else. We try to avoid the hypocrisy of saying 'The boys make all the rules', and then expecting them to make only the rules *we* want to see made. Where a clear law must be laid down, the adults lay it down and no monkey business. We (the staff) lay down the bedtimes, we made the rule 'No bathing except under adult supervision.' We explain the reasons for these rules, but we are not so dishonest as to explain the need for a rule and then say, 'So shall we make a rule about it?' when we know perfectly well that a rule must be made whether the meeting wants to make one or not. Outside authority says (in effect) 'You must go to school',

---

From *The Barns Experiment*, George Allen & Unwin, London, 1945 and although we should, on the whole, prefer voluntary lessons, authority relies on the adults to see that their order is obeyed. But although adults or outside authority make some rules, the enforcement of those rules has usually been taken on by the democratic governing machinery of the House. And because we have always been perfectly honest about what matters were, and what were not, within the jurisdiction of the Meeting, we have never had to deal with the grouse which I believe is not uncommon in some 'self-governing' schools. 'We're supposed to be self-governing – why can't we please ourselves' about this or that. In fact, we rarely use the phrase 'self-government' because it is not self-government, and I very much doubt whether there is any school where – if the adults are quite honest with themselves – there is complete self-government.

Where, then, there is no choice, the adults make the law; where there *is* a choice, the meeting makes it. True, the adults have a right to attend meetings, say their say, and use their votes, but in practice we try not to influence a decision unless, as I have said, it is something which concerns our relations with the outside world, or something which is likely to affect vitally a boy's happiness. Even when we do that, we are most careful to see that the boys understand the justice and rightness of the course we favour – indeed, if we do not, the voting will go against us. That is another reason that we are sparing with adult influence. If it begins to be suspected that adults are influencing too many decisions, the time will come when any course recommended by an adult will be voted against, just for that reason. Indeed, that happened at our very first meeting when – as everyone was new – it was taken for granted that anything suggested by an adult was suggested with some ulterior motive, and should, therefore, be voted against. It was over the question of orderly duties. I explained that paid adults had been appointed to do most of the housework, but there were various jobs which no one was paid to do, and for which we should have to make arrangements between us. Those jobs were bed-making, dish-washing and potato-peeling, and I asked how they were to be done. As at first no suggestions seemed forthcoming, and as I have had a great deal of experience of arranging orderly duties, I put forward a scheme, 'but Bruce Cobber said he had a better idea . . . After a lot of talk we decided to have Bruce's idea, beginning next Sunday.' This was not the last time that orderly duties were discussed, and that last time is not yet. A few weeks ago, someone got the idea that the system then in operation let off the staff too lightly, so another scheme (the nth) was devised which seemed to achieve the objective of making it rather harder for the adults. Since it involved the adults all working together (instead of being distributed among the boys), it also made things much harder for everyone else! But never mind – the adults aren't getting away with anything! I have explained that the new scheme is much easier for the staff, but the boys think that is just sour grapes.

At the early House meetings I was self-appointed chairman and secretary, but after a few weeks, when we had begun to fill up, I said it was time the meeting chose its own officers. So they elected me as chairman, my wife as secretary, and Kenneth Roberton as treasurer! Such timidity astonished me, but I let it pass – I knew it would not last long and I insisted that the term of office should be for one month only. As a matter of fact this timidity (which I hasten to add, expressed itself in no other aspect of the life of the establishment) lasted longer than I expected, and although they rang the changes among the adults, it was not until three months had passed that they elected a boy as chairman – Gilbert Rivers – with myself as secretary. The final minute on that occasion reads 'Jacob Everson said he would not obey the instructions of the new Chairman, so it was decided he should not attend School meetings.' Jacob (though none of us suspected this at the time) was to become one of our most distinguished chairmen, and his name stands out in the annals of Barns like a Cecil or a Chatham or a Churchill in the history of England. Two weeks later we read 'Jacob Everson sent a request that he be permitted to attend House meetings in future. He was brought into the meeting and asked whether he was ready to promise to obey the Chairman in future. He said he was, so he was allowed to attend meetings again.'

As one looks through the minutes, they give the impression of having been very orderly, well-conducted meetings. But it is a profoundly misleading impression. The minutes record merely decisions, with, perhaps, a few notes describing how the decision was arrived at. Disorder is not usually recorded, but there was plenty of it, and we do occasionally find an entry like this – on 9 December 1940 'After this, the meeting became disorderly and David [I was Chairman then] dismissed it.' What the secretary meant was that after 'this' (whatever that may have been) the meeting became just *too* disorderly, and it was impossible to carry on.

So we went on from week to week, arranging and re-arranging the orderly duties, discussing the care of the games equipment, talking about trespassing, arranging parties and concerts, arguing about the inter-dormitory competition we had in those days, appointing a committee to buy a vase for the postmistress, in return for the sweets she sent us from time to time – and so on. There were also very many items of this kind:

> Molly [cook] reminded us of the possible consequences of playing about with the food lift. There was a lot of talk about this, but no definite decision was made.

> David Wills raised the question of the electric light bulbs that were missing, but everyone said they knew nothing about it.

> The Chairman complained that on certain evenings when painting and handwork were being carried on, boys were in the habit of disturbing these quiet indoor activities by careering through the house, slamming doors. Bobbie Dodd suggested that these boys go outside or stay in the play-room. Chairman suggested that one night might be set aside for chasing. Wally Straight suggested that there should be no chasing while indoor activities were being carried on, and this was carried, with the proviso that Tuesday evenings and Sunday afternoons should be reserved for chasing about the house.

And so on.

It was one thing to make all these rules and prohibitions, but it was quite another to see that they were kept, and before long this became one of the principal preoccupations of the meeting. There was not only a matter of seeing that *statute* law, as we may perhaps describe it, was carried out; there was also the question of what, on the same analogy, we may describe as common law (and even, after a time, something very much like case law). We have no rule in the minute book forbidding stealing, and for a long time there was none prohibiting assault. But they, and many such thing, are by common consent regarded as improper, and there were many boys seeking redress and protection. All such cases came before the House meeting and indeed they took up most of the time. We therefore set up, eventually, a committee to deal with charges. It consisted of one boy from each dormitory (five in all) and one adult, and it met more or less every day.

I regard this court (for so we may regard it, though it has never had that name) as one of the most important aspects of shared responsibility. In any community – whether of children or of adults – there is (or usually has been so far in the history of man) a tendency, however slight, for the strong to exploit the weak, and it is necessary to have some form of protection against this. Most schools have their bullies, and in the orthodox school they often have a pretty free hand. A boy who appeals for adult aid against the aggressor is considered a sissy, and not only by the other boys! In any case, the chances are that after he has sought aid he will get a worse pummelling than ever for being a sneak. We have all read the autobiographies of sensitive boys who have endured the privilege of a public school education, and although there are perhaps not so many autobiographies of elementary school boys, I can assure my readers (for I was one) that it is just about as bad there. But I will resist the temptation to anticipate a chapter of my own autobiography, enlightening though it might be, in this context. Our court does come, I believe, as near to solving this problem as it is possible to come short of curing the bullies – a process which is being carried on at the same time by other agencies than the court. In the first place, if a boy brings a charge to the committee he is not sneaking – or clyping, as they say in Scotland. A clype is a boy who crawls up to some adult and surreptitiously whispers his tale of woe into his ear. Bringing a charge to the committee is no more clyping than is calling in the police if your house is robbed. That is clearly understood and accepted by all – so charges are brought. (We sometimes have over a hundred in one week!) Where restitution or compensation can be ordered, that is the usual course. If A steals B's toffee, he is made to replace it. If B breaks C's roller skate he is ordered to get it mended (he may have to ask an adult to do it for him, but that is neither here nor there – he gets the damage repaired); C has knocked over the gang-hut that D has spent several days constructing, and is ordered to build it up again. 'Och, never mind,' says D, 'I'll build it ma sel'.' He realizes suddenly that most of the fun of the gang-hut was in the building, and he doesn't want to give C that pleasure! But – and here is the important point – he is quite satisfied, and the breach is healed. Often there is very little the committee can do, except to hear the case – both sides of the case – and express an opinion as to who is in the wrong. But equally often that is all that is needed. If the frustrated boy who has had something unpleasant done to him, feels that he can explain his situation to a sympathetic audience, receive a measure of condolence and be assured that he is in the right – that is all he needs, more often than not. If, on the other hand, he has to suffer the minor annoyances of some petty bully, or some merely thoughtless bigger boy, and be unable to do anything about it at all, he is liable to become warped and embittered and be continually whining. I have noticed repeatedly that a boy will come to the Committee boiling over with a sense of frustration and injustice, and leave the Committee perfectly happy, though nothing whatever has been done! That is almost impossible in a normal school – it would be sneaking! It is an everyday occurrence at Barns.

'But is it good for the boys not to learn to stand up for themselves?' some people ask. And sometimes a new boy will disdain to use the court, saying 'I can stick up for myself.' There are two answers to this. One is that in seeking legal redress a boy *is* standing up for himself, and successfully, whereas very often the attempt to stand up for himself in the other way is the merest futility. The other reply is in the nature of a *tu quoque*, but is not without point. Do *you*, dear superior adult, always 'stand up for yourself'? Or do you send for a policeman? One of the things which principally distinguishes civilized from savage society is the willingness of individuals to surrender the right to 'stick up for themselves'. When that right is equally surrendered by the nations . . . But I will not digress.

Even, however, in the cases where nothing seems to have been done except comfort the aggrieved party, something else has in fact been done, and often a very important something. Public opinion has been expressed. When the headmaster stands before the school at assembly, and verbally castigates a boy or a set of boys, he may make a few people feel a little uncomfortable for a little while – perhaps for as long as he is speaking – but he is unlikely to have any permanent effect on the persons concerned. He is an adult, and adults have what seems to children a cross-eyed view about pretty well everything, and after all the Old Man's paid to stand up there and make orations. Even if the castigations take place in private, the effect is pretty much the same, except that there is less chance of the victim feeling himself a bit of a hero. But if the other boys are heard to say, 'That's a pretty lousy thing to do', the effect is totally different. This is an expression of real opinion, not another manifestation of adult prejudice. It goes home.

27

RESISTING THE SYSTEM

MAGGIE POTTS and REBECCA FIDO

This extract comes from an oral history of a mental handicap colony, 'The Park'.

The institution regulated everything and in this respect The Park was little different from the sort of total institution described by Goffman (1968):

> The patient's life is regulated and ordered according to a disciplinarian system developed for the management by a small staff of a large number of involuntary inmates. In the system the attendant is likely to be the key staff person, informing the patient of the privileges and rewards that are to regulate his life and arranging with the medical authority for such privileges and punishments.

To run efficiently, any large institution not only has to have rules but also has to have ways of ensuring adherence to these rules. This philosophy is summarized in the 1949 Park Annual Report as follows:

> The payment of conduct and industry rewards continued to encourage habits of regular work and good conduct. The rewards were graded according to the mental state of the patient and the type of work performed and were reviewed regularly by the medical staff. The money was spent on purchases of sweets and tobacco or were saved for purchases made on shopping expeditions to town.
>
> Trustworthy patients were granted increased freedom within the colony and were later allowed to make unescorted visits to town. The hope of securing these privileges stimulates good conduct in the more intelligent and stable patients.

Rules and regulations were designed for the smooth, efficient running of the institution: they did not allow for individual self-expression nor did they permit some basic human rights to be respected. The institution controlled everything, including contact with parents and relatives and the world outside. 'Leave is a privilege which is earned by obedience to the regulations.' This system was vividly recalled by Ernest:

From *A Fit Person to be Removed*, Northcote House, Plymouth, 1991

Patients had to be careful how they behaved in their work and on the villa or wherever they were 'cos there was strict staff in those days and any offence, they used to be up before one of the senior doctors. In the case of first offences, they were warned of the serious nature of the offence and what would happen if that or anything like it was repeated. Then they were placed before the doctor and they lost all their privileges for a certain length of time. As far as privileges were concerned, [they] used to be going to films and concerts and in the hospital grounds, recreation hall and money included.

The hospital rules euphemistically referred to the necessity of watchfulness at all times as demanding 'a high standard of tactful guidance by the nurses'. What constitutes 'tactful guidance' is not specified but staff were no doubt aided in their work by the payment of conduct money. The colony operated a system of conduct money payable each week to patients. The purpose of this money was to encourage obedience to the rules. In practice, the operation of this system went well beyond the rules; it was intended to develop and maintain a respectful attitude to authority.

> You know being really rude to staff and swearing. They'd go in front of Matron and Dr Black and all them. They used to get into right trouble. They really got into bother then . . . They couldn't go t' pictures or anything like that, concerts, where I was saying we go, until they learnt to behave themselves. (Margaret)

> Put them to bed just for swearing. (Grace)

> You got your money stopped for two months or three months. You didn't get a penny. For being cheeky or anything like that. Sometimes you'd stick up for yourself like mad, you were on your own! (Grace)

Obedience and respect were the order of the day.

> They were strict though. They used to tell them to put them to bed without supper if they didn't do as they were told. They used to try and take them upstairs to bed, make sure they get in and take their clothes away.

Staff had their own way of dealing with minor problems. Problems such as incontinence created extra work and could lead to punishment even when a person's physical handicaps prevented them from having control of their bladder and bowels. Grace tried to forestall trouble on her villa.

> I used to tell 'em who to excuse and who not to excuse. Well there were some that couldn't help themselves. I told her which ones had to go to t' toilet. They had to keep changing them 'cos they kept being wet. When they got bathed, they changed their clothes 'n that. If they couldn't get there quick enough they used to do it on 'floor. Staff used to get mad with them. They used to say, 'What've you done that for, you dirty thing!' (Grace)

Margaret, who is unable to walk and has little control over much of her body, has first-hand experience of such treatment.

If you were bursting to go somewhere and you wet yourself, you know like with me, you got punished. Say you were in a wheelchair and you couldn't talk to tell them, you still got punished – couldn't go out, couldn't see your visitors.

Margaret also recalls staff's attempts to get her to eat all her meals.

Shall I tell you something else – if you leave your food, you know what they used to do? If you didn't eat your dinner – leave it for your tea. And if you didn't eat it for your tea, you had it for your supper and if you didn't eat it for your supper you had it for your next meal. It's true!

Joe, seething with a sense of injustice, recalled with relish his one successful attempt to get his own back on a member of staff who was trying to force him to do something that he did not want to do, namely scrub the floor. Because he refused, he was given 'the treatment'.

I said, you do it yourself. So they grabbed me and got a bucket [of cold water] and poured it on top of your head to make you do as you were told.
So I thought to myself. 'Right, I'll get my own back' and I did it on her.
I got sent to Dr Black. He said, 'What's happening here?'
I said, 'She threw that cold water on top of me.' He said, 'Yes, why?'
'She wanted me to scrub the floor, so she threw a bucket of water on me and I got a bucket of water and poured it on top of her.'
He said, 'You shouldn't do that.'
I said, 'She threw it at me first so I threw it back.'
He didn't know what to say himself.
I slung the bucket down then said, 'She can clean up any mess herself.'
They couldn't do owt. What could they do? (Joe)

Punishment varied according to the severity of the offence. The most often employed was the control of money, 'they'd stop your money'. Restraint and physical punishments were frequently recalled as consequences for more serious offences such as any attempt to meet a member of the opposite sex or for absconding from the colony. Often both restraint and physical punishment were combined. A period of being locked in a side-room was often followed by some penance such as being made to scrub floors in pyjamas or underwear.

If you got caught doing summat to a girl, they used to lock you in a side-room. They used to run away did some of them and they had to bring 'em back and put 'em in a side-room. And scrubbing – used to have shorts. Same wi' girls. They used to do the same on the female side. We used to go round and see girls just in their knickers scrubbing floors. Villa 8 was their locking-up villa. (Horace)

John, he went on to villa 17, locked up in the side-rooms with no clothes on. (Horace)

They punish them. Put 'em in the side-room until they behaved. It were awful. They didn't use to have pyjamas on then. They used to have short pants on. That's what they had. (Henry)

They put you in pyjamas for scrubbing and that. You would be put in pyjamas. (Frank)

They used to make you scrub from one end to t' other. And if you didn't do it proper, you had to do it over. Sometimes, if we didn't do it, we didn't get anything to eat. They once put me in bed without any tea. (Sally)

Absconding was the direst of offences. However, this illegal freedom was very easily obtained.

It were easy. Go into 'wood down there and you were away. Just wandered about. Out for a few days. Sleep anywhere. Caught up with by the police – brought me back. Used to be awful when you were fetched back here. (Frank)

I used to sneak out from open bedroom window – where you come down 'stone steps. I used to open 'window that opened at bottom. We used to get out at night. (Grace)

Relatives and other people worried about the closure of institutions and the shortcomings of care in the community often picture the hospital or institution as a safe place, a haven where people can be cared for and protected. Hospital scandals in the late 1960s raised public awareness of conditions and some improvements were made. There is now a belief that such things no longer happen. While it may be true that some of the worst physical punishments do not now occur, punishment is an integral part of any institution. Like many people with a mental handicap, the people in this study are still subject to a system of rewards and punishment which we would find unacceptable for ourselves. Today, people in institutions who infringe regulations for whatever reason are just as likely to have their privileges (such as visiting relatives or going to the cinema) curtailed, their drugs increased and/or their money withheld.

Reference

Goffman, E. (1968) *Asylums: Essays on the Social Situation of Mental Patients and Other Inmates*. Harmondsworth: Pelican.

28

ANITA'S STORY

ANITA BINNS

Anita Binns, a woman with learning difficulties living in Newcastle-upon-Tyne, describes how she learnt to be a self-advocate.

Well, the Manager turned the meeting round, it was supposed to be about me attending, but when it came down to it what he was on about was that I been offered a place in the sheltered housing and workshop at Cramlington.

And I said I didn't want to go because I was not told that me name had been put down by the social worker, and I didn't want to give up this security so as to share with three other people who I didn't really know. And I might not get on with.

I lost all control of the meeting and I broke down, and like me social worker took me out and told me to pull meself together, and I went back in and the Manager turned around and said: 'You don't want to go.' I said: 'No, I don't and I don't see why I should give me security up', and he was really nasty after that. And then the Deputy Manager said: 'Oh, I think we'll suspend her for three months', and the Manager said: 'Well, what do you think about that decision?' I said the decision was taken before this meeting.

And like I stayed away for four months, and I went out and I told them that I wasn't going back and it's the best decision I've ever made. I've been talking to some of the people who go there now and they hate it, I mean it's just the management's attitude.

Well, I first got involved with Skills for People when I was asked to give a presentation at the Newcastle Voluntary Forum and the Newcastle Partnership . . . that was the start of me involvement with them . . . I was doing voluntary work at Mencap at the time, but I was unhappy there because they had residential workers and they were all putting on us and getting at us, and on a lunch-time they'd have their lunch and leave me downstairs on me own to have me lunch.

Tape transcript from D. Atkinson and F. Williams (eds), *Know Me as I Am*,
Hodder & Stoughton, Sevenoaks, 1990

Now, I felt really out of it so it all came to a head when the District Officer was on holiday and Roy Bradshaw the Divisional Officer was there and I said: 'Roy, I want to leave', because the day before I was really upset because they were trying to make us scrub floors, and to me that was not on because they'd made a mess of the floor.

I waited a while and then I started as a volunteer for Skills, and I used to go to the office and help out and I still go and help out now, but I go out and about now. I done some advocacy courses – I actually taught one at Aycliffe – and I've helped put on a self-advocacy course at Prudhoe Hospital, I've tried to involve consumers and I'm helping out with the latest one, and I've been down to Nottingham where I met Ian Pickering and Ian Pearson and I helped start up the Nottingham Advocacy Network. Well, I helped start that up and I was asked, on the strength of that, I was asked to go and lead a workshop in Derby with one of the other volunteers, Phil Parkin. And I mean the amount of work that I've done, I mean I've done presentations to home helps, I've done presentations to the CQSW students at the Polytechnic, and I've done presentations to graduate social workers at the Newcastle University. So the range is so varied.

What do you think self-advocacy does for people?
Well, it's certainly for me; it's helped me to stand up for me rights and it's helped me to be more confident, and I'm not frightened of confrontation now.

I mean, at one time I would sit back and take it, but now I won't. I'm also involved with Gateshead Council for the Disabled; I've just been re-elected on to the Executive Committee for the second time and I'm involved with another group in Newcastle which is similar, run on similar lines, it's called InterAct. It's been going for quite a while, it's a group of disabled and abled-bodied people – it all started off socially like meeting in the pub and then there were different things. And now we have offices in the house, which is in Newcastle, and I've been on the third management committee of that. But that isn't as good as the others; I mean, I was on the programme committee. At one stage I was on that many committees, I had to give one up. And I've been on a management committee which is a group of all kinds who like to do work with people like meself, and other disadvantaged groups you know.

They've actually made a video of me when I was on the Gateshead Co-ordinating Council, and I've seen it twice since they shot it. Some of it's done down at the ATC, and other people who've seen it said mine was the best one.

You said that self-advocacy helped increase your confidence, it helped you stand up for your rights. Could you tell us a little bit about how it does that? How does it help you do that?
Well, I really can't explain it, but it just helped me to be more confident about these things like rights and responsibilities, and it's helped me like put them into perspective, and I mean for all I've told them I've never actually

been on a self-advocacy course, it's as I got more involved I got more and more confident because at one time I was really shy and I just wouldn't say boo to a goose, but now I'm very, I mean I don't mind confronting people.

I was in a conference in Gateshead last year, and one of the people who works for Social Services was sitting and he was laughing at us. Well, I knew this bloke fairly well so I just turned around and said to him: 'Look, don't you laugh at me.' I thought that'll teach you for laughing at us. I only got five minutes' notice that I was wanted to stand in for someone.

So it's the actuql involvement and responsibility it gives you that gives you confidence and helps you do things?
And assertiveness.

What is assertiveness?
Well, being sure, knowing you're right and just being really, really confident.

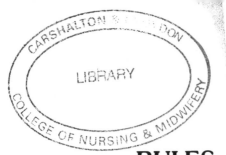

29

RULES, ROLES AND RELATIONSHIPS

SHEELAGH STRAWBRIDGE

All the world's a stage,
And all the men and women merely players;
They have their exits and their entrances;
And one man in his time plays many parts.
(Shakespeare, *As You Like It*, Act 2, scene 7)

The paradox of the self

The concept of 'role' is one which can fascinate and tantalize, perhaps because it presents us with an enigma which is at the very core of our sense of 'self'. We can feel with Shakespeare the hollowness of being mere players of parts, cast in roles to act out predetermined plots and relationships. To be truly oneself, 'authentic' and 'autonomous', is a high ideal in modern Western societies, and this is contrasted in everyday language with 'play acting' and 'putting on a show'. Similarly, our most valued relationships are those which are seen as satisfying in themselves, those in which we can be our real selves, valuing each other 'for ourselves' rather than for the roles we play and the functions we fulfil.

Paradoxically, we feel most comfortable, 'at one with ourselves', when we have a role to play and know that we can play our part. When we 'feel at a loss', 'have nothing to offer', 'are unable to relate', we might say 'I feel like a spare part', 'I don't fit in', 'I no longer have a role'. To have roles to play is tantamount to being at home in the world, to having an identity in a real world structured by recognizable relationships. Common expressions such as 'knowing the ropes' and 'street wise' convey the satisfaction in slipping easily into a role, and express a sense of the unspoken rules governing our social and personal relationships. When we step 'out of character', break the rules and behave unexpectedly, others are disturbed and we may feel very uncomfortable. In strange situations with unfamiliar rules and expectations we may feel 'like a fish out of water'.

This paradox highlights the usefulness of the notion of 'role'. It can provide a conceptual bridge between personality and culture or social structure, between the 'subjective' (me 'in here') and the 'objective' (society 'out there'). Roles are subjective and integral to our personalities because the roles we play become part of our personal identities, the way we see ourselves and the way others see us. They are objective, part of culture and social structure; because they are handed down from generation to generation, we get our roles 'off the peg', together with the cultural 'scripts' attached to them.

Social structure, culture and identity

Social structures and cultural patterns can be seen as rule-governed structures of roles and relationships. All our relationships carry role expectations and are governed by rules. Sometimes these can be more or less explicitly stated. For example, codes of professional practice, such as those of social work, counselling and nursing, lay down expectations and rules for professional roles and relationships. However, even our most intimate roles carry expectations and rules relating to particular cultural contexts and, like most cultural expectations, these are largely unstated and may be complex, ambiguous and even contradictory. Sexual roles and relationships are a good example and one task of sexual and relationship counselling is to facilitate awareness, communication and negotiation around conflicting, unstated expectations of partners.

The demands of becoming a socially competent person, someone who fits in, feels at ease with others and relates to them in acceptable ways, seem quite daunting when we consider the vast range of situations and relationships that the average person must cope with. In a fairly ordinary day, my own roles include those of wife, daughter, teacher, friend and counsellor. Each role expresses a particular kind of relationship with its own expectations. Each has its sub-roles and boundaries and may overlap other roles. As a wife I may play the role of cook, sexual partner or friend, and as a friend I have to take care not to slip into my counsellor role, or worse, my teacher role!

Seeing social worlds as patterns of rules, roles and relationships draws attention to the way they are constructed out of social action. It is people who create, or change, roles and, however strong social expectations may be, people are constantly rewriting the rules: 'Because they are historical products of human activity, all socially constructed universes change, and the change is brought about by the actions of human beings' (Berger and Luckmann, 1971: 134). Social worlds are inherently precarious, and are continuously constructed and re-constructed in the same process in which we are constructed as persons with recognizable identities.

Role theories posit an intimate connection between the formation of personal identities and the reproduction of social realities. Some of our roles are worn lightly, and may be taken on and cast off with ease, but we can see that others are rooted very deeply and are closely linked with our sense of identity. While studying, I had a number of temporary jobs: waitress, filing clerk, traffic census enumerator; but I defined myself as a 'student', not in terms of these roles. However, when I talk about my teaching or counselling roles I am inclined to say 'I *am* a teacher or a counsellor.'

Language, culture and socialization

We can say, then, that each role is played according to a basic 'script' and situated in a set of culturally defined social relationships. For instance, one classic study describes American marriage as:

> a dramatic act in which two strangers come together and redefine themselves . . . [Its] dominant themes . . . (romantic love, sexual fulfilment, self-discovery and self-realisation through love and sexuality, the nuclear family as the social site for these processes) can be found distributed through all strata of the society : . ..
>
> The chief protagonists of the drama are two individuals, each with a biographically accumulated and available stock of experience . . . Their society has provided them with a taken-for-granted image of marriage and has socialised them into an anticipation of stepping into the taken-for-granted roles of marriage. (Berger and Kellner, 1979: 30–5)

The stage is set, the basic script is written, but there is room for interpretation and negotiation as each partner contributes particular experiences and expectations of friends, family members, household organization, sexual fulfilment and so on. Berger and Kellner see marriage (or any other relationship) as constructed during the course of conversations in which common definitions and meanings are sought. For example, in conversations about in-laws, about who to share occasions such as Thanksgiving with, about friends and so on, couples work to define their shared meaning of 'family'.

This highlights a key assumption in role theories. Human social life is essentially concerned with the creation and maintenance of meanings, and language is central in this process. Different kinds of conversations – greeting friends, arguing, consulting a doctor, praying, giving advice, making love – have different rules. However, we slip easily from one familiar form of conversation to another and, for the most part, do not confuse them. Harold Garfinkel (1984) carried out some studies which demonstrate the power of the culturally defined rules of everyday conversations and the strong feelings evoked when the rules are transgressed. Experimenters were asked to insist that friends or acquaintances clarify everyday conversational remarks. The results were sometimes explosive:

> S: [waving cheerily] How are you?
> E: How am I in regard to what? My health, my finances, my school work, my peace of mind, my . . .?

S: *[red in the face and suddenly out of control]* Look! I was just trying to be polite.
Frankly, I don't care how you are.
(Garfinkel, 1984: 44)

Fortunately, given the complexity of the rules of conversation and social life in general, we largely acquire and apply them unconsciously. We 'know' the rules but would find it hard to describe them.

Socialization is a general term used for the process by which we acquire the 'culture' of the society and specific social groups we are born into and of which we become members during our lives. Cultures are structured systems of meanings, 'symbolic systems'. They include patterns of beliefs, attitudes, values and expectations; ways of feeling, thinking, speaking and moving; using objects, space and time; and so on. In recent years, studies of language, culture and socialization have increasingly informed each other. Languages, like cultures, are symbolic systems, and modern studies have focused on how they exist as structured systems independent of their use by individual speakers. In fact, these 'structuralist' studies show how our ability to speak, to understand and to be understood depends on the fact that languages are systems. They help us to see how our subjective experience, if it has meaning expressible in words, gestures or some form which can be understood by others, is less private and individual than we might think. This is because patterns of cultural meanings and values are internalized as we acquire language. So, for instance, in learning 'family' words we internalize, and identify ourselves in terms of, the structure of relationships, cultural expectations and values expressed in the roles of sister, brother, mother, daughter, husband, wife.

We are usually unaware of the extent to which our culture defines our personal identities. However, Eva Hoffman (1989) describes how the experience of immigration made her acutely aware of this normally unrecognized process. Her sense of self was profoundly assaulted when she was wrenched at fourteen from her native Poland, and had to construct a new identity in the alien language and culture of Canadian teenagers in the 1960s: 'What has happened to me in this new world? I don't know. I don't see what I've seen, don't comprehend what's in front of me. I am not filled with language any more . . . I don't really exist' (Hoffman, 1989: 108). One of several Polish ladies who had been in Canada long enough 'to consider themselves as well versed in native ways' shaved Eva's armpits. Others plucked her eyebrows; tried various shades of lipstick on her face; initiated her into 'the mysteries' of using shampoos and hair lotions and putting her hair in curlers; and, suggested to her mother, 'in an undertone', that she should start wearing a bra:

My mother obeys.
I obey too, passively, mulishly, but I feel less agile and less confident with every transformation. I hold my head rigidly, so that my precarious bouffant doesn't fall

down, and I smile often, the way I see other girls do, though I am careful not to open my lips too wide. . .

Inside its elaborate packaging, my body is stiff, sulky, wary. (Hoffman, 1989: 108–10)

Essential 'self' or relational 'subject'

All this stresses the cultural nature of the roles and relationships out of which our personal identities are constructed, but it leaves us with the sense of hollowness, of being mere players of parts, that we started with. What of being truly oneself? We seem to have lost any sense of an 'authentic', 'autonomous', 'real' or 'essential' self with a core of identity. Role theories seem to convey a disturbing picture of individuals comprising many selves, switching identities according to the roles we play. Peter Berger (1973: 124) describes the self as: 'no longer a solid, given entity that moves from one situation to another. It is rather a process, continuously created and re-created in each social situation that one enters, held together by the slender thread of memory.' This links to how Berger and others see modern social life as fragmented. Benita Luckmann (1978) has described it in terms of a range of 'small life-worlds' which lack the connecting sense of meaning given, in more traditional societies, by a cosmic or divine order in which life experience and eventual death make sense. All this can be very threatening. Indeed, from a different perspective, R.D. Laing (1965) has connected the insecurity of experiencing the self as tenuous and unreal with the development of schizophrenia.

The idea of an 'essential self', a core untouched by the social, often seems crucial to the quest for authenticity, autonomy and genuine personal relationships. 'Self' and 'society' are frequently opposed, with the latter seen as overlaying the former with a false, damaging, often oppressive, social form. The goal of much modern counselling and psychotherapy is expressed in terms that suggest seeking and developing the true self. Person-centred therapists talk of 'self-actualization', while Eric Berne (1969) has written, from a more psychodynamic viewpoint, of the destructive 'games people play' and of the 'life scripts' we enact. He describes the goal of therapy as the liberation of the *originally* autonomous individual from the inhibiting influences of parents and others.

The essential self, however, remains elusive. The deeper we dig, the more we find the social. Even the unconscious, according to much modern psychoanalytic thinking, is structure by relationships and by language.

Marxists have argued that the very idea of an 'essential self' is a 'bourgeois', 'individualist' notion, and some feminists would add 'masculine'. It denies that we are, in the very roots of our being, social, depending from the start on relationships with others and gaining a sense of separate identity in and through relationships. Some writers, particularly those who have been influenced by structuralist theories of language, have preferred to use the term 'subject' in order to contrast this view of a self, constructed at its deepest levels in relationships, with that of an essential self (for example, Henriques et al., 1984). Personal identity, seen as centred in a 'self', is often opposed to 'society', whereas 'subject' 'decentres' personal identity, emphasizing 'subjectivity' which is produced socially, in relationships, through the systems of meaning of language and culture.

Is it possible then to retain, in this notion of the 'subject', a sense of authenticity and autonomy? George Herbert Mead, whose work influenced the development of role theories, suggests an answer. He says that what is crucial is 'self-consciousness', consciousness which always includes, at least implicitly, a reference to an 'I'. He distinguishes the 'I' from the 'me', or socially acquired identity, and the 'I' becomes conscious of the 'me' in the course of development. Mead says that self-consciousness is *fundamentally social*. It develops out of relationships with others. An individual's experience as a self: 'is one which [s]he takes over from his[her] action upon others. [S]he becomes a self in so far as [s]he can take the attitude of another and act toward [her]himself as others act' (Mead, 1962: 171). If we think of 'I', not as an *essence* or *entity*, but as a *capacity* to reflect on ourselves, then we might understand authenticity and autonomy in terms of this self-reflective capacity of human consciousness.

The development of a 'self' can be seen as a project for which the individual becomes responsible. Autonomy and authenticity do not depend on the existence of a *non-social* 'essential self', but on the capacity of the *fundamentally social* 'subject' for self-consciousness. As we become more aware of how our personal and cultural histories shape our lives, we can develop the power to choose our roles and relationships and write, or at least edit, our own scripts. We can become what we make of ourselves.

Ideology and relations of oppression

Readers will have to judge for themselves whether this resolves the paradox of the self with which we began. The usefulness of 'role' as a conceptual bridge between the 'subjective' and the 'objective' is less disputable. We can also begin to see how it helps us to make links between differing perspectives on social life and personal relationships, such as structuralist studies of language and culture and Marxist and feminist viewpoints. In recent years these approaches have informed each other and contributed much to our understanding of ideology and relationships of oppression.

Work in this area has been influenced by the Marxist philosophy of Louis Althusser. Like most Marxists, Althusser concentrates on the broader structures of society. He has focused on how 'ideology', sometimes defined as those aspects of culture embedded in the social relations of production (the economy), works to reproduce class relationships. Role theorists, in contrast, tend to focus on interpersonal and group relationships. Nevertheless, although Althusser does not use 'role' explicitly, he employs the metaphor of an 'authorless theatre'. He says that ideology works through the subjective consciousness of individuals, forming us as identities and calling us out to play our parts in society (Althusser, 1971).

In so far as our parts are cast in structured relationships of oppression, between people in different class positions, women and men, black and white people, these oppressive relationships are reproduced as they are internalized, forming our identities as women, men and so on. Later 'discourse' theories have developed our understanding of ideology to include relationships of power and oppression in what appear to be politically neutral areas. Like role theories, they concentrate on conversations or 'discourses' in small-scale social situations. In particular, they have drawn our attention to areas of culture, defined as 'knowledge', where there are 'experts' and 'professionals', and they have shown how professional roles and relationships can control and oppress people. For instance, Michel Foucault (see Rabinow, 1986) has studied the historical development of the 'knowledges' of the medical and social sciences, and shown how they have constructed our concepts of normality and deviance. These affect all sorts of ideas that we have about ourselves and can set oppressive standards for: 'a healthy body'; 'a stable personality'; 'sanity'; 'a normal family'; 'a proper man or woman'; 'normal sex' and so on. They also institute new ways of exercising power, through disciplinary mechanisms embedded in the culturally defined professional practices of teachers, doctors, nurses, psychiatrists, social workers and others. At the same time, Foucault reminds us that discourses are cultural practices, and that people are created by cultural practices. Foucault's ideas impute a degree of powerlessness to human beings. Nevertheless, you the reader can reflect upon the extent to which cultural practices can become the object of self-conscious reflection, challenge and change.

Conclusion

This article began with a paradox highlighted by the ideal of autonomy and authenticity. This is a historically recent and Western ideal which has the important moral and political force of stressing the value of individual human beings. I have argued, nevertheless, that the paradoxical dichotomy between individuals and society that it seems to imply is misleading. We might also see the highly competitive 'self-seeking' individualism, characteristic of modern Western societies, as the other side of an ideal which emphasizes the value of the 'true self' to the detriment of socially defined roles and relationships.

I have suggested that linking personal identity to cultural patterns through rules, roles and relationships offers an interesting resolution to the paradox. In my view, autonomy and authenticity can be meaningfully preserved while shifting the emphasis to our fundamental interrelatedness. It is this, after all, that underpins the values of altruism and social responsibility central to our roles in the health and social welfare professions.

References

Althusser, L. (1971) 'Ideology and ideological state apparatuses', in *Lenin and Philosophy and Other Essays*. London: New Left Books.

Berger, P.L. (1973) *Invitation to Sociology: A Humanistic Approach*. Harmondsworth: Penguin.

Berger, P.L. and Kellner, H. (1979) 'Marriage and the construction of reality', in P.L. Berger (ed.), *Facing up to Modernity*. Harmondsworth: Penguin.

Berger, P.L. and Luckmann, T.L. (1971) *The Social Construction of Reality*. Harmondsworth: Penguin.

Berne, E. (1969) *Games People Play*. Harmondsworth: Penguin.

Garfinkel, H. (1984) *Studies in Ethnomethodology*. Cambridge: Polity Press.

Henriques, J., Hollway, W., Urwin, C., Venn, C. and Walkerdine, V. (1984) *Changing the Subject: Psychology, Social Regulation and Subjectivity*. London: Methuen.

Hoffman, E. (1989) *Lost in Translation: Life in a New Language*. Alexandria, VA: Minerva.

Laing, R.D. (1965) *The Divided Self*. Harmondsworth: Penguin.

Luckmann, B. (1978) 'The small life-worlds of modern man', in T. Luckmann (ed.), *Phenomenology and Sociology*. Harmondsworth: Penguin.

Mead, G.H. (1962) *Mind, Self and Society from the Standpoint of a Social Behaviourist* (ed. C.W. Morris). Chicago: University of Chicago.

Rabinow, P. (ed.) (1986) *The Foucault Reader*. Harmondsworth: Penguin.

SECTION 4

REFLECTING ON PRACTICE

The term 'practice' often seems to conjure up the idea of aspirations, as in the old joke 'She's practising law', 'Oh yes, when will she be able to do it?' 'Good practice' and 'bad practice' are common terms and imply that practice can be carried out in a superior or inferior way.

Clearly, people have criteria against which they judge both their own practice and that of others. However, not everyone is able to articulate how they go about their practice whether to themselves or other people. Donald Schön, in another part of the Reader talks about knowing-in-action: this may consist of everyday things we can do expertly but are not necessarily able to articulate. A simple example of this is riding a bicycle, a complex skill whose component parts are difficult to describe for someone else so that they can do it too. Schön also talks about reflection-in-action where we consciously think about what we're doing when we are doing it. Schön refers to phrases like 'thinking on your feet' to describe this phenomenon. The concept of reflective practice which emerges from these ideas is based on a belief that the application of technical know-how is not enough to ensure good practice. There is confusion in the changing world of practice: the rules change, the goal posts shift. Practitioners need to be able to accommodate this uncertainty and think on their feet and this is what reflective practice is about.

This final section looks at a number of accounts which reveal the reflections of the authors about practice. It gives us some insight into how they have been able to articulate their knowledge-in-action through the process of reflection-in-action. For some people writing is itself a form of reflection. But in the act of writing all of the authors have decided to share their reflections with others. The writings are framed, in the sense that they relate to reflections on specific roles and situations. In some senses the writers expect the reader to share some of their knowledge-in-action, they assume a shared concern for the area of practice. Barbara Webb writes for an audience who will identify with sociological concerns; Tom Heller writes for medical colleagues; Liz Lloyd writes for her tutor and expresses the concerns of the occupation of social work. What they share is an overarching concern with encounters between workers and users. Reflective practice challenges the primacy of a technical rational know-how. So the concerns of individual articles should be of interest to you in thinking about your own personal engagement in practice, whether as a user of services or as workers. The concerns of the writers can throw light on your own experience.

The section reflects a variety of areas of practice: social work, nursing, medicine, the probation service, child care and AIDS. The areas of practice are by no means exhaustive. They have been chosen because they provoke an interesting and stimulating set of reflections. Moreover, the writers all base their reflections in some kind of tension or problems of practice or role. Reflective practice is not then in situations but something which can be used to address problems.

The articles are grouped according to areas of practice. The first group relate to reflections on health care. Barbara Webb is a sociologist. Despite the difficult experience of her child's stay in hospital, she was able to reflect on power relationships between nurses and parents. On nurses' territory parents learn to modify their behaviour, to change their own practice to conform to the role that is expected of them. Another side of the coin is revealed in the article by Gillian Chapman who reflects on her role as a nurse doing research and on the way that nurses handle the anxieties of an occupation which is constantly near disease and disorder of various kinds. The juxtaposition of the two articles presents the role of nursing from two different points of view.

Naomi Craft and Tom Heller are both doctors. Naomi Craft reflects on the way medical students are taught to deny their emotional response to human suffering and argues that this makes for bad practice. Tom Heller recalls the Hillsborough disaster and describes the terrible discrepancy between the demands on ordinary occupational competence and the response that a tragedy of such magnitude requires.

The next articles examine residential care. Graham Connelly's article on key workers in residential child care discusses conflicts within their role between perceptions of themselves as caring for the emotional well-being of young people and the control function they are expected to discharge. John Simmonds takes a psychoanalytic perspective on residential care for young people. He argues that workers are inclined to avoid addressing painful issues – endings, loss, sexuality – because they themselves fear them. But this is detrimental to young people and hinders their ability to move out of care and into adult roles. Both Graham Connelly and John Simmonds have taken a step back from the face-to-face experience of residential work and begun to abstract and organize that experience into more general models.

Like Craft and Heller, Liz Lloyd and Tara Mistry provide examples of workers reflecting on aspects of their own work, although perhaps both are more based in the *relationship with users* rather than the nature of the occupation. Liz Lloyd wrote her article as a social worker student. She shows how a reflective approach on the part of the worker can tap the service user's personal strength and enable her to articulate her own needs.

Tara Mistry's account of the probation service group is an example of progressive practice within the confines of the traditional probation order. Using feminist groupwork proved an effective alternative form of supervision which allowed both users and workers to develop confidence in themselves.

The article by Robert Bor, Lucy Perry and Riva Miller shows the importance of reflective practice in the relationships between providers of care. If helpers are not sensitive to the service users' own perceptions of themselves and their situation they can act to disable rather than enable.

30

TRAUMA AND TEDIUM: AN ACCOUNT OF LIVING ON A CHILDREN'S WARD

BARBARA WEBB

Admission to the ward

At the age of eleven months my son was badly scalded on both arms. The day after the accident, he was admitted to a local hospital. We were discharged four days later on the decision of a junior doctor who considered that a skin graft would not be necessary. While receiving outpatient treatment, a consultant referred us to the Burns Unit of a hospital some distance from our home for a second opinion. On our second visit to this Unit, we were admitted on the initiative of a junior doctor there, who decided that a skin graft was advisable. The time taken for the injuries to heal was approximately three months. In all, one month of that period was spent in hospital.

There were certain dramatic features of the admission procedure which tended to accentuate the crisis dimensions of the situation. In our case, it was not an emergency admission, yet to our combined distress, the child was whisked out of our arms by a nurse who sped down the corridor to the dressing rooms, to await inspection of the injuries by a doctor. Parents, we were told when we asked to accompany him, were not allowed in the dressing rooms, but we could wait in the visitors' room at the other end of the ward. From there, our son's unremitting screams could be heard for the next hour and a quarter, due to the fact that 'the doctor was longer than expected coming up from theatre.'

Our emotional distress was heightened by the sights and sounds provided by a ward of children and adults, in individual cubicles, having sustained serious thermal injuries; in some cases these injuries were exposed. Visitors, parents and staff all wore gowns and masks, which added a further dramatic

From G. Horobin and A. Davis (eds), *Medical Encounters: The Experience of Illness and Treatment*, Croom Helm, London, 1977 quality to the setting. The distress evidenced by other parents whose children were being admitted was equally disquieting; nervous pacing up and down the corridor, openly weeping or talking compulsively about how the accident had occurred, were common expressions of grief. The nursing staff avoided contact with the parents during this waiting period.

The decision that our child was to be admitted came as a shock. The accident, its implications and consequences had to be reassessed. Guilt experienced when the accident occurred led to our now perceiving admission as some form of punishment – the final cruel blow in a series of incidents in the preceding weeks that had been mentally and physically exhausting. Installed in a cubicle on the ward, wearing the appropriate masks and gown, my initial feelings of desolation were intense; I reacted defensively and viewed with suspicion the smiles and friendly approaches made by the staff to the children and mothers on the ward. My maternal instincts, which had previously shown great reluctance to reveal themselves, became inflamed.

Yet these problems of emotional adjustment were soon superseded by a different set of problems: how to survive socially in the hospital environment. Defining the situation, acquiring information about routine practices and planning ways in which the system could be made to work for you, were some of the few mental preoccupations which provided some relief from the suffocating boredom of living on the ward. 'Negotiation' and 'bargaining' were no longer concepts which were of interest sociologically, they were vital resources to be used in managing everyday encounters.

Defining the situation

All mothers were given the opportunity to live in with their children. At this particular hospital it involved coming 'on duty' at 7.30 am and leaving the ward at 6.30 pm; no parents were allowed on the wards after these hours. Sleeping accommodation for the mothers was provided in a separate building. The mothers' timetable was as rigid as that of the shifts worked by the staff, with meal and coffee breaks taken at set times. Living in on the ward was perceived by staff and mothers as a privilege, not an automatic right. It was a privilege that could be taken away: the Sister spoke of a previous group of mothers who had been told to leave because 'they took to going out drinking at nights and bringing men back to their rooms and generally treating the place as a holiday camp.' Living in was an occupation to be taken as seriously as nursing duties among staff; it was a privilege that mothers could show gratitude for by being sensible, cooperative and abiding by the rules.

The newly admitted mother had to learn what was involved in being a 'good mother' on the ward. This process of identity management was made more difficult by the fact that there was no direct socialization of the mothers by the staff; mothers were not informed about what they could and could not do on the ward and yet were expected to know what the appropriate modes of behaviour were. The mother acquired knowledge of the rules and routines of ward life through observation, experience and discussion with other mothers once off the ward. An awareness of what some of the rules were, however, emphasized the ambiguity surrounding many other activities, which the staff appeared unable or unwilling to define. It was never made clear, for example, whether a mother could enter the cubicle of a child whose mother was not staying, and talk to, play with or comfort him or her. Demarcations of territory were not established; should a mother return her child's plate to the kitchen once the trolley had gone, should she go to the linen cupboard herself or ask the nurse to go for her? It seemed vital to acquire knowledge of accepted practices in order not to spoil your identity as a 'good mother' in the eyes of the staff; fear of making a fool of yourself, of annoying the staff, being told off by them, or appearing stupid frequently inhibited action. Learning by making mistakes was often a painful and humiliating procedure. For example, it was not explained to me after my son had had a skin graft exactly what I should allow him to do by way of moving around. A week after his operation I let him walk around the cubicle holding my hands because I had seen another child doing this; a nurse passing the cubicle said, 'He shouldn't be walking around like that on his donor area, you know.' This practice on the part of staff of exerting control by negatively sanctioning others' actions had the effect of inducing a passive parent population.

Yet the learning process was not entirely a passive one involving an assimilation of accepted practices which then allowed the performance of the correct activities; perceiving and experiencing ward life, often being made aware of the gaps between theory and practice, led irrevocably to the participant's formulation of his own set of definitions of what was appropriate, possible and feasible in any given situation. Schutz (1971) argues that 'reality is developed out of shared access of members of a society to stocks of knowledge which define events as typical, usual, and routine.' Each member may differently perceive aspects of that reality as having most relevance for him, and also be aware that these actions impinge on and influence that reality; he is engaged in role-making as well as role-taking (Cicourel, 1973). The ability to negotiate is enhanced in a situation where it is noted that those who enact the routines most efficiently and are believed to be best acquainted with the rules of the game seem to be acting in many cases by rule of thumb. *Ad hoc* decisions were made with surprising frequency by staff while maintaining the outward impression that there was a well-established pattern of normative rules governing all action. Mothers concurred with staff in this complicity, so that when some rule was breached, some strategy successful in altering the accepted practice, the mother was careful not to have won – to 'have got over' on the staff. Mothers became skilled at formally acknowledging the staff as the decision-makers, while among themselves sharing knowledge about how to work the system.

'Bargaining' is perhaps too crude a form to describe the subtleties of nuance, changes in tone, looks, gestures and stance which characterized strategic interaction in these situations.

On the second day after being admitted, the weather was extremely hot and during afternoon visiting, we asked the Sister if we might take our son out for a while. She responded with the words, 'I *do* allow children from my ward out sometimes, when the weather's fine,' emphasized in such a way as to imply that this was exceptional. It seemed to us that we had then to convince her that the circumstances were appropriate for the rules to be waived. We achieved this by taking her words to indicate a positive response and expressed our pleasure and thanks; we immediately dressed our son in his outdoor clothes. The Sister on seeing this: 'You will just be taking him round the hospital grounds, won't you?' A question stated in a way that pre-empted the reply. 'We thought of taking him out for a ride in the car.' Silence. 'A ride in the car?' We avoided looking at her. 'Make sure you're back for tea then.' 'We have to be back for tea?' 'Oh, yes.'

The following day I chatted to Sister about where we had gone, how much we had enjoyed it and how beautiful the surrounding countryside was. Both she and the nurse making the bed discussed the areas we should visit on our next excursion. That afternoon we prepared to leave the ward and said to the Staff Nurse on duty, 'We'll give him some tea while we're out, all right?' She nodded. On every subsequent occasion that we went out, I always checked that it was all right to do so (having dressed him in outdoor clothes first), and received an 'Of course' reply as though I need no longer have asked.

Not all strategies achieved their desired aims. Success was often due to making the appropriate appeal to the appropriate person at the right time. This involved mentally rehearsing the approach and deciding which line of attack was the most promising, selecting and 'catching' the person who it was imagined would be sympathetic and who had the authority to grant requests of this nature. Sometimes such approaches were the culmination of great mental preparation and required a certain degree of skill and judgement in their execution; at other times they arose spontaneously from the situation, and relied a good deal upon chance. For example, it was a general rule, as stated by ward and dressing room staff alike, that parents were not allowed to accompany their children to the dressing rooms where dressings were changed and wounds cleaned. These were often frightening and painful procedures for the children, evidenced by their screams both during, and in the case of my son, for some time after his return to the ward. Often the sight of one of the dressing room staff in the corridor would provoke a hysterical reaction in the child. On virtually every occasion during the first two weeks I asked either the nurse from the dressing room or the ward Staff Nurse or Sister if I could go with my son and the request was always refused with the words, 'I'm afraid parents aren't allowed in the dressing rooms.' One afternoon two weeks after admission, the junior doctor and consultant were passing the entrance to our cubicle and I overheard them stating their intention to 'take a look at this one'. I made my usual request and almost before I had finished phrasing my appeal, the consultant with a wave of his hand said, 'Yes, of course you may come my dear, if you think it will help the child.' The dressing room staff were extremely pleasant to me, allowing me to hold and quieten my child and this prevented their having to use gas to make him compliant, a practice which seemed to increase his alarm. On other occasions when I asked to accompany him, the staff always gave a casual affirmative reply.

Contradictory information about what was permissible and what was not inhibited the learning process. The mother's position was particularly vulnerable because if she used the strategy of appealing, in defence of her actions, to the fact that 'the other nurse/doctor said I could', she was in danger of causing greater conflict and alienating both parties. Giving accounts of what had been said or done by other staff members was construed by mothers as 'tale-telling' and acted as a further restraint on the passage of information. A nurse who was new to the ward to which children moved after their operations, where there were four cots to a cubicle, was making up the cot of a two-year-old, David, who had lain prostrate for four weeks. Turning to the three mothers in the room she commented that it was terrible for a child to be in a cot for such a length of time. She then encouraged David's mother to support him in taking a few steps around the room. Both mother and son seemed exhilarated by this brief excursion. Some time later the boy's mother repeated this during bed-making and was reprimanded by one of the nurses. She did not reply to this rebuke at the time, but afterwards in the company of the other mothers was profuse in her criticism: 'One tells you to do one thing and another something else. I wish they'd make up their bloody minds. I ask you – it wasn't hurting to let him up for two minutes, was it? But I couldn't tell her the other nurse had done it first – you can't go telling tales, can you?'

There were limits to strategic interaction, bargaining and negotiation. There was a tacit acceptance of a structural framework of non-negotiable or agreed rules, and an awareness of the way in which the balance of power and the position in the hierarchy determined the degree to which negotiation was permissible and possible. The staff derived their authority from their ability persistently to apply their definitions of the situation, based upon seemingly clinical values of what it was right or wrong for sick children to do in hospital. These medical or clinical perspectives and definitions defied any argument based upon lay common-sense criteria.

The risk of infection was another frequently used appeal to an overriding value which stifled all argument. As Hawthorn (1974) observed, the definition of this risk depended more upon the way the staff wanted their ward to be run than any more scientific criteria. Siblings were not allowed in the ward because of the risk of infection, yet consultants rarely wore masks on the ward – their position in the hierarchy allowing them immunity from following such procedures (Roth, 1957). Parents were not allowed in the dressing rooms because of the infection risk, yet ants were witnessed crawling up cot legs in one of the wards; one mother picked up her child's feeding bottle, which had been sterilized and placed on a locker by a nurse, to find ants covering the teat.

Parents never used their observations of 'irrational actions' to contest the medical definitions of the staff. After all, you were there voluntarily, in the belief that the hospital could bring about your child's recovery. If you contested and denied all the rules, what alternatives could you provide? As lay people you did not have the skill to perform skin grafts. There was a feeling, produced as a result of staff controls and sanctioning of behaviour, that if you, as the patient's representative, acted in too critical or questioning a manner then you were acting in a way which was detrimental to the child's recovery. You came to equate helping the child to be a good patient and being a cooperative and compliant mother, with the physical improvement of the child. One mother who had an argument with the ward Sister in front of the child was held responsible for the child having a raised temperature that evening: 'Now look what you've done.' All mothers wanted their children well – it was the ultimate restraint on behaviour.

References

Cicourel, A. (1973) *Cognitive Sociology*. Harmondsworth: Penguin.
Hawthorn, P. (1974) 'Nurse – I want my mummy!', *Royal College of Nursing*, series 1, no. 3.
Roth, J. (1957) 'Ritual and magic in the control of contagion', *American Sociological Review*, 22 (3).
Schutz, A. (1971) 'The problem of social reality', in *Collected Papers*, Vol. I. The Hague: Martinus Nijhoff.

31

RITUAL AND RATIONAL ACTION IN HOSPITALS

GILLIAN CHAPMAN

This brief extract of a much fuller article has been chosen for the insights it offers into the practice of nursing. The author reflects on both the role of the nurse and of the participant observer. The article is based on empirical material collected during three five-month periods of participant observation in five hospitals in South London.

As an Agency Staff Nurse I was as much a participant as an observer of the social situation I was studying. The positive side of this was that I had access to aspects of nursing practice I may not have seen, by adopting a more observational role. On the negative side, my access to social settings I was not directly allocated to work in was limited. Therefore a degree of bias was inevitable.

It was my growing understanding that the ritual elements of nursing action unified an otherwise disparate experience, which led to the use of this perspective in this article. It is not claimed that this account describes or explains the totality of nurses' experience.

Ritual and rational action: sociological model

The ideology of the healthcare professions may give the impression that actions taken are rational actions. If we look more closely, however, we find that this is not always so. Weber (1964) has noted that human action can be described as belonging to one of four ideal types. First, *traditional* action in which behaviour is determined by action or habit. Secondly, *Zweckrational* action, that is, purposively rational conduct in which there is a technical relation between means and ends. 'The individual rationally assesses the probable results of a given act in terms of the calculations of means to an end' (Giddens, 1975).

Abridged from *Journal of Advanced Nursing*, 8, 1983, pp. 13–20

Thus a surgeon might calculate whether or not an operation will improve a patient's health and balance the possible harm against the possible good of his actions. The third type, *vertrational* action is also found in hospitals. Here the means and ends of the action taken are not always empirically provable, although, it is based on a systematic set of beliefs or ideas. Psycho-therapeutic techniques might be a good example of this. The fourth and final type is *affective* action 'which is carried out under the sway of some sort of emotive state' (Giddens, 1975). Such actions are on the borderline of meaningful and non-meaningful conduct. Bocock (1974) has defined rituals in the following way: 'Ritual is the symbolic use of bodily movement and gesture in a social situation to express and articulate meaning.'

He argues that these acts may be either non-rational or irrational:

> Ritual action should not be seen as necessarily irrational or non-rational. Irrational action is action to which certain rational criteria could be applied, and which fails to meet criteria. Some magical action may be of this kind: this type could be replaced by technological action if and when rational action were applied. Non-rational action is action which cannot be assessed by any rational criteria because they are inapplicable, for example the feeling involved in loving a person. Ritual action is best seen as to some extent rational, and also non-rational at times.

It is important to distinguish between irrational and non-rational action, if we are to understand the function of any given ritual. Bocock quotes Jung who said 'The rational differs from the irrational ritual primarily in its function, it does not ward off repressed impulses but expresses strivings which are recognized as valuable by the individual. Consequently it does not have the obsessional-compulsive quality so characteristic of the irrational ritual.'

In one of the hospitals observed in this study there was a striking example of a whole system of behaviour centred around irrational actions. This was in a private nursing home where the staff occupied the major portion of their time cleaning and tidying immaculate cupboards. The domestic workers and nurses shone and polished gleaming brasses and furniture. The nurses patrolled the corridors, often avoiding eye contact, only occasionally speaking with patients. The patients were admitted to this 'home' to die and the irrational ritualistic nature of the cleaning seemed motivated by the sort of anxiety that Menzies (1970) mentions.

Empirically, it is at times difficult to describe any given action as being a non-rational or rational ritual action. This is because any action may have mixed components. A common example of action with mixed components is the taking of temperatures. This routine is *Zweckrational* aimed at assessing the state of a patient's health. The more dangerously ill the patient, the more frequently the temperature is taken; pyrexia is a warning sign that certain therapeutic measures might become necessary. It becomes a non-rational ritual when it is clear that the patient is well. For example, the day before discharge, or in those people with psychiatric illnesses which do not have a physiological base, the taking of temperatures serves no rational purpose.

In one hospital in the study I noted that nurses were in fact making up the temperatures. This did not appear to be a meaningless act: the dots on the temperature chart indicated the well-being of the patient to anyone interested. The nurses took a calculated risk in not taking the temperature, but they only guessed when they felt the patient was well. One might ask why the nurses bothered with the deceit. I believe this non-rational ritual had something to do with an attempt to communicate concern and healing to significant others.

Rituals, then, are not only used as a defence against anxiety but are intended for social effect. Non-rational rituals which seem to reflect distinct cultural values around the helping and healing of the sick, and the differing status of staff in healthcare organizations, are now described more fully.

Ritual and rational actions observed in London hospitals

Ethnomethodologists have noted the greeting ritual which begins: 'Hello, how are you?' and the response 'Alright, thank you, and you?', etc.

This has a different meaning in an institution in which illness is paramount: the format changes.

> *Nurse: [to patient]* Hello, how are you?
> *Patient:* Alright, thank you.
> *Nurse:* And how is your stomach?
> *Patient:* Oh, that's still a bit sore.

The nurse's second response gives the patient permission to say how he really feels. This may seem trivial, but nurses can use their knowledge of greetings rituals to contain a patient who is a habitual complainer. This interaction was observed between a nurse and an elderly patient who usually listed one complaint after another.

> *Nurse:* Hello, how are you?
> *Patient:* Alright, thank you nurse.
> *Nurse:* That's good *[as she moved on to the next patient]*.

That this greeting can become a non-rational ritual embued with social but not technical meaning is supported by a comment by a ward Sister. She said: 'It makes me feel dreadful when I stand at the bottom of the beds each morning and ask "How are you", because, do you know, I really don't care, not any more.'

Zweckrational components have gone. She no longer asked the question to ascertain nursing or medical information, but used the greeting ritual to convey concern she apparently no longer felt. It was notable that the greeting ritual was often followed by a specifically nursing/medical ritual. This was the laying on of hands. Laying on of hands may or may not have *Zweckrational* components. Nurses and doctors may be observed placing their hands on the arm/wound/sore area to undertake a technical procedure, but they may also be observed simply touching patients with the apparent intent of signifying care, concern or healing. Taking a patient's pulse when he or she is anxious, but the member of staff is not, seems to be one such medico-nursing non-rational ritual.

It is important to acknowledge the psychosocial background against which these ritual actions are played, if we are to understand them fully. Nursing and medical staff are acutely aware that the penalty of a serious mistake may be the death of another person. It is in the framework of potential death and the presence of this elementary fear that so many routines in hospitals are instituted and performed so 'religiously'.

Concealment rituals

Concealment rituals can appear to be grotesque. At one hospital I noted that babies who died were carried away in a wickerwork travelling cat basket. The clerk who was concerned with the registration of deaths in the hospital thought the siting of the mortuary at the entrance to the car park 'tactless'.

In their analysis and description of the behaviour of staff and relatives around dying patients, Glaser and Strauss (1965), by implication, suggest that this behaviour is to do with resistance to the disruption of the sentimental order of the ward by the staff. I would suggest that a more convincing explanation of these social interactions lies in a combination of social and psychological disruption of the participants' internal and external worlds.

Kubler-Ross (1969), Parkes (1975) and Hinton (1978) have studied the way grief affects the bereaved. The feelings of loss, sadness, grief and anger are often accompanied by painful self-questioning. After the death the standard of self-conduct is often questioned, especially in relation to the inevitability of the death and the care provided by the hospital. The hospital staff in this study often felt this way too. It is perhaps as a defence against such feelings that social rituals occur.

Lifecycle rituals

Another area of interest is hospital-specific lifecycle rituals. For clarity, although it may distort the meaning, I will refer to these as *rites de passage*. The hospitals' *rites de passage* are associated with initiation into the professions. Although the actual ceremonies are not always public, the symbols associated with them do appear to be important to the participants. Nurses, as they proceed with their training and grow into professional maturity, are awarded certain symbolic objects. Seniority is acclaimed by the wearing of different coloured belts, dresses or different shaped hats. It is fairly typical for Sisters to wear frilly lace caps, while other nurses wear paper disposable ones. State registered nurses (SRNs) are permitted to wear silver buckles, whereas the lower ranking state enrolled nurses (SENs) wear bronze ones. These material symbols are jealously regarded.

At times a specific symbol can appear ridiculous if it is taken out of the social or cultural group for which it has meaning. As a member of an outside agency, I was entitled to wear whatever uniform I might buy. At one hospital this coincided with that of the cleaners, which seemed to cause consternation. First, I was not always given the deference due to someone of my rank; secondly, I caused unease because I performed tasks normally allocated to a nurse in a blue uniform. These symbols are powerful; at the same hospital a consultant hesitated before he spoke to me, and said 'I never talk to people in white dresses only blue dresses count. I don't trust people in white dresses.' Doctors also have rituals associated with seniority in the profession, for example consultant surgeons relinquish the title 'doctor' when they become a Member of the Royal College of Surgeons (MRCS).

The most striking, perhaps, of all rituals associated with the medical profession is the deference ritual. The deference ritual is both recognition of the power which a medical woman or man holds, and maintenance of that power by symbolic acts and ritual deference. The ceremonious obsequiousness displayed by junior doctors and nurses towards a consultant illustrates this. It involves physical actions such as standing up, if sitting, and modestly placing hands clasped in front or behind the body. An interesting variant of this is that doctors may more readily fold their arms over their chests in the presence of the consultant, perhaps because they are nearer the consultant in status than are the nurses. There is an immediate and attentive positioning of the head, questions are responded to with a 'Sir'. The consultant may stand slightly apart from the juniors, who may stand quite close together. He is not touched by them.

The following is an example of a ritual humiliation procedure from this study. The consultant arrived on the ward in a perfectly tailored suit. The senior nurse, wearing a cotton denim dress and paper collar, stopped what she was doing, serving patients dinner, and approached him. Although interrupting patients' dinners and although the consultant was two hours late, the nurse approached him respectfully and did not complain. He stood next to the note trolley. It was the nurse's responsibility to indicate his patients and what the current concerns were. Sometimes the houseman helped with this. The nurse found the notes, the pages of relevance and made phone calls at the consultant's request. In this incident the consultant then indulged in some ritual humiliation procedures.

The senior nurse was asked to do four things at once, each with conflicting priorities. She had to make a phone call, lift a patient on a bed for examination, find a lost X-ray in the office, and find the page in the notes indicating a pathology laboratory result. While she attempted to do all these things, the consultant showed by his demeanour that she was failing to meet his requirements. He scowled, sighed, leaned negligently on the trolley, tapped his fingers and looked out of the window. These actions seemed effective in producing a loss of face and a feeling of shame in the nurse who flushed and apologized for being slow.

Menzies (1970) suggested that nurse sickness rates and student nurse drop-out rates were associated with the failure of the structure to modify and resolve primitive anxieties. It is tempting to suggest that being at the receiving end of ritual humiliation procedures is not an experience guaranteed to enhance the morale of nurses. It is a social ritual based on the undervaluing of female nurturant and caring roles, and the overvaluing of male, instrumental and technical roles in the health service.

References

Bocock, R. (1974) *Ritual in Industrial Society*. London: Allen & Unwin.
Giddens, A. (1975) *Capitalism and Modern Social Theory*. Cambridge: Cambridge University Press.
Glaser, B. and Strauss, A. (1965) *Awareness of Dying*. Chicago: Aldine.
Hinton, J. (1978) *Dying*. Harmondsworth: Penguin.
Kubler-Ross, E. (1969) *On Death and Dying*. London: Macmillan.
Menzies, I. (1970) 'The functioning of social systems as a defence against anxiety', Tavistock Pamphlet, no. 5. London: Tavistock Institute.
Parkes, M. (1975) *Bereavement*. Harmondsworth: Pelican.
Weber, M. (1964) *Basic Concepts in Sociology*. New York: Citadel Press.

32

A FEELING FOR MEDICINE

NAOMI CRAFT

Naked bodies featured heavily in my first weeks at medical school – not only in the bar after the pub games had gone too far, but also in the dissection room, where they were pickled and covered by white sheets like extras for a Hitchcock thriller.

Pulling back the sheet for the first time was an unnerving experience. Lying there on a cold metal table was a human body, identified as 'female, 75y, d. bronchopneumonia' by a brown label stapled to her ear.

It is not something that you easily forget, and yet there was no preparation for it. A room full of dead bodies apparently required no explanation. It was assumed that we would get on with the dissection as if nothing could be more normal than cutting up human beings. Silly me for thinking otherwise.

By week two the atmosphere was flippant. Loud gossip and jokes were exchanged across the heavily laden tables. The body became no more than an anatomical structure – a convenient bench for idle doodles.

It is here, in the dissection room, that students begin to learn about the intricacies of the human body, gradually unravelling the mechanics of all its working parts. They also begin to see diseases as malfunctions in the machine and are taught how to find and treat them.

The machine is, of course, a human being who is unwell. Someone else's mother, brother or sister. Rarely in the medical curriculum are doctors encouraged to relate to patients in this light.

Later, during my first days as a clinical student, I met George in casualty. He had a painful leg. Later on that night, the leg was amputated. I was devastated. Through my tears, I talked about George with my friends. They unanimously agreed that I could not allow myself to be emotionally affected by my patients or I would not be able to do my job as a doctor.

Seduced by their argument, I tried not to react emotionally. But, far from finding things easier, I felt worse. How could I empathize with a patient coming to terms with something unpleasant, when all I did was to suppress my own feelings?

From *BMA News Review*, May 1990

I am now sure that what my friends advised, although well intended, was wrong. We should learn that we can react in moderation, without impairing our ability to help others in distress. And that it is essential to do so if we are to care for them sincerely.

Broken parts

Doctors cultivate unemotional ways of talking about people's bodies. They study diseases and organs in depth, often in isolation and usually in medical jargon. Doctors, as scientists, are trained to approach all problems by division: the aim is to find the smallest single offending member which can be held responsible for a broken part.

Doctors sometimes talk about patients (or even to them) in this reductionist way. As an occasional patient myself, I dislike the thought of being referred to as a 'fractured finger' or a 'query appendicitis'.

Once patients are seen as pathological specimens, the doctor is on a slippery slope. At the bottom lies insensitivity and, perhaps, loss of effectiveness.

One friend described with embarrassment how she was instructed to lift her skirt to the waist and stand on a chair in front of the consultant and his entourage of medical students. The consultant then spent ten minutes looking at her legs and talking to the medical students about varicose veins, while they all stared with expressions ranging from enthusiasm to apologetic or total disinterest. The *coup de grâce* came when, one after the other, they pressed and stroked her groin and legs, sometimes tentatively with clammy hands, sometimes more roughly. When the examination was over, she was so disturbed by the experience that she was reluctant to follow the consultant's advice.

Medical schools are neglecting an opportunity to teach trainee doctors a fundamental skill: how to absorb and inwardly digest upsetting and frightening things without them having an incapacitating effect. How this should be taught remains an open question – it is high time that it was answered.

33

PERSONAL AND MEDICAL MEMORIES FROM HILLSBOROUGH

TOM HELLER

Outside every public house and on every verge on my way home there were relaxed groups of young men chatting and joking in their 'uniforms' of tight faded jeans, off-colour teeshirts, and something red and white. Were these the people whom later I saw laid out on the floor with life just pushed out of them? There were so many I didn't dare to count them. They looked as they had in life, not disfigured; they were just lying there, not quite the right colour. Not much to identify them on that sports hall floor. Who were they? What had gone wrong? Who was to blame for all this?

Call for help

I was on call for a practice adjacent to the Hillsborough ground for the weekend of Saturday 15 April. My home is one side of the ground and the practice is on the other. On the 15th the atmosphere was special for the semi-final; people were parking their cars miles away from the stadium and walking to the ground many hours earlier than the crowds usually do for home games. I remember being especially cheerful (despite being on duty) and proud that Sheffield was the centre of the sporting world that day.

I switched on the television just after 3 pm and saw the coverage of the snooker being interrupted by scenes from Hillsborough. Like almost everyone else, I imagine, I thought that there had been a pitch invasion and worried about how this might affect the chances of English clubs being allowed back into Europe. I then got into my car and took my daughter to a party that she was due to attend. At about 3.20 pm I heard on Radio Sheffield the call for doctors to go to Hillsborough, so I hurried to drop off my daughter and go to the ground. The stadium was familiar to me as I had often been to matches there. The concrete beneath the grandstands is unusual: it is stained grey, cold and unyielding; the light is always poor

Abridged from *British Medical Journal*, 299, 23–29 December 1989, pp. 1596–8 beneath the stands, even on sunny afternoons like that one. As we rushed along, the atmosphere was all wrong: there were lots of people but there was no noise. We got to the sports hall in about two minutes, and I entered by stepping through a cordon of police officers who were holding back people who were crowding around the outside of the door.

Bodies everywhere

Nothing could have prepared me for the scenes inside. I had thought vaguely that there might be a couple of members of St John Ambulance standing over a man with his head between his knees, telling him to take deep breaths. This was not normal though. There were bodies everywhere. Who was alive and who was dead? They couldn't all be dead. It had to be a mistake; this just didn't happen on sunny afternoons. Blotchy faces against the floor, not disfigured but apparently peaceful. Bodies higgledy-piggledy just inside the door, the line stretching over to the far wall. I asked a policeman what was to be done. Thankfully, he pointed away from the bodies to a section of the hall that was separated from them by a long, low screen of the type used to divide sports halls when two different sports are being played at the same time. There were more bodies here though. My God, what could I do? Who was going to tell me what to do?

Without directions I ran along the line of crumpled bodies. At least this lot were alive. I stopped between two bodies, took out my stethoscope, and lifted up a teeshirt and listened, grateful to have the time at last to do something that I knew how to do. I often use 'stethoscope on the chest time' to think during consultations. It's a good ploy really; the patient thinks that I am being ever so thoughtful and thorough, and I have time to think about what the hell to do next. Panic overtook me on this occasion. How could I be sure that this person was the one who needed help most? What was going to happen to all of the others if I stayed with this bloke? I could hear his heartbeat and breath sounds. For some reason I took my stethoscope out of my ears and crawled up to his face.

'What's your name, mate?' I asked.

'Terry' was the reply.

'OK Terry. How are you feeling?'

No answer. Silly question really.

How could I help?

His leg was at the wrong angle somehow, and so was one of his arms; he looked terrible, and where I had rested my stethoscope earlier was obviously not all right at all: it was moving wrongly and was not the right colour either. Although I could hear breath sounds, they were hard to interpret. [. . .] What medical equipment could enable this man to survive? If only someone would arrive who knew what to do. What did I know about anything? I turned around and looked at the man behind me; he was immobile and a terrible blue-grey colour . . . and so it went on.

I had taken my bags full of the equipment and drugs that I usually use. Not much call for antibiotics or infant paracetamol this afternoon. After some time – how long? – I became aware of a friend of mine going between the bodies doing the same as I was. Another general practitioner. We had worked together in the past but not on anything like this, nor are we likely to again. A smile of recognition. I wonder if I looked as lost as he did.

The first large-scale equipment arrived, and we started working together, putting up drips on everyone. We intubated as many patients and established as many airways as we possibly could. We needed scissors to cut through clothes. Why didn't I carry them in my bags? We started giving intravenous diamorphine, and some sort of routine and organization began to be established. I'm quite proud in a funny sort of way to be able to put up so many intravenous drips so quickly without missing a vein. More doctors had arrived by now, and around every body there was a little huddle of workers. Someone said that he was an anaesthetist – a man of gold dust. Come over here and look at Terry for me, mate. He's still alive, but he keeps stopping breathing. 'Hang on, Terry.' The anaesthetist took out the airway, and it was blocked with blood. Not a good sign. One rib seemed to be almost through the chest and was certainly at the wrong angle. The ambulance stretchers arrived, and we put in a passionate bid for Terry to be taken off first. By now six people were around him, holding the drip bottle, his head, and his legs, which were at all angles. He was rested on a low trolley. I checked that the ambulance was waiting and could get through to the hospital. The anaesthetist went with Terry to the ambulance. Thank God for anaesthetists. I'll never tell an anti-anaesthetist joke again.

Comradeship amid the horror

Now that I had no one to work on I wandered around and could see the dead bodies again at the other end of the sports hall. Among the doctors I recognized many of my friends and colleagues who had also answered the call of duty. One of them gave me a hug, bless him – a friend for life after what we went through that day. The police were much in evidence, but nobody was in charge of the medical tasks. What should I do next? Where would I be most useful? I decided to use my newly refound skills to put up drips on everybody who was going to be transferred to hospital. I somehow remembered that this was the thing to do in case the patients suffered more collapse on the way to hospital. It was also a sign to the hospital doctors that we general practitioners could do something right after all. I used up all of my diamorphine on those in need. By this time the routines were more established. Someone was writing down the obvious major damage to each person and what he or she had received in the way of drugs, etc. Then suddenly there was nobody left in the hall who was in need of attention and who wasn't dead.

I noticed a close friend amid the sea of dead faces. He was comforting someone who was leaning over a body. I stepped over some bodies to speak to him and offer some help; there weren't any words, just a look of rare empathy and comradeship.

Not knowing how to react

The doctors in the hall grouped together, almost silent, all wondering what to do next. I left the hall and walked through the silent crowds back to my car. I went home stunned and numbed. My children were playing in the garden; it was all so lovely and normal. Sandpits and skipping ropes. I had not known any of the dead or injured. Why is a major disaster so important for the people who participate as helpers? I meet death almost every day of my working life. Was this worse or was it just larger numbers? Everyone sort of expects that an event like this will be upsetting. But why is it that more attention is focused on the feelings of helpers in such disasters than on those of people concerned with upsetting events that happen every day? For me it seems to have been a major shock to my system in a general sort of way. I was grumpy, washed out, and flat for a couple of weeks. Passing Hillsborough shocked me again when I had nearly rebuilt my professional defences.

All of us general practitioners who were there met a few times to talk about our experiences and to support each other. Why are all the others so articulate about how they are feeling whereas I'm just sort of non-specifically upset? I can't remember what I felt like at the ground and can't describe to the helpful counsellor how I'm feeling during the group sessions. I know all the theory, but I can't get it together for myself – the plight of the modern professional. It's three weeks since the disaster now, and I'm feeling OK again; I make jokes at work and have lots to be thankful for. I've been enormously well supported through all this by family, friends and colleagues. Time has passed and lessons to be learnt are being thought about. Perhaps British football has changed because of these events, and perhaps major disasters will be better dealt with in the future.

I'd like to tell the official inquiry in a systematic way what I think went right with the medical response that day and what I think could be done better next time. I don't know what training should be given to general practitioners and why none of us took charge of the medical happenings in the sports hall and was prepared to be the coordinator. I've got strong views about the counselling that is necessary and appropriate after the event for helpers at disasters. I'd like to do physical damage to the person who took the pictures for the *Daily Mirror* and reserve a special act of aggression for the person who allowed them to be published. But most of all I'd like to find out what happened to Terry.

34

CONFLICTS IN THE RESIDENTIAL KEYWORKER ROLE

GRAHAM CONNELLY

During an interview which I conducted with an 18-year-old woman living in a centre for young homeless people, I asked what her keyworker, a middle-aged woman, meant to her. She told me that this worker was like the mother she never had for large parts of her life, and that what she wanted from their relationship was a keyworker who was willing to 'be there for me'.

This article explores in some detail the various roles implicit in being a residential keyworker, and some of the conflicts which can be experienced by care staff in performing these roles. To investigate the perceptions of keyworkers themselves, I used a simple questionnaire and invited workers from different establishments attending a day-release college course to respond to a number of questions. This modest survey was not intended to provide results of scientific value, but merely to guide my own thinking. I refer to the results of this survey and to the relevant literature simply to illustrate my points.

Defining the keyworker role

How is the term 'keyworker' used? Two quite different meanings are in common use. One refers to the largely administrative functions of coordinating the assessment of needs and planned intervention in caring for a young person. The other summarizes the close relationship which develops between the worker and the 'keychild', which is seen as vital to raising self-esteem and a sense of security. Both interpretations were referred to by the keyworkers who responded to my questionnaire. However, where only one aspect was mentioned by respondents the befriending role was the more common. This is, perhaps, not particularly surprising. Many workers who have described to me their reasons for being attracted to residential caring say that it affords an opportunity to influence young people through the use of special talents, or by strength of character. Being a 'befriender, helper, a special person' was how one respondent in my survey described this role.

Millham et al. (1980) distinguish three types of role available to residential workers. The first two indicate the complexity of the 'helper' aspect of keyworking: 'instrumental roles which facilitate the transmission of skills to clients' (teaching about basic personal hygiene, for example); and 'expressive roles which promote in the clients some desired end-state' (like using personal relationships to emphasize a client's worth as a person). The third type refers to the administrative and coordinating functions of keyworking: 'organizational roles which are concerned with the maintenance of social work service'. Another way of expressing these roles is perhaps to describe them as teaching, supporting or counselling, and coordinating.

Roles by definition imply expectations, both in the workers who carry out the required tasks and in the clients who relate to them. As an effect of these expectations workers may experience conflicts in the form of competing demands or in resolving inner tensions. If we understand something of the nature of these conflicts, we ought to be able to appreciate better the complexity of the residential task. We can discuss some of these conflicts using Millham's role-types to structure the discussion.

The teaching role

Workers provide help and guidance to vulnerable young people in many ways. Particularly where they have special skills, for example in craft or sport, care staff will feel comfortable in passing these on to young people, and will usually experience great satisfaction in doing so. Conflicts can arise, however, within this role. Older workers with their own teenage children have described to me their frustrations in coming to terms with rules for conduct in establishments which are more relaxed than they permit in their own homes.

One aspect of residential life which appears to be a source of particular conflict for workers concerns the educational needs of children in their care. In my experience, residential workers often underestimate their capacity to provide intellectual stimulation for young people in care. Out of sixteen respondents to my questionnaire, only two mentioned this aspect of the work, one of these specifically referring to providing assistance with school work. Two possible reasons for the neglect of educational needs of young people in residential care emerge. First, as Millham et al. (1980) discovered, only 32 per cent of residential staff surveyed had enjoyed their own school days, and most had generally 'mediocre' academic attainments.

Understandably, such staff are likely to shy away from defining their work in terms of providing educational support and, worse, may even express negative attitudes to learning. Secondly, as Jackson (1987) observes, many residential workers tend to see educational experiences in instrumental terms, perhaps to secure promotion, 'not as something which pervades all aspects of life'.

Another aspect of the teaching role involves training for social and life skills. Workers at the Strathclyde Independent Living Project, evaluating their own project, interviewed twenty former residents (Hughes et al., 1990): 'Only one person described herself as "well prepared" for independence.' Preparation mainly 'consisted of programmes of practical skills training, such as cooking, cleaning, shopping and budgeting. A small number of the group had not even been given any practical tasks such as cooking.' Significantly, the authors report that little attention was given to the social and emotional aspects of independent living skills, such as dealing with loneliness, or being assertive with visitors. Those young people who had lived in residential centres which had independent living units felt better prepared, but only in relation to practical skills.

The supporting role

Most residential staff emphasize the supportive aspects of their work with young people. These include a whole spectrum of behaviours from providing a listening ear or giving encouragement (helping), to setting clear limits on behaviour or dealing firmly with misbehaviour (controlling). This aspect of caring has been studied by researchers. Clough (1988) noted a discrepancy between different research reports investigating the day-to-day experience of young people in care. For example, Berridge (1985), in a survey of children's homes, had concluded that 'workers were generally sensitive to children's needs and problems and revealed an admirable degree of tolerance.' However, Whitaker et al. (1984) observed that young people very often suffered stress arising from their relations with fellow residents, and Fisher et al. (1986) found that parents often wished centres would place more constraints on their children. Clough (1988) writes that 'young people liked control which was firm but flexible, consistency of approach amongst the staff team and disliked arbitrary action.' Students on placement in residential centres have described to me entirely the same preferences when explaining what makes a satisfactory training experience.

All too common, however, is the environment where, as Clough found, 'Staff are uncertain of their task, of their aims for particular children, of what makes a successful day and of their ability to control the young people.' Clough argues that 'The core task is for staff in the residential centre to develop a clear strategy in which aims and methods are specified.' This clarity of purpose is more likely to exist where centre management are themselves secure in their understanding of the service they can provide and feel empowered within a supportive policy framework. For example, at Glengowan House, a hostel for homeless young people run by the Catholic Archdiocese of Glasgow, the centre director has complete autonomy to manage a service within the funding and general policy constraints of his agency and the local authority social work department. However, all staff and young residents are able to exercise real influence over decision-making through House meetings (Glengowan House, 1990), operating on lines similar to the therapeutic community model.

The keyworkers who responded to my questionnaire were invited to distinguish between the 'controller' and 'helper' aspects of their role, describing typical behaviours characterized by each. They were also asked to indicate their perceptions of the relative importance of each aspect, and estimate the proportion of time in a typical shift spent controlling and helping young people. In this small sample, though there was much common ground, each individual respondent referred to at least one behaviour not mentioned by others. This indicates that residential staff often hold a very personal view of the nature of the job. Such an observation is perhaps not surprising, given that workers tend to be recruited from a wide range of backgrounds and experience, rather than directly from college courses.

Most respondents stated that they believed both aspects of their role to be equally important; no one mentioned control as being more important. However, about a third of the keyworkers indicated that the controlling aspect of their role accounted for substantially more of their time during a typical shift. The most commonly mentioned behaviours were 'imposing sanctions' and 'setting limits'. Other examples mentioned by more than one person were 'implementing agency policy', 'confronting behaviour' and 'organizing chores'. The discrepancy between those aspects of the caring role which workers believe they were employed to perform (i.e. helping), and those which occupy considerable amounts of their time (i.e. controlling), is a significant source of dissatisfaction for residential staff. This is undoubtedly due to the stress that results from repeated confrontation, but it may arise because workers feel temperamentally unsuited to the 'harder end' of the work or because they lack training.

Keyworkers replying to the questionnaire were asked to describe incidents where they had experienced conflict between the controlling and helping aspects of their role. Aggressive behaviour, often accompanied by verbal or physical violence towards workers, is typical of situations where residential staff experience conflict between roles. The following description was provided by a 25-year-old houseparent working in a local authority children's home:

> Having to restrain a young boy who was attempting to assault me after I confronted his unacceptable behaviour. I felt confident that I was responsible for controlling him as he had lost control . . . of himself. This was linked to helping him to realize the consequences of his behaviour. I did not like having to do this but knew that I was responsible for controlling and helping the resident . . . No support is available as it is seen as part of my role to take these situations on board and deal with them appropriately. I find this unsatisfactory.

In this incident the worker felt personally equipped to deal with the crisis, but hinted at the isolation often felt by residential staff who see themselves as having been abandoned by their managers. Many workers describe feelings of anger: a woman assistant officer-in-charge described to me how she found herself having to administer a 'grounding' sanction imposed by a fieldworker on a boy who was constantly absconding. The anger was caused by her feelings of powerlessness and an awareness that the sanction was inappropriate, particularly since no attempt had been made by the fieldworker to explore why the child was absconding. Many workers also experience feelings of guilt, associated with their inability to deal with a situation to their own satisfaction, like the woman who told me: 'there are many occasions when a young person has needed time to talk but due to staff shortages I have been unable to spend time with them.'

This worker's comment indicates another source of dissatisfaction for residential staff: their belief, borne out of experience, that time spent listening to, and talking with, an individual young person is beneficial. Yet the nature of group living (and staffing ratios) can make this individual work appear a luxury. Time spent by a worker in developing a relationship with a young person may well be the key to reducing the likelihood of violence erupting. Good communication between colleagues, and between workers and young people, is clearly a vital component of effective residential work.

The terms most commonly used by respondents to the questionnaire to refer to helping behaviours were 'counselling', 'listening' and 'sustaining', the latter two being skills which are obviously important elements of counselling. I was interested to find that counselling was listed so frequently, although I have heard it argued that this form of intervention is not practised by residential staff or that it is an inappropriate method for use by non-caseworkers.

My impression, however, is that residential workers generally think of counselling in a different way from fieldworkers. Residential staff sometimes describe counselling as taking place 'on the hoof', often during a shared recreational activity. This use of the term 'counselling' is unacceptable to many people, who argue that residential staff are most usually engaged in the use of counselling 'skills' within the context of a helping relationship. My experience in working with Certificate in Social Services (CSS) students has been that planned counselling sessions, sometimes with formally agreed contracts, have often been associated with coursework, such as case studies, where extra time has been allocated to individualized work. One common spin-off, however, is that a student learns skills which can then be applied in the more unplanned situations.

Time allocated by workers to listening to individual young people is clearly important, though good communication on its own is not sufficient. The combination of effective communication with shared agreements for acceptable group living and valuing individuals is a theme expressed in a letter from a worker in a girls' hostel, quoted by Brown et al. (1986):

In my 15 years' experience working with teenagers I have never experienced violence against staff. I believe this is because:

1 It is made clear from the beginning that violence is not acceptable either in the group or against staff – it only leads to further trouble and is therefore wasted energy.
2 Every child is respected as an individual and is treated as such.
3 A personal weekly opportunity [is given] to air grievances . . . in private or in the weekly group meeting where all girls and staff are present.
4 Time is always given to listening to a child when this is required.

None the less, even very experienced workers have been assaulted by children with whom they have built up close supportive relationships. A personal friend successfully completed professional social work training, substantially increasing his confidence as a residential worker, and was soon promoted to team leader in another residential school. A short time later he was seriously assaulted by a young person, spent a number of weeks off work, and finally left the work disillusioned. Obviously, workers themselves need support: both emotional support to help them deal with crises, and supervisory support to provide advice and direction in their interventions with young people and their families. Support and consultation can take many forms; Berry (1989) advocates the use of an 'external consultant' who 'by virtue of coming from outside and having no direct responsibility for inmates, is not bogged down in the unit's daily pressures, and therefore is free to empathise with whatever the staff choose to present as being uppermost in their minds.'

Residential workers often speak positively about the quality of support they experience from colleagues. However, this support is more likely to consist of a kind of fellow-feeling, than structured assistance to reflect on events to help the worker improve future interventions. In some situations, workers experience conflicts between loyalty to colleagues and responsibility to clients, like the male houseparent responding to my questionnaire who recalled occasions when 'two or even three members of staff have spoken to a client simultaneously when the client is obviously uncomfortable in the situation.' The conflict between controlling and helping aspects of the work can be quite complicated. Sometimes a worker will feel that colleagues use controlling actions in a counterproductive way. A woman assessment officer described her conflicting feelings to me as follows:

[The] client was really acting out but calmed when I spent time with her even although I strongly confronted her about her behaviour. Rest of staff had obviously had to deal with the client over much longer periods than I had but I felt frustrated and useless when they took control of the situation and ignored my offers of assistance. I felt I could have used my relationship to alleviate the situation and try to come to some sort of situation where some constructive work could have been carried out. I could understand how frustrated the other staff felt due to her continual misbehaviour but felt their practice could have been less heavily weighted towards control.

A quite different form of conflict is the internal struggle experienced by some care staff when considering their own preferred styles of working, and described here by one of my respondents: 'The difficulty arises due to personality. I dislike confrontation and feel more confident within the helping role, although my training has allowed me to identify that not all confrontation can be negative.' This worker makes an important point: children are very often in care precisely because controlling actions by caring adults have been absent. Replacing controls may lead to confrontation, and this is not necessarily a bad thing if handled calmly, and without the attitude that the adult must win at all costs.

The coordinating role

The third aspect of the keyworker's task in residential care described by Millham et al. (1980) is an organizational role. Typically, this includes collecting information about clients from different sources and using this to draw together a coherent care plan, writing reports and advocating on behalf of clients with teachers, DSS officials and at case conferences. My own discussions with workers and their supervisors indicate some considerable personal conflict for many in this general area. Another effect of the limited educational background of many residential workers referred to earlier is one of difficulty in meeting the more administrative demands of the work. Two aspects are of particular significance here. The first is the ability to research and write reports, a critical skill in preparing assessment reviews. Understandably, many otherwise confident workers experience personal anguish at the thought of putting pen to paper. The second is the confidence to express opinions at meetings and case conferences. I have regularly heard residential staff describe their frustrations and disappointments at their own inability to contribute to discussions about clients for fear of being shown to be 'unschooled' in the presence of 'qualified' professionals. These frustrations are often compounded as workers lacking in confidence hear others, with limited contact with the child being discussed, offering unchallenged opinions.

Conclusions

Earlier in this article I said that the roles performed by residential workers also create expectations in clients. What roles are open to young people in their relationships with care staff? One possible role emphasizes powerlessness, variously expressed as unhealthily compliant behaviour or negativism. Given that young clients are vulnerable and tend to be poorly educated, it is not surprising that they often feel unable to exercise control over their own destiny. None the less, keyworkers, adopting the teaching role, have a major responsibility to ensure that young people learn appropriate skills in independent thinking and action. Parsloe (1988) argues that this requires workers to begin to think of knowledge of human behaviour in terms of its application to themselves, their families and people in general, rather than to a different species called clients.

If this can happen, a more partnership-based role can become available to young people. An example of a partnership approach is the regular House meeting (a feature of group living in Glengowan House, referred to earlier) where young people and workers feel they have equal rights to raise issues and equal responsibilities to listen to others. Partnership is also evident where workers encourage participation in case conferences and reviews, making use of Access to Records legislation, and participating in self-advocacy groups.

Inevitably, young people who enter residential care arrive emotionally scarred and a period of dependence on a keyworker is necessary, the length of time varying with individual needs. Restoration of self-esteem and development of a true sense of identity can be achieved within an atmosphere of caring which encourages good communication and allows young people to participate in the decision-making process. Effective caring seems to need all three elements of the residential keyworker task: teaching, supporting and coordinating. Conflicts for workers are often evident between these roles, and these cannot easily be resolved without clear guidelines for work, support mechanisms and access to training.

Acknowledgements

I would like to thank the residents of Glengowan House, Glasgow, and the Director, David Ramsay, and his staff, who gave me time and answered my questions patiently, and many workers attending courses at Langside College who have described to me their experiences as keyworkers.

References

Berridge, D. (1985) *Children's Homes*. Oxford: Basil Blackwell.
Berry, J. (1989) 'Daily experience in residential care for children and their caregivers', in S. Morgan and P. Righton (eds), *Child Care: Concern and Conflicts*. Sevenoaks: Hodder & Stoughton.
Brown, R., Bute, S. and Ford, P. (1986) *Social Workers at Risk: The Prevention and Management of Violence*. Basingstoke: Macmillan/British Association of Social Workers.
Clough, R. (1988) *Living Away from Home*. (Bristol Papers in Applied Social Studies 4.) Bristol: School of Applied Social Studies, University of Bristol.
Fisher, M., Marsh, P., Phillips, D. and Sainsbury, E. (1986) *In and Out of Care*. London: Batsford/British Association for Adoption and Fostering.
Glengowan House (1990) 'Annual Report 1990'. Glengowan House Centre for Young Homeless.
Hughes, F., McCulloch, P. and Murphy, M. (1990) *Independent Living Project: A Survey of Consumers' Views*. Glasgow: Strathclyde Regional Council.
Jackson, S. (1987) *The Education of Children in Care*. (Bristol Papers in Applied Social Studies 1.) Bristol: School of Applied Social Studies, University of Bristol.

Millham, S., Bullock, R. and Hosie, K. (1980) *Learning to Care: The Training of Staff for Residential Social Work with Young People*. Aldershot: Gower.

Parsloe, P. (1988) *Social Workers and Children in Care*. (Bristol Papers in Applied Social Studies 7.) Bristol: School of Applied Social Studies, University of Bristol.

Whitaker, D.S., Cook, J., Dunne, C. and Lunn-Rockliffe, S. (1984) *The Experience of Residential Care from the Perspectives of Children, Parents and Care-givers*. London: ESRC.

35

THINKING ABOUT FEELINGS IN GROUP CARE

JOHN SIMMONDS

In this extract from a longer article, John Simmonds discusses the relationship between personal anxieties and the workings of an organization, with specific reference to residential care for young people.

Failure to appreciate unconscious defences in organizational matters can make many well-intentioned changes simply the object of powerful resistance and in consequence fruitless work. There are two theoretical and practical traditions that have most tried to evolve a psychoanalytic view that combines both organizational structure and of the individual with an inner unconscious world. The first not surprisingly is associated with a specific movement in the mental health field – that of the democratic therapeutic community (Jones, 1955, 1976). The second has had a more general application to commercial, industrial as well as human service agencies and is exemplified in the work of the Tavistock Institute of Human Relations and more particularly that of A.K. Rice (cf. Miller and Rice, 1967).

One of the main arguments of organizational analysts like Rice and psychoanalysts like Jaques and Menzies is that the importance of objective and rationally conceived notions of task and structure, must be complemented by an understanding of the place of emotions and particularly unconscious motivation in organizational life. This is unambiguously put by Jaques (1955) when he says 'One of the primary cohesive elements binding individuals into institutionalised human association is that of defence against psychotic anxiety. In this sense individuals may be thought of as externalising those impulses and internal objects that would otherwise give rise to psychotic anxiety, and pooling them in the life of the social institutions in which they associate.'

In comparison to the model of organizations which starts with task and

Abridged from G. Pearson, J. Treseder and M. Yelloly (eds), *Social Work and the Legacy of Freud*, Macmillan, Basingstoke, 1988 derives structure from a rational appraisal of that task, this picture of organizational functioning is inside out. However, it is important in understanding the psychoanalytically informed model of organizations, that this does not of itself reduce task and structure to a secondary position in such a theory but that task and structure cannot be fully understood without also being aware of what these come to represent to members of the organization. When Menzies (1960) traces the structural problems of the nursing service in a teaching hospital back to institutional methods of dealing with individual nurse anxiety, it does not place the objective need for nurses or a structure to deliver their services in a secondary place. However, it does draw attention when looking at the concepts of task and structure to the deeper and dynamic significance of these terms. It also demands that we consider these dynamic aspects when looking at the processes which interfere with an organization's successful pursuit of its task.

Britton (1981) adds another dimension to this theme when he explores the Freudian concept of repetition and re-enactment not just in relation to individual or family dynamics but also in relation to the way that professionals handle these dynamics both inside and among themselves. He is concerned therefore to demonstrate the way in which patterns of relationships in one situation can be transferred into a different situation 'in which new participants become the vehicles for the reiterated expression of the underlying dynamic ... The basic situation remains unrealised and unchanged whilst new versions of it proliferate. The cast changes but the plot remains the same' (Britton, 1981: 49). Britton suggests that 'the intensity of feeling aroused by a case; the degree of dogmatism evoked; of the pressure to take drastic and urgent measures' together with inappropriate unconcern, surprising ignorance, undue complacency, uncharacteristic insensitivity or professional inertia (1981: 48) are all possible indicators that such is happening. The uncontained and unwanted feelings in a case therefore come to dominate and dictate professional thinking and consequent action in that case. When thinking is divorced from the painful emotional reality to which it relates then unhealthy and inappropriate action can result. However, this is not only a possibility in individual cases and therefore peculiar and confined to individual instances for, as Menzies makes clear, the actual structure and practices of the professions and organizations themselves may take on these unconsciously determined themes. This is discussed by Miller and Gwynne (1972) in their study of long-term residential establishments for the physically handicapped. Here defences against the emotional and social anxiety of the primary task give rise to what they call humanitarian and liberal defences. From this they derive two models of residential care – warehousing and horticultural – both of which seek to deny some important aspect of the reality of the task of these establishments.

What I am arguing therefore is that developments in psychoanalytic thought suggest that every aspect of organizational life from task, structure and culture to individual decision-making and case management can express the basic problem human beings have in facing emotional pain and learning from experience. In so doing not only are there socially structured mechanisms for the defence against anxiety but each situation has the potential for expressing an underlying and unconsciously determined emotional dynamic.

However, rather than this theory being a negative expression of the potential of organizational life, it opens up the possibility of organizations becoming more sensitive to the emotional reality of human problems. In so doing they can develop descriptions of their tasks and corresponding structures and work practices that relate to the necessity of understanding and working with the underlying anxiety and dynamics of the task.

This is exemplified in a residential establishment that helped young people who had been in long-term local authority care to establish themselves independently. A crisis had occurred in the establishment over staffing and shift rotas. While on paper there were adequate people to cover shifts in the establishment itself, it was difficult when preparing rotas to allow staff to have the time necessary to support those residents who had actually left. Because of these difficulties, the quality of the after-care work had in fact diminished and those staff who were following up on residents were largely doing it in their own time. The crisis had also deepened as the management group had tried to deal with this problem by quantifying present demand for after-care and also anticipating future needs for those residents about to leave. These figures showed that an increase of some 30 per cent would be required to meet this demand. This figure was not only rejected by the senior managers of the organization but started a questioning of the necessity of doing after-care work at all. This was greeted by considerable anger in the staff and over time a marked drop in morale.

In discussing after-care with the staff of the establishment, it became apparent that the issue as presented – staffing – was in fact only one aspect of a problem that there was considerable feeling about. Not only were staff concerned about what happened to residents when they left, they were also worried about what was happening to residents while they were actually resident. After some time, it became clear that the principal issue that linked both areas of concern was the question of separation: separation for the young people from an uncertain past into, for many, an uncertain future. For the staff this was also important as it meant the breaking of important relationships with residents which had been built up over time and with considerable effort. As this was discussed in more detail, it became clear that many staff found the aims of the establishment difficult to relate to in that so many of the young people that were referred and accepted had needs and problems that were far deeper than two years' stay could deal with. The staff felt that for many of the young people, it could take two years to build up any kind of trusting relationship. The focus on this aspect of the work tended therefore to push the other aspect of the work – preparation for leaving – into the background. While, therefore, it was not absent from discussions during a person's stay, it was something that was discussed with considerable ambivalence on the staff's part. I had the impression that for some young people there may well have been an air of some unreality about the plans for the future and their need actively to engage in work on it. The point at which it was actively discussesd could therefore be only weeks and in one instance three days before the move to a flat was planned. In that time, the emotional atmosphere could easily be dominated by panic in the resident and guilt on the part of the staff. Preparation itself was often focused on practical matters with little consideration being given to the feeling content of what was happening. A culture seemed to have developed in the establishment based on the difficulty of both being in a close relationship and at the same time dealing with the complex issues of separation and independence. The residents' anxiety about this latter issue caused many of them to deny completely the reality of what they were facing and forced them into expressing a powerful and often a negative dependency on the staff. As a consequence of this, the period of after-care was at its best often used to deal with some of the issues which might more usefully have been focused on during the period of residence. It was at these times that the demands of after-care on staff resources became particularly acute but even then the anxiety of bringing the work to an end and transferring the responsibility elsewhere caused the work to go on for longer than appropriate. In a number of instances where after-care was not used to recoup the lost work during residency, the young person's previous poor experiences of separation were re-enacted in a mixture of rejection and neglect. It was often these young people that had the most difficulty in coping with independence and over time of needing a further period of residential care, although this time it could be in a mental hospital or prison.

The focus of the work with both management and staff group was in the first instance not so much in finding a way of increasing staff resources. Rather they needed help in developing their own emotional resources in order to understand the emotional content of the task and the corresponding culture that had developed in order to cope with the anxiety of that task. In so doing, the staff's deepened understanding of this task and of their own subjective responses to it became the most significant point in the development in the original problem and the work of the establishment. By both experiencing and reflecting on the pain of separation, and it was quite clear that at the point of deepest understanding the staff most directly experienced this pain inside themselves, the staff found a way of becoming more openly sensitive and receptive to the problems and anxieties of the residents. This in turn enabled the staff to help the residents confront more directly and in a more helpful way both their past and future while they were in residence and as a preparation for leaving.

In the current debate in social work, therefore, much more thought needs to be given to the impact of the very powerful feelings that I have discussed than currently seem to be in vogue. Whether in theory or in practice, what we feel and often want to ignore may be the basis for building a social work less dominated by the present climate of insecurity, guilt and tragedy.

References

Britton, R. (1981) 'Re-enactment as an unwitting professional response to family dynamics', in S. Box, B. Copley, J. Magagna and E. Moustaki (eds), *Psychotherapy with Families*. London: Routledge.

Jaques, E. (1955) 'Social systems as a defence against persecutory and depressive anxiety', in M. Klein, P. Heimann and R.E. Money-Kyrle (eds), *New Directions in Psychoanalysis*. London: Tavistock.

Jones, M. (1955) *The Therapeutic Community: a New Treatment Method in Psychiatry*. New York: Basic Books.

Jones, M. (1976) *Maturation of the Therapeutic Community*. New York: Human Sciences Press.

Menzies, I.E.P. (1960) 'A case study in the functioning of social systems as a defence against anxiety', *Human Relations*, 13. Reprinted as *The Functioning of Social Systems as a Defence Against Anxiety: a Report on a Study of the Nursing Service of a General Hospital*. Tavistock Pamphlet, no. 3, 1970.

Miller, E.J. and Gwynne, G.V. (1972) *A Life Apart*. London: Tavistock.

Miller, E.J. and Rice, A.K. (eds) (1967) *Systems of Organisation*. London: Tavistock.

36

REFLECTIONS ON SHORT-TERM CASEWORK

LIZ LLOYD

This article is an edited version of a piece of work done by a student for a social work course. The account is written for an assessor and the author is careful to present a 'comprehensive case' of the history of her relationship and her practice with the user. Reflections in practice are often not only for the personal benefit of the worker, but part of the account of her own work that the worker presents to others.

---

1   Initial referral

Ms M was referred by the community occupational therapist who asked for a visit with information about community groups, particularly health-orientated groups. Ms M was referred as a 'West Indian' woman of 33 who was disabled.

2   First visit and assessment

Ms M is in fact from West Africa. She has lived in England for five years. Three years ago she was injured in an industrial accident which has left her with severe pain in her shoulders and arms. She has been unable to work since the accident and receives Invalidity Benefit. She has all the necessary practical aids and adaptations in her house. She was rehoused last February to her present home where she lives with her husband. I got the impression that he is away a lot of the time. She has not had a social worker since being rehoused. She received no compensation for the injury as her employers could not be proved to have been negligent. Her job was kitchen assistant.

Ms M wanted to make contact with the local community and to be able to contribute to community life as a valuable member, not as an object of sympathy. She wanted to get back to work, to be retrained in a job which would be within her capabilities physically. She wanted to break out of her isolated, housebound existence and put her injury and subsequent problems behind her.

She was very shy and reticent about relaying all this to me and her voice was practically inaudible at times. It was clear to me that her self-image was extremely poor and her morale very low. She seemed quite depressed and very lonely.

3 The plan

The plan we worked out together was based on:

(a) Ms M's own definition of her problem

It seemed vital to me that I should accept this and not attempt to probe any deeper into underlying issues. I was aware of difficulties in her marriage but she was clearly not keen to talk about this. It seemed to me that she had set realistic and appropriate goals for herself and I felt that contact with community groups might well provide a positive step towards the wider goal of improving her confidence and morale.

(b) Agency role

The Health Project has wide contacts with community groups which may be able to offer support to Ms M in combating her feelings of isolation. The goal of retraining and improving employment prospects was also something with which we could provide practical support.

(c) The temporary nature of my involvement

I knew that Ms M's limited time with me would place restrictions on the methods of work available to me. While there might have been some benefit in long-term individual work, there seemed no possibility of this from statutory agencies.

Community groups appeared to be a viable form of long-term support. *The goals,* then, were:

1   Establish social contacts.
2   Tackle Ms M's difficulty in getting out of the house.
3   Find a suitable course as a step towards improving Ms M's job prospects.
4   Build up Ms M's morale and self-confidence.

4 The process

Over the next three weeks I visited once a week with information about community groups and training courses. Gradually, Ms M began to make contact with agencies herself and to make appointments. My role was to encourage and validate her strengths. In fact, there were a number of hurdles and difficulties in finding suitable groups and in getting information about training courses, but Ms M's determination in carrying on was a strength which impressed me greatly. We went out together to the appointments and she became more confident in walking around.

We discussed the kind of work she would like to do and I discovered that she was well qualified in her country of origin as a civil servant. Her talents had been wasted since coming to England. The more time I spent with Ms M, the more I realized the extent to which the racism she had experienced had contributed to her present difficulties. Quite apart from the practical issue of employment, I felt her contact with medical, legal and welfare professionals had increased her feeling of helplessness and dependence.

About four weeks after my first visit, Ms M asked me to come and see her. She told me with some difficulty that she had had a miscarriage two days previously and had told nobody about it, except her husband. She had not been to see a doctor and wanted to. She was clearly in a state of crisis and I took her to her GP. After this, Ms M was more confident in talking to me about herself, except that she still would not mention her husband and deflected any reference that I made to him. I decided to wait until she was ready to open up on this.

Over the next few weeks I found myself becoming involved in discussions with other professionals who had contact with Ms M. I was being given information I hadn't asked for and being asked for information I didn't want to give. Although I had at times felt frustrated by Ms M's reticence, I felt I should respect Ms M's own judgement about what she wanted to tell me and when. At times I felt in a dilemma as the new information on offer might have shed light on areas where I was in the dark. I still believed that what I was doing was useful to her and that I didn't actually need to have a fully illuminated picture based on other people's judgements.

A breakthrough came when Ms M made and kept an appointment in the city centre, travelling alone by bus: something she hadn't done for three years. My support in such practical matters is now minimal.

5 The outcome

The likelihood is that Ms M will start a course in computer programming as soon as she has sorted out a grant through the Manpower Services Commission. She has made some social contacts through attending the Local Neighbourhood House. In addition, she has talked to me about her need for support in dealing with her depression. Through marriage guidance counselling, she has reached the conclusion that she needs to change and that her mental state has been a major factor in her marriage problems. She is going to attend a group at the women's mental health project to give more long-term attention to this.

6   Evaluation

Contacts with community groups for social purposes have been of limited success. Ms M has enjoyed attending a day centre, but it probably won't be a long-term involvement, as her interests are developing in other directions, especially in work. There is a notable lack of groups in the community for younger women with no children.

My view is that Ms M will benefit from being enabled to deal with her depression through being a member of a mutual support group. Perhaps the single greatest achievement of our relationship has been that she has recognized her need and been able to communicate it. I feel that my approach in validating her strengths has made it easier for her to ask for help, and I feel that having reached this position at her own pace will give her a positive view of what she can go on to achieve at the women's mental health project. She is more able to make choices about her priorities and trusts her own judgement.

It might have been possible to reach this position earlier if I had not spent so much time on practical issues. However, my role was largely determined by the agency remit. I also feel sure that my role as supporter has contributed to her increased self-confidence. She told me that I was the only person to have given her such positive encouragement and made her believe she could do things for herself. The support of the women in the women's group will ensure that this encouragement continues as she continues the effort of shedding her isolated, housebound identity.

37

ESTABLISHING A FEMINIST MODEL OF GROUPWORK IN THE PROBATION SERVICE

TARA MISTRY

This article describes a probation women's group which was set up in the inner-city area of Bristol in 1983.

Women and the probation service

Women are proportionately more likely to be placed on a probation order than men. In 1985, 7 per cent of male offenders received probation compared to 17 per cent of women (Home Office, 1986). Despite this, provision for women on probation has been limited mostly to a 'one-to-one' individualized response which is often based on a notion of 'women needing help'. Because women form a relatively small percentage of the probation caseload, they have been continuously marginalized, reflecting both their position in society and the dominant power position of men in the criminal justice system, particularly the probation service hierarchy.

The probation service is predominantly run by men with most of the female workforce concentrated at the main grade level. This reflects an attitude which permeates the treatment of women clients by managers and, subsequently, by main grade practitioners who 'absorb' the culture of the agency – initially during practice placements while on training courses, and later as employees.

Historically, women clients have been 'social worked' and pathologized by social workers and probation officers on the basis of whether they were good wives, mothers, daughters, sisters and so on. If they failed to fit the gender-specified role, both male and female workers would undertake to supervise them individually in order to 'support, guide or prepare' them more usefully for the feminine role. Women who offended had after all

Abridged from *Groupwork*, 2, 1989, pp. 145–58

stepped out of their natural place. When groupwork began to make an impact in the probation service, some women's groups were organized, but these often took the form of *ad hoc* arrangements with poor facilities for child care; using inexperienced workers to run crèches without proper toys; and with everyone huddled together in one room. Discussion and activities often focused on good grooming, cooking and sewing, and suffered from the 'coffee morning syndrome'. These types of groups perpetuated the image that women could make do with poor provision, and they also reinforced the role stereotype of women needing to prepare to fit into their 'rightful' feminine role, for example learning to budget effectively in order to stay out of trouble.

It seemed from my own experience as a worker supervising women on probation and observing colleagues' work, that social workers and probation officers, and those in other state institutions, colluded with the view that women are subordinates, and were slow to respond to the challenge of feminist thinking in their social work practice. It was against this background that our desire to empower women offenders, albeit under a probation order, resulted in the establishment of the women's group in the Easton probation office.

The case for a women-centred group

Questions have regularly been posed by practitioners and magistrates as to why there needs to be a separate group for women. As the potential co-leaders of the pilot women's group, my co-worker and I made certain assumptions that women working together would naturally develop a support system. Our experience also indicated that the degree of emotional and practical support derived from an all-women group would be more constructive, relevant and practical than in a one-to-one client/worker relationship.

From our observation of women's participation in the mixed sex 'induction group' model (Brown and Seymour, 1983), it seemed that the combination of the structured framework and the proportionally small numbers of women in any one group (usually two women to eight to ten men), women's needs were 'submerged'. Women often enabled, accommodated and assisted the male members to understand their offending behaviour. In effect they helped 'service' the group without getting much for themselves. In my discussions with women clients over the years, it was also evident that a structured group such as the induction model did not help to pin-point their offending behaviour, nor did it show them a way forward to stop offending. This was because the focus often shifted to the dominant problem behaviour in the group and that was dictated by the men's reasons for offending.

We were also unhappy about using breach (of probation) proceedings and the courts as a 'stick' for non-attenders, as we thought that this ran counter to feminist philosophy and would not create an alternative model for the women. Although the group had to be a credible option for the courts and the probation officers, we felt that women had to have a choice as to whether or not they attended the group. It could not, however, be regarded as a totally voluntary group, because it was part of probation supervision and they had to give a commitment to attend for a certain number of weeks on a basis negotiated between themselves and their respective probation officers. If women chose not to continue coming after the minimum negotiated time, then the supervising officer would explore other avenues. Many people argue that this principle does not apply only to the feminist group model but should apply equally to all groups. However, I think that many male colleagues found the lack of clearly defined boundaries difficult to accept, which may say more about the nature of the probation service and its relationship with the courts than it does about an attitude typical of male probation officers!

In summary, we described our model of groupwork as having a feminist perspective because:

- the group is run for women by women only;
- it has a value base that does not assume women are subordinate or fit the stereotype of 'feminine' women;
- it seeks actively to promote women taking control of their lives by methods devised through collective discussion (and action, where appropriate);
- it views the offending behaviour of women within their socioeconomic position in a patriarchal society;
- it starts from the point where women (in the group) choose to start and seeks to build on that rather than adopt a 'baseline' which the group leaders define as the 'norm'.

The group

The group was 'open' with the exit and entrance of members phased. For the first two years it ran every week throughout the year except for statutory holidays. After that, it ran only in school term time as the crèche was not available in school holidays. Also, as workers, we needed to reappraise our aims and objectives frequently and spend some time away from the group to evaluate and develop our own styles and skills.

The main recurring themes of discussion were motherhood, child care, relationships, sexuality, health, poverty, status, class, welfare rights, racism, sexism, family, criminal justice system, offending, coping alone, domestic violence, portrayal of women, stereotyping and power. These discussions gave rise to various dynamics within the group. In the early days the leaders played an active role in getting the women to address and challenge each other. As each particular group membership cohered and developed its own momentum, we had a correspondingly reduced role in directing the group. The programme of discussion and activities was always negotiated with the group, but sometimes the direction would move away from the original plan if the group dynamics needed exploring or external problems encroaching on the women members' lives arose; for example, problems with children, relationships, violence at home, an outstanding court case, or possible risk of re-offending. Ironically, in view of earlier criticism, this flexibility made the group both demanding and stimulating for the leaders and the members.

On one occasion, when £400 was granted for an activity, the women wanted to use the money for a three-day residential trip to a Butlin's Holiday Camp. This was demanding for me as my co-worker could not attend, but it proved to be a most rewarding experience. Nine women and six children went on the trip, and events over the three days revealed that despite the positives we felt about the group, the issues of discrimination, lack of status, rivalry for men and resources, racism and lack of money had not been addressed in a manner which was pertinent to their lives. One evening, I attended a dance with other women in the group and we were set upon by white women holidaymakers. I was terrified, but the other black women (having always been on the receiving end of this type of behaviour) dealt with it in the most skilful way possible. It demonstrated to the white women in our group how racism worked against the black women, and reminded me as a middle-class black woman how I had been protected from this in recent years since the change in my status. There were occasional rivalries between the younger women over men, and much of this shared experience formed an important focus for group discussion in the next twelve months in the group. This trip also provided a useful lesson for me about the importance of probation officers being in touch with the experiences of women who become clients.

Evaluation of the group

The process of the group bore out our initial assumption that women would naturally draw together and develop their own support system. They were generally prepared to talk about themselves and their families once they had had adequate time to get to know each other. There was often a sharing of intimate personal details, particularly with reference to relationships with men and motherhood. These two factors often caused stress and worries which were alleviated by the offer of active practical support from other women within the group; for example, volunteering to baby-sit, inviting isolated women to their homes and, on occasions, providing accommodation in the event of physical abuse from male partners. There was ample evidence of physical and emotional support both inside and, more importantly, outside the group. This went beyond the hopes and expectations we had expressed when we originally set up the group.

Some women learned to use their skills of listening, understanding and counselling with each other, and were able to extend their support beyond the boundaries experienced by us as co-workers and probation officers. One problem which can and sometimes did arise was that this type of supportive relationship makes it difficult for group members to challenge each other. When this happened the group leaders had to take up their responsibilities, and use their skills and position to direct the group to challenge in a constructive manner. As in any group, the co-workers also had to be sensitive to general groupwork processes; for example, dealing with scape-goating, engaging the quiet member, controlling the more dominant member.

Overall, in making a process evaluation of the group, we can say with confidence that the women's group had portrayed levels of self-disclosure, nurturing and emotional and practical support of a quality which we had not experienced as workers in other mixed groups or in individual work with women.

Eighteen months after the group started, a student from Bristol University undertook an independent consumer study of women who had been through the group. Her findings confirmed our own positive views. They showed that the women had felt safe to talk about themselves and did not feel judged. They felt more supported than in one-to-one settings with their probation officers, and welcomed the regular meetings with other women in the community setting. For some, it was nice just to get out of the house for an hour and a half while their children were being looked after! It may be worth repeating this monitoring of consumer feedback with a larger sample now that the group has been in existence for six years and more than 120 women have been through it (by January 1989).

Demands on the co-workers

For us as workers, this type of group made tremendous demands on 'self' because it was not possible to maintain a distant, 'professional' stance. As women we all shared common experiences, and as a black woman I had the specific experience of racism which could be shared with other black group members. However, it has to be acknowledged that as probation officers we were often in a more privileged position, and there was a clear power imbalance (although not as marked as in the one-to-one client/worker relationship) because we 'ran' the group.

My co-worker, Carol, and I felt that it was important to acknowledge our differing positions, but utilize our skills and knowledge to facilitate the group where and when it was needed (especially at the early stage of a new term). However, at certain stages of group development the boundaries between 'worker' and 'client' were often blurred, especially if certain shared experiences were being discussed (the role of mother, daughter, girlfriend, lover etc.). Sometimes Carol and the other white women would be discussing the experiences of racism as expressed by myself and other black women. One of the clear recollections I have of this is black women (in the majority at that session) challenging and then explaining that stereotypes of 'dirty black people' were ill founded and not based on facts but on distortions. I am sure that the white women too remembered the collective voice of the black women from that session! For many working-class white women, this was the first time that their stereotypes of black people had been challenged by their black friends.

In our co-working relationship, Carol and I spent a lot of energy developing a strong partnership in order to work effectively together as black and white co-workers. We also had different class backgrounds and sometimes we clashed due to the differing positions of black and white feminists on certain issues. We felt, however, that this was a healthy sign which acknowledged that having a feminist perspective is not enough. As workers we had to be open and responsive to our own history and the needs of the group.

This qualitative evaluation of the outcome makes it clear that most of the aims and objectives of the group have been met, and the arguments for establishing a women-centred resource have been validated by the effectiveness of the group. A further positive indicator is that regular attendance was never a problem: in fact, persuading women to leave the group proved to be the difficulty!

Other issues

While we had no doubts that the women's group was a worth-while project, we recognized that there were some shortcomings. Even though black women were getting a better service in an all-women group, my own growing awareness led me to believe that their needs could be met more specifically, for example, through the establishment of an all black women's group. Most of the black women I spoke to felt uneasy about this but, like the issue of black and white co-workers, this issue needs another article which could explore the race dimension and the contradictions that the feminist model throws up for black women leaders and members in a racially mixed group.

Another limitation was that people referred from the Central team were not meeting within their own community setting, although this did not seem to worry the women unduly, preferring sometimes not to be in their own neighbourhood. Our original wish to help them move on to community-based groups or projects did not materialize and the voluntary 'move-on' group seemed a better alternative.

Conclusion

The most significant learning points were that, given the opportunity, a women's group consisting mainly of working-class black and white women who had been caught up in the criminal justice system and placed on a probation order, could develop members' self-confidence and increase their self-esteem. Self-disclosure and the sharing of personal, social and economic problems in a safe comfortable community setting with adequate child-care facilities, and sensitivity to a feminist philosophy, allowed the women to explore their own positions within society. This inevitably helped the group to achieve a framework of practical, physical and emotional support. Although I personally have reservations about the term 'empowerment', there is no doubt in my mind (having run groups of various types over the past eight years) that we did see women helping each other to take control of their lives in a manner I had not witnessed in other probation group settings. For myself as a worker, this piece of practice was the most stimulating and personally fulfilling of all.

For the courts and the probation service, the scheme proved that an all-women's group is successful, not only in terms of the low re-offending rate, but also because it demonstrated that attendance does not have to be a problem if the needs of clients are being met in a constructive way which is relevant and pertinent to their lives. The feminist model, with flexibility for women to explore the concept by reference to the effects of offending on their lives, was the key to this group's existence. The fact that after six years the group is still running, with regular referrals and commitment from probation teams, is evidence that collective single-sex groups within the structure of the probation order are a viable method of supervising women offenders.

In the climate of *Punishment, Custody and the Community* (Home Office, 1988) and greater 'packaging' of probation orders, it will be very interesting to see whether the group can continue to survive without controls imposed by the courts. It augurs well that, despite the change in the political climate of the probation service, a group based on a feminist ideology has so far succeeded in keeping to its principles and diverting more women away from further offending. It continues to provide a relevant and useful facility where women are not seen to be consistently in need of help but where they can understand why they have been caught up in the criminal justice system, and seek to find their own short and long-term solutions, even if they are not in a position to challenge the whole structure of a patriarchal society.

References

Brown, A. and Seymour, B. (eds) (1983) *Intake Groups for Clients: A Probation Innovation.* Bristol: University of Bristol.

Home Office (1986) *Criminal Statistics for England and Wales, 1985.* Cmnd 10. London: HMSO.

Home Office (1988) *Punishment, Custody and the Community.* London: HMSO.

38

WHEN THE SOLUTION BECOMES A PART OF THE PROBLEM

ROBERT BOR, LUCY PERRY and RIVA MILLER

This article examines the psychosexual management of AIDS patients.

For any problem to exist, it must (a) be defined by someone as a problem, and (b) this definition must be accepted by at least one other person (Maturana et al., 1988). In a counsellor's conversations with patients, the counsellor has the opportunity to confirm or disconfirm problems. Thus, if a counsellor says to a patient, 'I do not think there is anything wrong with you and I see no point in our meeting', this is a message to the patient that in the counsellor's view the patient has no problems. If, on the other hand, the counsellor says, 'Yes this is a very serious problem and I will need to see you on a regular basis for several months', he or she confirms that a problem exists.

In making a referral, a professional defines at least three things. First, a statement is made about the *nature* of the problem. The referrer may, for example, mention that the patient is 'depressed'. Secondly, the professional indicates *for whom* this is a problem, be it the patient, a family member or a member of the health care team. Thirdly, the referrer indicates what should be *done about* the problem. If the referrer, for example, suggests that the patient sees a psychiatrist, the message may be conveyed that there may be an organic basis to the behaviour, whereas if the referral were made to a psychotherapist, there may be the belief that there were problems in the early development of that person. No referral is therefore a completely neutral gesture.

This is not altogether a new idea. New problems will, however, arise over time in new and developing fields, such as in AIDS counselling. In this field,

Abridged from *British Journal of Guidance and Counselling*, 17 (2), 1989, pp. 133–7 the counsellor and medical practitioner often work closely together for the benefit of patients and their families. AIDS is a new problem for both counsellors and medical practitioners. The definition of the purpose of counselling and the management of psychosocial problems may not always be clear.

A case study

Gregory, a 44-year-old man with AIDS, was regularly seen by the physician in one of the medical outpatient units. He had been diagnosed with AIDS over a year beforehand. He was being treated with Zidovudine (AZT, an anti-viral drug) which had been of benefit to him. He was, however, beginning to become unwell and it was believed that an opportunistic infection was imminent. The counsellor had been seeing the patient every three months for a review in order to assess how he was coping with his diagnosis, treatment and relationships with others.

At his most recent counselling session, Gregory walked in, sat down and said to the counsellor: 'Dr Stephens says I should see a psychiatrist.' Apparently, Gregory had described himself to Dr Stephens as being 'paranoid' and 'depressed'. He qualified this with the doctor by saying that he also thought that his being moody was a natural response to his illness. Gregory disagreed with the physician that he should discuss this with a psychiatrist. He said that he had financial and physical considerations and limitations in his life. These prevented him from going out as much as he would like to. His having to go to a psychiatrist would, in his view, change his view about himself: 'I would be a real nutcase.' He did not have that view of himself in that meeting. Additionally, he stated that it would make his ordinary problems seem all the more complex.

This situation presented the counsellor with a dilemma. On the one hand, the counsellor agreed that some of the patient's depressed behaviour was probably a consequence of his being ill and some of his social problems. The patient was no longer able to work and he felt so disfigured that he did not want to see any of his friends. On the other hand, the patient agreed that he was depressed but did not want to take up a referral to a specialist as he believed that this would compound his problems by making him view himself as a 'nutcase'.

In one sense, the patient was happy being unhappy. He had acknowledged that he would have to face many personal problems through the course of his illness. Had Dr Stephens said: 'Gregory, you tell me that you are 'paranoid' and 'depressed'; what do you think could be of help to you in managing these feelings?', the patient might then have said that he was prepared to be depressed on his own, or he would make contact with some of his friends, or he would find another way of helping himself out of his misery, or he may have even asked for a referral to a psychiatrist.

After a long session in which many issues were discussed, the patient finally turned around to the counsellor and said, 'I feel that I'm managing. I may not have many friends; I may not be able to go to work; I guess I don't have the support of my family . . . but now I am really concerned about what the doctor had said. He thinks that I am not managing. I think I am managing. But now he says I have got to go to a psychiatrist. He makes me feel that I'm not managing, I feel maybe I am also going crazy.' This illustrates that it can be helpful to ask patients how they think their problems might best be solved.

The counsellor's options

The counsellor might agree with the view of the doctor and suggest that it is a good idea for the patient to consult a psychiatrist. There might then be several levels to the psychosocial management of the patient. These might include a psychiatrist, a counsellor and others all working with the same patient. A second option may be for the counsellor to agree that Gregory should see the psychiatrist but to decide to hold off counselling sessions until such time as the sessions with the psychiatrist come to an end. In that way there would not be several levels of patient management. The third option could be to disagree with Dr Stephens about the need for a referral to a psychiatrist. This might have put the counsellor in conflict with his medical colleagues, which could have serious ramifications for the patient.

A further option, the one we prefer, is to intervene in the referring system. One way to do this was to go back to the physician and discuss the case with him. In this case, they examined how the patient was managing, what specific psychosocial problems had arisen, and what should be done about these. From this, some consensus followed as to how the patient should best be managed. There was then less disagreement over the definition of the problem. In addition, they were able to defuse any possible conflict between the two professionals. At that point, the main counselling activity is with the referring system rather than with the patient.

In similar professional liaison meetings, the counsellor might ask the doctor: 'How do you think the patient's problems should best be managed? If the patient were to see a psychiatrist, how do you think this might affect his view of himself? What problems do you see arising from having a psychiatrist involved in this case? What advantages might there be? How do you see the work of a counsellor in relation to that of a psychiatrist with such a patient?', and so on. By asking questions such as these, it is possible to begin to examine the doctor–patient–psychiatrist–counsellor interfaces and the task of counselling as it is defined by others.

Some counsellors might wonder why the counsellor in this case example did not discuss the different views of the problems with the client. The authors believe that through the counselling context the definition and re-definition of the problem will unfold. Thus, while the presenting problem may be 'depression', it may later be seen as a symptom of marriage difficulties or, as is frequently the case in AIDS, a symptom of not being able to talk to others about the diagnosis because of fears of ostracism and stigma. It would therefore be entirely appropriate to discuss this with the client from the first session. In a clinical setting, and in relation to a problem both as complex and as compelling as AIDS, some counsellors are 'seduced' by one view or another and fail to note the professional conflict this may cause. In turn, clients become confused and complain of uncoordinated care. The idea is neither complex nor new, but warrants re-stating in the context of AIDS counselling where no one should claim to have a monopoly of ideas about how best to counsel or manage clients.

Conclusion

This brief article has described the important role a professional has in defining the nature of psychosocial problems with patients. An example has been described in which the solution to a problem becomes a part of the new problem for the patient. That is, referring a patient to a psychiatrist defines the patient as being 'crazy' and not coping, in the patient's view at least. The counsellor may feel that the patient is coping despite his unhappiness. Referrers may want some patients 'off their back' in their busy clinic and so suggest that patients see another specialist. The patient may express feeling unhappy, but be content to do nothing significantly to change this. The psychiatrist in turn may be faced with a 'resistant' client rather than one who is 'paranoid' or 'depressed'. It is argued that a lack of consensus over the nature of problems and how they should be treated can lead to particular difficulties in the management of a patient. These differences between professionals should be addressed at the outset. This is 'counselling business' which should in the first instance be dealt with between professional colleagues.

References

Maturana, H., Coddou, F. and Mendez, C. (1988) 'The bringing forth of pathology', *Irish Journal of Psychology*, 9 (1): 144–72.

CONCLUSION
WHY STUDY ROLES AND
RELATIONSHIPS?

KATE LYON

The fact that we sometimes spend time thinking about ourselves in relation to the other people in our lives suggests that we can and do engage in thinking in terms of roles and relationships. More than mere curiosity, however, should induce workers in the health and social welfare fields to acquire a clear understanding of roles and relationships. The development and maintenance of a relationship with the client is one of the major tools or skills of such work. Moreover, health and social welfare workers are often called upon when something has gone wrong with roles and relationships.

The helping relationship rests on specialist knowledge and professional skills and the role of the practitioner is very specific, with rights and duties (or role expectations). But, at the same time, it is unclear because it reflects more general values about altruism, caring and a commitment to the well-being of others (Watson, 1980). Without a clear sense of their roles and relationships, practitioners risk either the loss of their specialized knowledge, or the danger of a narrowly defined 'overprofessionalized' response. The first can lead to confusion about the boundaries to responsibility, and may lead to the unfocused 'helping' that encourages dependency. The second can stifle skills by an emphasis on professional detachment, and can be experienced by users as a lack of interest.

Practitioners need to underpin their systematic knowledge in order to establish a link between social structure and the individual human being – between the purposes of the organizations they work in and the users they serve. By making use of models developed in the social sciences, such links can be established.

Common-sense knowledge

In common-sense understanding there are two diametrically opposed views of roles and relationships. The first is that role-playing is somehow inauthentic, and that those who are seen to be so engaged are putting on a performance designed to mislead other people. Such misrepresentation, it is believed, can distort relationships because we present ourselves as other than we really are. Behind this view is an assumption that there is a 'real' person hidden within the role. The second view is that most people have very limited choices in life and that this is a reflection of the need for social order, rules and regulations. More a form of fatalism than social analysis, this view sees human beings as puppets whose strings are pulled by others ('them', the boss, the government, the powers-that-be).

As with all generalizations, there is some truth in both of these views, in some situations. But as explanations of roles and relationships they are crude and offer little real understanding of how the individual behaves as a member of a social group in relationships with others. These two models alert us to the fact that there are difficulties in distinguishing who we 'really' are from the roles we play. Is there something more to human nature than the roles we play, our 'social identity'? And can we speak of *an* identity or does *every* individual have *many* social identities which are brought into focus in the widely differing spheres and contexts of social life? How congruent are the various roles we perform and how aware are we of the positions that we occupy?

Social science knowledge

In order to make sense of what our social world is and how it influences us, we need to approach human social behaviour in a more systematic manner. By using concepts such as 'role' and 'relationship', abstractions developed by role theorists, we are likely to achieve a clearer understanding of the links between society and the individual human being – in other words, how the social is constructed within the person.

First developed by social anthropologists studying non-Western societies, role theories have been further developed by social psychologists and sociologists. A broad distinction can be drawn between theories which emphasize the contractual dimensions of roles and relationships, and those which are more concerned to demonstrate the fluid, negotiable nature of social interaction. The first set of theories assumes consensus, that there is agreement about what kind of behaviour is to be expected of the incumbents of particular roles.

The *structuralist–functionalist* framework approaches role in terms of reciprocity, with an emphasis on rights and duties, a sort of contract, where there may be little scope for choice in how the role is performed. This framework was most extensively developed by Talcott Parsons, and although oversimplified by later theories, his analysis provides an under-standing of the social system as a network of interactive relationships (1951: 24–67, 201–43). Some roles are instrumental or task orientated, such as work, and some are expressive and more concerned with emotions or feelings, and both kinds serve societal functions. If individuals behave deviantly, and do not fulfil role expectations, social control may come into play to bring them back into line, in order to maintain the social system.

Another set of theories points to the ambiguous nature of social interaction, and to the possibility of disagreement and conflict about how roles should be performed. Theorists such as the symbolic interactionists (Rose, 1962; Strauss, 1969) emphasize the 'making' as well as the 'taking' of roles, that role expectations can be negotiated and that there is creativity and choice in how people perform their roles and relate to others. Goffman (1959) too, emphasizes the performance of roles, using analogies drawn from the theatre. Although his *dramaturgical* model is more concerned with social structure than are the symbolic interactionists, none the less he draws attention to symbolic aspects of role behaviour.

However, we must be aware of the limitations of such social science models. Each model has its problems and all have been criticized because they assume either too much conformity to expectations or too much choice. For Giddens (1984: 83–6) role is too 'given', with little scope for individual preferences and no recognition of the different meanings that people attach to their behaviour. In other words, the contractual model is criticized for depersonalizing role. Similarly, interactionist models are criticized for ignoring the constraints of social structure, and often providing little more than information about the minutiae of small-scale encounters.

Role theory is no longer a fashionable topic in social science and, if discussed at all, it is quickly dismissed in favour of apparently weightier topics such as power and oppression. In place of role, *discourse* theorists have concentrated on ideology (or systems of belief), expressed in both language and action. However, there are some situations where we can only understand what is going on by means of the concepts and models developed within what is broadly defined as role theory.

Concepts of role and status

We all occupy certain positions or statuses in society which locate us in relation to other people. Each status can be thought of as giving rise to certain expectations (rights and duties), which are translated into role performance, with role being the active expression of status. Particular kinds of behaviour are thought to go with particular positions, and the concept of role is used to describe the expectations that are attached to a position and expressed in role performance or behaviour. We make assumptions that the occupant of a particular status will have certain goals (or aims) and motivations which will lead to certain patterns of behaviour.

Although apparently straightforward, the ways in which roles are performed suggest that social interaction is far from unambiguous. While status (position) and its accompanying role (expected behaviour) seem to be separate easily identifiable aspects of social life, the reality is that behaviour which expresses role is often far from straightforward, and so it is useful to distinguish between role and role performance. In other words, although individuals must operate within the constraints of social structure, there may be scope for variation in role performance, depending on the context and the nature of the particular status and its corresponding role. For example, there is assumed to be clarity about the status or position of a parent, and yet when we examine what we mean by parenting we find it hard to be precise about what kind of a role a parent is expected to perform: what is desirable, tolerable, unacceptable or forbidden in the behaviour of a parent? What difference is there for mothers and fathers, for parents from particular cultures, for parents of younger and older children? What is prescribed and what proscribed in terms of relationships with children? When we use the term 'parent' what kinds of values are we using, what kinds of family structures are we assuming, how do we arrive at the idea of the status and role of 'parent'?

Some of the variation in role performance will reflect the meanings that are attached to a particular status: both our own personal meanings, and those that we share with others as part of a common culture. But our judgement of a particular role performance as a parent will be very different if, for instance, we work as a health visitor with preschool children, or as a residential social worker in a home for adolescents, or as a member of a community mental handicap team. What is assessed as being perfectly appropriate parental behaviour in one context could be seen to be smothering, inconsistent or overcontrolling in others. It is essential not only to be sensitive to how the role of parent is defined in other cultures than our own, but also to be aware of the complexity and variation in the meaning attached to a role by the people who carry it out – parents.

Role theory suggests that the many roles we engage in are not all of equal importance and that some have very little impact on how we see ourselves – our sense of self. Key roles are those that are most important to us. We may decide for ourselves what is important and what unimportant, but usually those roles to which we give most weight have already been defined as important for us by society. A distinction can be drawn between basic roles (sex, age), general roles (work, family) and independent roles (leisure activities) (Banton, 1965), and between those roles that are ascribed or inherited (for example, through kinship) and those that are achieved (for example, through education). For some people, occupation and the work role that goes with it may be simply a way of earning a living, and of little intrinsic importance. For many, however, the work role is crucial and can give meaning to life outside work. Our occupation can determine our standard of living, our sense of self-esteem, the degree to which we can exercise power and autonomy in our life and our physical and mental health. Even if we thoroughly dislike our work it can have far-reaching effects on our life.

Relationships

Like role, 'relationship' is a word used freely in everyday life, and its meaning can be elusive. Just as status and role vary with context and the social meanings that are attached to them, so too do the kinds of relationships that we establish with other people. In some social situations there is no need to be conscious of our own or others' behaviours. Erving Goffman describes the fleeting social contacts we have with others in public places, on the street, in the bus, in shops, as requiring no more than 'civil inattention' (Goffman, 1971: 214–21). Such simple interactions, where we are aware of but barely acknowledge another's presence, work best because we engage in them unthinkingly. But even this area of seemingly unself-conscious social interaction is something that we have been taught as young children.

Interactions can be at different levels of meaning and intensity, and it is possible to distinguish between routine, ritual and drama. Morris (1972) suggests that routine is what maintains everyday life, that ritual sustains our ordinary interactions and that drama is the channel for change. Thus we live by the first, remember by the second, and survive by the third of these kinds of interaction.

Relationships are shaped by and expressed through interaction, and how we behave with other people reflects the meaning we attach to our relationships with them, and in turn is confirmed or altered by their behaviour. We learn how to relate to other people through the processes of primary socialization, by which, as small children, we learn to share in the cultures of our society. Our social self or identity, the sense of belonging to our social world, is confirmed in relationships with others. 'Like a good conscience, identity is constantly lost and found' (Berger, 1966).

Just as some roles are more important than others, so are some relationships. In part the importance we attach to certain relationships is shaped by the cultural meanings they have. Intimate relationships within the family or with friends carry different meanings, and therefore require different ways of interacting from relationships with colleagues, for example. This generalization needs qualifying, of course, and has to take account of the different sources from which people derive their sense of social identity. Family relationships, supposedly the most intimate, include instrumental (task-orientated) expectations: a clean house and children, the money to live on, and so on, often divide along gender lines (Parsons and Bales, 1956). Conversely, relationships at work often supply the expressive (or feelings) components of affection, warmth and support. And those relationships that we value most are where we invest most.

The investment we make in key relationships, and particularly in intimate and/or family relationships, is a reflection of the ways in which they contribute to our sense of identity. The strength of a relationship depends on a balance of shared understandings and the 'pay-offs' for each party. Social exchange theory (Blau, 1964) suggests that we remain in a relationship so long as it continues to give us what we think we want and are entitled to. This model of a kind of balance sheet of profit and loss perhaps offers too cynical a view of human nature: the closeness of our interpersonal ties to other people depends on a range of factors. These include ascription, for instance ties of kin or religion, and commitment, as in the legal and (sometimes) religious bond of marriage. There are other, less tangible factors: how much we feel we can rely on getting what we want from the relationship (reward dependability), the love we feel towards the other (attachment), and the investments we have made already, whether of time or effort (McCall and Simmons, 1966: 167–79).

We need to appreciate the complex web of motivations that underpins most important relationships. There is some truth in the ideas of social exchange theory because the greater the investment, the more vulnerable the relationship may be and the more we put into preserving it. The more willing we are to work to nurture a relationship, the less willing we become to let it go. And by doing this work we may simply be conforming to the social meanings that are attached to certain statuses and roles. Ties of blood, family, affection and long-term commitment to other people are all valued in our culture. The involvement of health and social welfare practitioners in helping to maintain these relationships provides further proof of the social value attached to these interpersonal ties.

Meanings and patterns

The study of role and relationship allows us to step back from our everyday world and see our behaviour and that of others in terms of the links that exist between the individual and society: between ourselves as social beings, in interaction with other social beings, located in particular social structures, sometimes constrained and sometimes enabled to behave in particular ways. With this knowledge we may be better able to understand the meanings that we and others attach to relationships and the rules or discourses that shape them, and to perceive the pattern of our lives.

Hughes (1959) used the term 'career' to describe the way in which each of us seeks for meaning in our life. He suggested that it has two aspects: the subjectively experienced patterns (personal experience), and a sequence of statuses. A career is not necessarily a smooth progression, and may be shaped by chance and contingency. None the less, we seem to need to have a sense of a pattern in what we do, a sense of continuity between the different spheres and phases of our life. Assuming that there are life patterns (and sometimes they may be more desired than real), then an appreciation of the extent to which we make choices, the kinds of choices that are open to us, and the constraints that limit choice, is illuminating. The career of a mental patient, as Goffman (1961) demonstrates, is imposed rather than embraced. Similarly, the choices perceived by an older person unable to continue to care for herself in her own home are likely to be limited, and the sense of the finality of the move into an elderly persons' home may help to explain why some residents are not very interested in reminiscence, preferring to concentrate on the present (Coleman, 1986). But with skilled assessment and planning, an older client facing residential care may be able to see some choices in her new life. The helplessness that Parsons described in his analysis of the 'sick role' (1951: 476–7) carries expectations for how the patient is expected to behave in order to continue to receive medical care. Some of these expectations increase the patient's powerlessness and may not always be to the individual's benefit.

The exploration of freedom versus constraint, of powerlessness versus resistance, can also encourage greater awareness of the complexity of social life. One person's 'reality' may not be shared by other people, and even where it is, may not be 'true'. The varieties of culture and sub-culture in large, complex societies throw doubt on the world-taken-for-granted that we assume we share with other people (Berger and Luckmann, 1966). For instance, juvenile delinquents often assume that the other members of the gang are much more committed to delinquency than they are, and sometimes law-breaking takes place because of this shared misunderstanding (Matza, 1964). As the pace and range of social change increase, so the need to take account of cultural diversity becomes more urgent.

Transitions

There are times we can become conscious of overwhelming change and the anxiety that it brings. We occupy a new status and are unfamiliar with the role performance that is expected of us. Most often this occurs at times of transition – of status transformation – when change forces us to become aware both of what we may have lost, the old patterns and relationships, as well as the potential of what we may gain. Status passage (Glaser and Strauss, 1978: 89–131) involves transformations of identity and the levels of anxiety experience are influenced by a range of personal and social factors. Anxiety may be less where the change is expected and shared with others. Some major transitions are marked by a 'rite of passage', such as weddings and funerals. These ceremonies can serve to reduce anxiety by offering a formal, ritualized set of responses.

An example of a status transformation is that of a new job. A change or transition in a professional or work role may appear to be relatively straightforward, not least because we often have a job description which tells us what role behaviour is expected of us as, say, a social care worker. Interestingly, however, what a job description rarely does is to set out the expectations which we can legitimately have of others with whom we will be working, such as colleagues, superiors and other professionals, as well as users and their families. While it may be clear what our duties are, we have to discover what kinds of relationships are possible and desirable, as well as required, in the new situation. The process of secondary socialization comes into play and we are exposed to the learning required of adults as they enter new roles. As we acquire the necessary knowledge, skills and values, so we learn to be what we are supposed to be, and the feelings of strangeness and unease may soon pass. However, even when completed satisfactorily, secondary socialization does not ensure that our role will be trouble-free thereafter. Conflict, role strain and the constraints imposed by the organization, our colleagues and the users we serve are all part of the everyday experience of work. By standing back from the world-taken-for-granted and attempting to understand our work in terms of role theory, we not only become aware of our own situation but also perceive the situation of others. These other people will include those in very different situations, with statuses different from our own. We may come to understand the situation of people who are unemployed, who have lost or retired from their jobs, or whose work is unpaid and perhaps hidden, in a society that values the individual's contribution primarily in terms of participation in paid employment.

Conclusion

The study of roles and relationships permits us to understand our own world and that of others. We acquire the ability to question, explore and, if necessary, de-bunk what we have previously taken for granted, and by so doing become active participants in our social world. We can become fine-tuned to the nuances and ambiguities of social interaction in organizations and may be better placed to act effectively for our own and others' benefit. Instead of hiding behind 'bad faith' (Sartre, 1956) by blaming external constraints for aspects of our lives, we can acknowledge choices we may have made and decisions taken which have given rise to the position we find ourselves in.

Many factors appear to be beyond our control – resource constraints, poverty, poor housing and deprivation – but by a critical appreciation of roles and relationships we become better able to see where social structure impinges on us and others, to recognize where power lies and where we and others may have a chance of influencing outcomes. When we have rigorously analysed what the constraints on us are, then we may be able to find some areas where we can gain some control over our situation. Examples may range from seeking information on welfare benefits to developing a self-help group or a residents' association. They may seem like relatively small moves, but they acknowledge people's capacity to learn new roles and to develop relationships. In place of 'everyday knowledge', or what everyone knows, which in the field of health and social welfare is increasingly depressing, we acquire the knowledge that comes from deeper understanding of ourselves and others.

If we make the connection between personal and social constructions of identity, we can understand that while we contribute to our own social worlds, we are at the same time shaped and determined by them. An understanding of the personal is only useful if it is informed by a complementary understanding of social forces and social constraints. The one without the other provides only a partial view. The study of roles and relationships gives us greater awareness of, and perhaps control over, the everyday experience of our lives. To appreciate that social life is ambiguous, open to a variety of different interpretations, and open also at times to negotiation, is to acquire power for ourselves and other people. At its most sophisticated, role theory can take account of the strength and pervasiveness of the social structure and offer the understanding of the relationships between 'private troubles and public issues' that C. Wright Mills (1959) urged as part of the proper study of sociology.

References

Banton, M. (1965) *Roles*. London: Tavistock.

Berger, P. (1966) *Invitation to Sociology*. Harmondsworth: Penguin.

Berger, P. and Luckmann, T. (1966) *The Social Construction of Reality*. Harmondsworth: Penguin.

Blau, P. (1964) *Exchange and Power in Social Life*. New York: Wiley.

Coleman, P. (1986) *Ageing and Reminiscence Processes*. New York: Wiley.

Giddens, A. (1984) *The Construction of Society*. Cambridge: Polity Press.

Glaser, B.G. and Strauss, A.L. (1978) *Status Passage: a Formal Theory*. London: Routledge & Kegan Paul.

Goffman, E. (1959) *The Presentation of Self in Everyday Life*. New York: Doubleday.

Goffman, E. (1961) *Asylums: Essays on the Social Situation of Mental Patients and Other Inmates*. Harmondsworth: Penguin.

Goffman, E. (1971) *Relations in Public: Microstudies of the Public Order*. New York: Free Press.

Hughes, E.C. (1959) *Men and their Work*. New York: Free Press.

Matza, D. (1964) *Delinquency and Drift*. New York: Wiley.

McCall, G.J. and Simmons, J.L. (1966) *Identities and Interactions*. New York: Free Press.

Mills, C. Wright (1959) *The Sociological Imagination*. Oxford: Oxford University Press.

Morris, J. (1972) 'Three aspects of the person', in R. Ruddock (ed.), *Six Approaches to the Person*. London: Routledge & Kegan Paul.

Parsons, T. (1951) *The Social System*. New York: Free Press.

Parsons, T. and Bales, R.F. (1956) *Family Socialisation and Interaction Process*. London: Routledge & Kegan Paul.

Rose, A.M. (ed.) (1962) *Human Behaviour and Social Processes*. London: Routledge & Kegan Paul.

Sartre, J.-P. (1956) *Being and Nothingness*. London: Routledge & Kegan Paul.

Strauss, A. (1969) *Mirrors and Masks*. Oxford: Martin Robertson.

Watson, D. (1980) *Caring for Strangers*. London: Routledge & Kegan Paul.

INDEX